THE
TRACK
OF
THE WOLF

THE

ESSAYS

ON NATIONAL SOCIALISM

AND   ITS   LEADER,

ADOLF   HITLER

BY

NORTHWESTERN

TRACK OF THE WOLF

JAMES H. McRANDLE

UNIVERSITY PRESS

EVANSTON, ILLINOIS

1965

THIS BOOK

HAS   BEEN   PUBLISHED   WITH   THE   AID   OF   A   GRANT

FROM THE PURDUE RESEARCH FOUNDATION

TO CAROL AND JOHN

ACKNOWLEDGMENTS

I wish to thank the libraries of the universities of Minnesota, Michigan, and Purdue, the Bayrische Staatsbibliothek, the Institut fuer Zeitgeschichte, and the Library of Congress for their generous aid to me in writing this book. My thanks also go to my wife Carol, to James Quirk, to G. G. Hatheway, and to my other friends who read portions of this work, listened patiently, and offered encouragement. It goes almost without saying that this book could not have been completed without the full support of Purdue University and its Department of History.

JAMES H. McRANDLE

CONTENTS

THE
TRACK
OF
THE WOLF

I

THE TRACK OF THE WOLF

In the winter of 1922–23, as Adolf Hitler tells the story, it became necessary to spirit Dietrich Eckart, who was wanted by the police, out of Munich to Berchtesgaden. It was a well-told tale, as were many of Hitler's anecdotes, replete with tricks played on the police and other examples of the resourcefulness and recklessness characteristic of his early band of comrades. The upshot of the whole incident was that Eckart, safely—though not too secretly—ensconced at Berchtesgaden in the Pension Moritz, invited Hitler to visit him in the spring of 1923. Since it was Hitler's first visit to the mountain town, Eckart was able to disguise the Fuehrer's true identity by introducing him to the townsfolk and the boarders at the pension as "Herr Wolf." The masquerade delighted Hitler—he could draw people out about their true feelings toward the Nazi leader, enjoying the sense of superiority that goes with anonymity and the subsequent looks of happy or anguished surprise when finally he did reveal himself some months later.[1]

Hitler craved anonymity. Time and again he would picture himself as one of the city masses or as an indistinguishable part of the front-line army. Yet he also had a hypersensitive awareness of his own uniqueness which contrasted strangely with this other quality. For all that he said "I am everything," he also said "I am nothing"; for all that he tried to create the image of himself as a "world-historical personality," he just as deliberately sought to efface and destroy that singularity in a series of identifications with the masses of ordinary men. It is the curious paradox of a man who encouraged an entire nation to shout "Heil Hitler" and yet was willing to hide his identity behind the quite common (and often Jewish) name of Wolf.

The choice is fascinating. "Wolf" was Hitler's party nickname in the early years and later recurred in the code names of several of his headquarters: *Wolfsschanze, Wolfsschlucht,* and *Werewolf,* for example. Perhaps he showed a predilection for this pseudonym because the name Adolf is derived from the Teutonic word meaning "fortunate wolf." [2] Certainly few would argue that it was inappropriate. The suggestion of power, destructiveness, and loneliness inherent in the wolf figure fits closely the facts of Hitler's life. [3]

From adolescence on, Hitler maintained a distance between himself and society. In Vienna he buried himself among those who were unable to achieve even minimal success in the Austrian society of the day; in the army he had no close friends; and as a revolutionist he obviously pitted himself against the society of the Weimar Republic. Again, in the last years of his life he withdrew into the seclusion of his headquarters, "Wolf's Lair." Hitler never, properly speaking, was a part of society. He manipulated it or allowed it nearly to crush him; but from the moment he dropped out of school he also, in a very real sense, dropped out of society. He was not so much lonely as alone, and if he shouted at even his closest associates it was because so great a chasm existed between himself and all others.

Yet if Hitler was asocial and destructive he was also anxious to establish his reputation as a creative personality. He considered himself an artist and gave artistic matters and the artistic pose great attention throughout his life.[4] At the height of his power he surrounded himself with people from the world of art: film stars, architects such as Speer, sculptors like Arno Breker, and frustrated novelists like Joseph Goebbels. He personally supervised the architectural planning of the National Socialist period and imposed upon it a canon as severe in its own manner as that of the Egyptian kingdoms. The constant repetition of folkish and classical themes in the art and architecture may have been tiring, it may not have suited the tastes of the artistic leaders of the Western world, but it did represent a taste. Hitler was not artistically insensitive nor, in general, was the National Socialist regime; in fact, this was one of the charges leveled by the National Socialists against the bourgeois world.[5]

Hitler was interested in emphasizing both the destructive and creative sides of his personality, and he was perhaps even more interested in presenting himself as a man of decision; yet one of his outstanding characteristics was a marked tendency towards procrastination. He was perfectly capable of dawdling endlessly over tea and cakes while the foundations of his power trembled and dissolved. This spirit of hesitation often drove his lieutenants to the brink of despair. But over and against this hesitancy must be placed his remarkable ability to forge ruthlessly ahead once the die had been cast, an ability not only amazing in one so given to indecisiveness but awe-inspiring in the precision with which he made his calculations during these periods of decision.

One might, indeed, conclude that there were two Hitlers—the one a dawdling dreamer with aspirations towards the artistic life, the other a ravening wolf hungering for, and attaining, political power. In many ways these two contrasting characters were complementary, and an understanding of both is necessary for a comprehension of the reasons for Hitler's successes as well as his failures. It was the dreamer who envisioned the successive goals of the National Socialist period; it was the wolf who broke the trail.

If this can be called the essential nature of Adolf Hitler it must also be said that these traits were seldom to appear in simple juxtaposition or nakedly alone, for Hitler was a master at revealing only fragments of his personality to those with whom he associated. In fact, this was so much the case that there is little resemblance among the portraits of the Fuehrer offered by his various acquaintances, and the obvious contradictions present a major obstacle to a full assessment of his character. To some who knew him he appeared to be a cheap opportunist, to others he demonstrated an overpowering personal magnetism, while still others found him vulgar and uninteresting. Some men saw a wide-ranging intellect—others were appalled by his crass and petty mind. To some a statesman, to others a demagogue, Hitler appears in the literature and memoirs of the period in a kind of haze, his face and personality changing as we watch. So varied are the descriptions of Hitler that it has been common for historians and biographers to assume that all of those portraits in which Hitler's nihilism is not clearly visible either are inaccurate or result from a deliberate masquerade on the part of Hitler himself. Compelling as is that interpretation which sees the Fuehrer as a simple nihilist, a view that can be supported by some striking quotations, it suffers from the weakness that almost all the quotations derive from one source: Hermann Rauschning. Without casting any doubts upon Rauschning's veracity, it nevertheless seems necessary to say that the quotations tell us more of Hitler's relationship with Rauschning than they tell us of his "true" nature.

The fact is that we cannot be certain that Hitler was telling the truth to one man and lying to all of the rest. Therefore it may be profitable to avoid labeling certain descriptions as true and others as spurious (or, what is worse, disregarding those which fail to concur with our preconceptions) and instead consider Hitler as the player of many roles. Role playing is fundamental to all human relationships. Jonathan Swift saw some of this truth long ago in his acid "philosophy of clothes," to which he gave voice in *The Tale of the Tub;* to a certain extent a man's personality is molded by the position he occupies. There is a strong tendency to act according to certain stereotypes set by conditions of the social environment. Thus a man may be a lion at the office and a mouse at home; he may be a frivolous freethinker in one group and a nominally serious churchgoer in another. With one friend a man may continually speak of his war experiences, with another he may talk of women; but he might feel himself unjustly handled if history were to describe him either as a militarist or a lecher. A good deal of self-deception of course is involved in role playing. A man may play many parts in his life and in each case feel that he is acting largely as "the real me." One should not be too harsh with this game of deception for we are all involved in it.

From his earliest days Hitler apparently possessed the ability to cast himself completely into the part which he had chosen to play. Thus, it is interesting to compare the young artist and dandy of "invariably spruce appearance" known to Hitler's boyhood friend, August Kubizek, with the carelessly dressed revolutionary of the days of the struggle for power.[6] That playing a part might even involve a physical change is indicated by the fact that Hitler, who as late as 1904 could be described as "strongly built" and of robust health, was pictured by his teachers a year later as "gaunt, pale-faced, almost like a consumptive." [7] This was the period when Hitler was changing from a gregarious schoolboy into a "solitary artist"—a romantic conception of himself which he never entirely lost. Franz Jetzinger, who has pointed out this change in physical appearance, has also convincingly demonstrated that it was not due to illness (as was claimed by Hitler), so we may conclude that these changes in habit and appearance were all fixtures for the new role Hitler was playing. [8]

In Vienna, the young artist-dandy of Linz changed into the artist-Bohemian and later into the "down and outer of the Home for Men." [9] Again, Jetzinger is able to show that this degradation was not due to financial necessity. Hitler had, during this entire period, an income which could have provided him with a more amenable life than the one he chose. [10] One cannot help but feel that there was something very appealing to Hitler in this life of self-imposed hardship. Just as we may suspect that George Orwell accepted the life of the tramp for a time, not out of absolute necessity or because he was gathering material for a book, but rather because it helped him to establish the point of view for his criticism of Western society, [11] so we may suspect that Hitler, through his apparently aimless existence in Vienna, was also establishing a line of departure for his attack upon society. Hitler lived the part he had chosen and felt the privations as deeply as if they had been due to absolute necessity. [12]

In a sense, these experiences were necessary, for all of the roles played by Hitler during his youth involved a large element of rebellion—rebellion against his father, against the provincial society of Linz, against the bourgeois, cosmopolitan society of Vienna. That this rebellion contained a tremendous amount of hatred, perhaps not least of all self-hatred, is manifest not only from his theories but also from all of the later statements which he made about his life in Vienna.[13] Rebellion and hatred do not of themselves necessarily lead to evil results; they have also been at the basis of many great works of modern art and have played a considerable role in political movements that have proved to be constructive in nature. But the existence of this rebelliousness and hatred does point to the conclusion that those who would see Hitler as a cynical opportunist are probably wide of the mark.[14]

Neither artist-Bohemians, nor dandies, nor tramps, no matter how attractive they may be as characters, really fit into the life of the community. They exist on its periphery as open rebukes to the society which they hate. Hitler had, up until his twenty-fifth year, lived a good part of his life in the interstices of society. There is no doubt that through his own experiences he had learned to feel deeply the longings, hatreds, and fears of the masses of men in the lower-middle and lower classes; but he had, up until that time, undergone no experience which gave him a real sense of identity with these masses. It was the war, in which he served as an ordinary infantryman, which provided that experience. It was the war which enabled him to become for a time "one of seven million," the "unknown soldier," the "face in the crowd." [15]

The poses—the artist-Bohemian, the derelict, the man in the crowd, and the simple soldier—proved to be basic for Hitler's political career. During the next twenty years he returned constantly to these themes or poses in his public addresses, written works, and private conversations. Certainly he embroidered upon many of the phases of his life, turned them into forms of self-justification, and tended to twist the facts until they became in some cases unrecognizable. Yet what man does not do the same? Certain experiences loom so large in our lives that they assume a greatness and grandeur which they may have lacked in reality. Instead of expressing shocked disgust at the idea that Hitler would lie about his past life, we should be relieved to find such an utterly human trait in his character.

However many roles Hitler may have chosen to play, they do seem on inspection to resolve themselves into two major categories: those that were predominantly creative and those that were largely destructive. As has already been noted, Hitler was not a simple nihilist but possessed real creative energies as well. He was *both* artist and wolf, and all of the roles which he acted out during his life were formed by one or the other of these basic drives. Insofar as he was creative he tended to view himself as unique, as a man who dominated events. His destructive urges were viewed by him as the workings of implacable "natural law." Thus the struggle against "the Jew" was joined below the conscious level, in the blood itself. Furthermore, he felt that the destructive activities were justified by the creative vision. The soldiers of the front army destroyed in order that they could rebuild society and the SA continued the war against a hopeless society for the purpose of building a "true" community. Seen in this light the warrior and the worker were twins, for the worker was necessary to justify the warrior's deeds. In an opposite fashion it was the revolutionary who made possible the artist's dreams.

Certain of Hitler's roles seem obviously creative in character. As the artist or former worker, now a leader of workers, he was concerned with the task of rebuilding. To the conservatives he was the "good" German bent on preserving the traditional values of the Fatherland. Certain foreign correspondents who were granted interviews in the early 1930's met with a surprisingly charming diplomat determined to find a "European" solution to the German problem.[16] Again, at the Nuremberg rallies he was the high priest of the National Socialist faith conducting liturgical ceremonies aimed at unifying the new community, while at Potsdam in March of 1933 he was the Reichschancellor uniting, through responsible leadership, the old Germany with the new.

Yet this same person was the coarse, crudely anti-Semitic Hitler of the *Secret Conversations*,[17] the embattled revolutionary, the terrorist, the destroyer. If, on occasion, he sought to act the part of the clear-headed statesman in the tradition of Bismarck, he could also play the *Feldherr*, the man who sought to solve his problems with a quick, clean stroke of the sword.[18] In his more fantastic moments he could even toy with the notion that he was the reincarnation of Frederick the Great.[19] Indeed, as the war drew to its close these allusions to Frederick became ever more frequent, culminating in the ludicrous scene in which he and Goebbels found a parallel between the death of Roosevelt and the death of the Russian Empress. Finally, he was the implacable judge, passing the death sentence upon millions of people for the good of the race.

Not all of these parts were played to the same audience for, as has already been remarked, most men change their character to fit their surroundings. To Hermann Rauschning he could appear as the cynic who craved nothing but power, while to many others he was an idealist. Thus throughout his life Hitler oscillated between creative and destructive roles, often combining elements of both types within the limits of a single conversation. He was the intellectual who could spend long hours proclaiming his views on art, music, and European life, and he was also the activist who with drawn pistol could break up a political rally or condemn his closest co-workers to death. He was both reasonable and hysterical, both clown and fanatic. He was, as General Guderian put it so dryly, a "most difficult man." [20]

Perhaps nowhere did Hitler have the opportunity to play a greater variety of public roles than at the yearly party rallies held in Nuremberg. It must also be added that nowhere did he have a more magnificent platform from which to exhibit his talents. Even when he was not physically present at the activities the force of his personality was felt, for the Nuremberg Rally was in a sense the personality and mind of the Fuehrer writ large. Certainly it was his artistic love of the gigantic which guided the construction of the massive buildings; it was his sense of the dramatic which drew together hundreds of thousands of uniformed men to stand in awesome silence before their leader—fierce sheep guided by a wolf-like shepherd.

In starkest terms, the deep contrast and necessary unity of the unique and the anonymous were expressed on these occasions. Yet this rally was also the most concrete expression of the idea of a German racial community. Here were gathered the elite: the men who had fought for, the men who would guard, and the young people who would build the new Germany. Military exercises, memorials to the "time of struggle," reviews of the labor battalions, and displays of folkish art and dances all had their place at this annual assembly. In time the party rally might have become an important element in the German governmental structure. Already several important laws, such as those concerning the Jews, had been announced here. The Four Year Plan was established at the rally of 1936, and in 1938 a loosening of rules on rationing was proclaimed. In effect, the party rally was becoming the popular assembly of this totalitarian democracy.

Some would argue that the Nuremberg Rally was merely a tawdry carnival backdrop for the obscene display of naked power. The obvious impact on foreign states of these exhibitions of military and political strength lend a certain verisimilitude to such statements. Yet to hold that the rallies were this and no more fails to explain why these meetings were so tremendously important to Hitler himself, why for seven days during the height of the Czech crisis in September, 1938, he was in constant attendance at the rally and completely out of contact with the diplomatic corps.[21]

A study of the structure of the party rally gives us considerable insight into its meaning for Adolf Hitler. From the moment when he alighted from his special train and marched past the guards of the *Leibstandarte* to be greeted by Mayor Liebel, he was not only the center of all attention but the ceremonial leader as well.[22] Always aware of his impact, he would assume purposefully dramatic poses such as fixing his left hand in his belt buckle and striding determinedly toward his car.

In 1938 the "First Party Rally of Greater Germany" officially opened with a dedication before the insignia of the First Reich, the imperial crown, the orb of empire, the scepter, and the sword, now back in Nuremberg for the first time in 140 years. These connections with the past seem to have held deep meaning for the Fuehrer. Seemingly he was trying by every means to establish the integral and mystic connections of the old and the new empires.

This contact with the distant past established, he proceeded to the Congress Hall where, following the presentation of the "Blood Flag," the roll was called of those who had died in the struggle for power, reminding one of the lines in the Horst Wessel song to the effect that comrades shot by the Red Front and the reactionaries still marched in spirit in the ranks of the SA. Again, this ceremony was intended to press home Hitler's special interpretation of history which held that all good men in Germany during the 1920's were engaged in the task of overthrowing the regime of the "November criminals" and reestablishing German honor. In his speeches and private conversations he would often include a long resumé of the events of his life and their relationship to the development and final success of the National Socialist Party. Repetitious as they were, these summaries of party achievement served to fix in Hitler's mind and in the minds of his listeners the special Nazi version of historical reality.

The "Blood Flag," so called because it had been dipped in the blood of those killed in the *Putsch* of 1923, occupied a central position among the ceremonial objects of the National Socialist German Workers' Party (NSDAP). All new banners were consecrated by touching them to this flag. This consecration took place once a year at the rally, with Hitler performing the sacerdotal functions. There was no trace of self-consciousness or dissimulation involved in his performance of these priestly tasks. They were of as great importance to him as any of his other duties.

In contrast to this scene of historical reminiscence and fabrication, Hitler the artist, the statesman, and the ideologist presided over the Cultural Session at which awards were presented for achievement in technology and socialism. In 1938 the recipients were Dr. Ferdinand Porsche (designer of the Volkswagen), Dr. Fritz Todt (Autobahn system), Dr. Wilhelm Messerschmitt (Me-109), and Dr. Ernst Heinkel (Heinkel fighter). The awards perhaps say something about the cultural tastes of Nazi Germany but there can be no doubt that the Volkswagen, the Autobahn system, and the Me-109 represented solid achievements. The Me-109 was one of the best fighters in the war, the Volkswagen continues to be the nearest thing to a "people's car" produced in Europe, and the Autobahn is still one of the best examples of a well-planned road system. Hitler ended the evening with a speech on the integration of science, art, and culture in the German people's community as opposed to the cultural isolation of the "Judaized" Western world.[23]

The third day of the rally was traditionally set aside for the young men of the Reich's Labor Service. Under the watchful eye of the Fuehrer, column after column of young men in uniform carrying shovels at their shoulders swung into the great stadium. It was assumed at the time that the Labor Service was intended as an introduction to the military life, but it is doubtful that this training really prepared men for the army or war. As a para-military force the Service was only a preparation in the sense that it served to imbue the young men with a soldierly attitude towards the problems of life (an approach paralleled by the Hitler Youth and the SA). It was not, however, properly speaking, pre-military training. The central purpose of the organization was to emphasize the dignity of labor in the national service. The close connection of the Labor Service to the military service in Nazi Germany stemmed from the conception in National Socialist thought that there was an integral relationship between the worker and the soldier centering on the struggle of man against his human enemies and against the power of nature. It was the soldier who destroyed the harmful human organizations; it was the worker who rebuilt the human society by cooperating with natural forces.

It is well to remember that the worker was one of the honored archetypes of Nazi society, whereas the financier definitely was not. Hitler's public espousal of the worker's cause (whether or not he gave it wholehearted support) constituted an important proof that he was a revolutionary, and though he was now head of the state he was loath to relinquish this image for it was one of the justifications of his power. The National Socialists argued that all were workers—"workers of the hand and workers of the head"—and just as they portrayed the entire German nation in one of its aspects as a community of soldiers, so in another of its aspects it was a community of workers. Class cleavages were denied in the interest of national unity.

As Hitler identified himself with the workers, so also he

identified himself with the soldiers and the veterans. What must have been the most impressive of all the Nuremberg ceremonies was the assembly of the political leaders, many of them veterans of the war. One hundred and forty thousand strong they stood before their Fuehrer in the dark with the flags of their detachments. Robert Ley stepped to the rostrum and announced to the suspense-filled audience, "My Fuehrer, I present your political leaders." At that moment, behind the tribune, searchlights shot straight columns of light into the night sky, forming at their apex a hugh dome of flooded light over the great field. The political leaders stepped forward, their black, white, and red banners waving bloodily in the back lighting. All was silent, and then a single voice was heard:

> We salute the dead of the World War.
> We salute the victims of labor.
> We salute, above all, the dead of the party struggle.

A hush followed, and then a full chorus and orchestra performed with solemn reverence the old soldier songs "Argonnerwald" and "Ich hatt' einen Kameraden." The crowd was touched and silent as the leaders assembled for the torchlight parade. In a sense they were holy, untouchable, for at this moment they represented the survivors, the men who had come back from the holocaust with a message for all Germans. And in a column of swirling light the evening ended.

It would be possible to suppose that this entire display had been coldly planned by Hitler to achieve the desired emotional response but it seems more likely that the occasion was supremely important for him. Standing with the other veterans of the war and the struggle for power, he could, for the moment, be again "one of seven million." Although he often harked back to the war he was seldom afforded precisely this kind of a setting. Perhaps the Nuremberg Rally was necessary to Hitler for his spiritual (if that is the word) rejuvenation. He could, for a week, give himself up to the pleasures of adulation, displays of power, and the sentimental re-creation of former stages of his life.

Lastly, the rally provided an excellent platform for the delivery of major political addresses. In 1939 Hitler launched one of his most ferocious attacks upon Czechoslovakia from this rostrum. Here before the multitudes of the faithful the national leader was able to express most forcefully the demands of the German state. His role changed from Fuehrer to Reichschancellor for the duration of the speech, though he returned to the more party-oriented pose for the closing ceremonies.

The strains of brutality and sentimentality so closely interwoven in these rallies clearly reflected the character of the party leader. The destructive threat and the creative promise alternated freely during the week, although to the outsider the over-all impression was one of immense and menacing power. In a very real sense the society of Nuremberg, this dream microcosm of the greater society which Hitler was trying to create, was wholly an extension of the man's personality. Unable to fit into ordinary society, he was forced to adjust society to his needs. Perhaps never before had this been done so brutally and successfully as in National Socialist Germany.

The imprint of Hitler on the Third Reich was everywhere visible. The public building style was to his taste. Auschwitz and Treblinka were the terrible reifications of his ideology. The Reich itself had become the great masterpiece dreamed of by the youthful artist. Yet, as the war grew more bitter Hitler dissociated himself from, and finally denied, this society created in his own image and likeness. From 1942 onwards he spent ever greater amounts of time in the sanctuary of his various "wolf" command posts, and during these years he seems to have become wholly destructive in character.

It is in this last period of his reign that Hitler, having lost the power to destroy his enemies, turned on his own people and his own creation. A series of statements and orders dating from the last months of the war show Hitler seriously contemplating the obliteration of the Reich. Though he was not able to accomplish this goal, his orders for a last-ditch stand certainly added much to the ruin of Germany. At last, Hitler could not spare even himself. The wolfish will which finally could achieve power only through senseless destruction was left in the end with but one target—Hitler himself. The repeated urge to reduce himself to anonymity, as characteristic of the Fuehrer as his assertion of uniqueness, now was realized in the most literal manner possible—suicide.

The wolf who had served the artist so well had never recognized him as master. The creative energies of this man, extraordinary as they were in some ways, were never equal to the task of curbing his demonic will to overpower and destroy. Whether things would have ended differently had this not been the case is impossible to tell, for then the projects might never have been launched.

We are left then with the question: wherein lay the attractiveness of this man? Certainly most Germans did follow him—and not through coercion alone. Without doubt naked destructiveness is appealing to some, but not many; nor can the dreams of an ineffectual man rouse great support. However, the volatile compound of artistic vision and destructive force has possibilities for attraction which have been effectively exploited in many eras of history. But perhaps never has this dangerous attractiveness been more convincingly demonstrated than in the unstable German society of the twenties and thirties. In attempting to understand Hitler's political success we have to recognize that he brought hope to millions of people who were not depraved. The hope for a solution to the economic crisis gave Hitler the leadership of a nation that had not bargained for war or for all of the despicable deeds of the Nazi era. One may even wonder to what extent Hitler envisaged the course he was to pursue. It is at least possible to suppose that he himself did not understand fully the savagery of which he was capable.

If this be true, however, it is also an indication of the frailty of his creative impulse and imagination, of the gap that existed between these capacities as measured against his truly monstrous capacities for destruction. For never, so far as we know, did he voice remorse, or even mild surprise. He made a cult of "responsible personality" but created one of the most irresponsible governments in the history of mankind. The lesser officials have transferred the blame to Hitler while he in turn ascribed responsibility to the "forces of nature." This denial of responsibility undercut Hitler's claim to a unique personality and allowed him to slip into that curious anonymity of the great who are everywhere and nowhere, who have overvaulted human limits and in the process have emptied themselves of human qualities, particularly those of pity and responsibility. Aristotle remarked that he who can do without society is either beast or a god. It can be said of Hitler, as it was once said of a Roman emperor, that because he could not become a god he of necessity became a beast.

NOTES

1. Adolf Hitler, *Hitler's Secret Conversations* (New York: Farrar, Straus and Young, 1953), pp. 173–76.

2. His favorite dog, Blondi, was an Alsatian bitch—in German, a *Wolfhund*.

3. One of the interesting vestiges of totemism left in modern society

is the tendency of populations to adorn their heroes and leaders with names drawn from the animal world. The "tiger of France," the "desert fox," the "conquering lion of Judah," and others have all taken their place in the history and folklore of the recent past. Just as interesting as the tendency to bestow these names is the willingness with which they are accepted by the leaders and in some cases even invented by the leader himself. For instance, Teddy Roosevelt's phrase that he was ". . . as strong as a Bull Moose" launched a political party.

4. Again and again in the pages of his *Secret Conversations*, Hitler returns to the artistic theme. At one point he says, "My dearest wish would be to be able to wander about Italy as an unknown painter." One need not take this statement too seriously but it does reflect one of his recurring daydreams. See *Secret Conversations*, p. 10.

5. The question of the artistic worth of the programs launched by the National Socialists may be left aside (although one would suspect that it would be worth serious study). It is quite possible that the various building programs would give the historian some indication of what Hitler's mental picture of the Reich was.

6. August Kubizek, *The Young Hitler I Knew* (Boston: Houghton Mifflin Co., 1955), p. 17.

7. Franz Jetzinger, *Hitler's Youth* (London: Hutchinson and Co., 1958), p. 95. It can also be supposed that this physical change was of the sort that often occurs in adolescence.

8. *Ibid.*, pp. 89–90.

9. The expression is Alan Bullock's.

10. Jetzinger, *op. cit.*, pp. 109–14.

11. See George Orwell, *Down and Out in Paris and London* (New York: Berkley Books, 1959).

12. All of Hitler's biographers readily admit the importance of the Viennese experience, but many of them are also torn by the desire to

prove that this showed Hitler to have been a ne'er-do-well. At a time when other young men were training themselves for a trade, Hitler was doing nothing but idling away his time. One often has the feeling that these writers are somehow angry with Hitler for not having been an ordinary man with ordinary ambitions. Had Hitler, instead of turning to politics, actually developed into an artist of real stature (although there is no reason for believing that such would have been the case), we would in all probability hear much of the rich experiences of the years in Vienna when the young Hitler, behind the mask of apparent inaction, was laying the groundwork for his future triumphs. The dream life that Hitler led in Vienna was important for his future development, so important that one has the impression that, far from being a ne'er-do-well, Hitler hardly wasted a moment of his time.

13. See his remarks in *Mein Kampf* (New York: Reynal and Hitchcock, 1940) and those recorded in *Secret Conversations*.

14. It is doubtful, for instance, that Hitler, with equal facility, could have constructed a philosophy which would have provided a defense for the upper-middle-class society or could have delivered the clarion call for a classless, internationalist society along the lines suggested by Marx. More than the cynical opportunist, Hitler resembles the juvenile delinquent of a later period of the twentieth century. Living in a private world, fantastic, colorful, impassioned, cruel, and superficial, he was able to develop an approach to the problems of society which was at once simple, attractive, and insanely consistent. (On the importance of "insane consistency" see Hannah Arendt, *The Origins of Totalitarianism* (New York: Harcourt, Brace and Co., 1951), pp. 341–43.

15. The remarkable accident which has preserved for us a photograph of Hitler in the cheering crowd gathered in Odeonsplatz to hear the War Proclamation read in August of 1914 may be more than sheer coincidence. That is, it is entirely possible that it is another man or that Hoffman, who took the picture, has doctored it (it will be noted, for instance, that the moustache is different from that which

Hitler wore in the drawing of 1908 and from the one which appears in his wartime photographs). But the fact that this picture, whether real or falsified, was widely reprinted indicates the importance which Hitler attached to the portrayal of himself as one of the anonymous mass, a simple man in the street.

16. See H. R. Knickerbocker, *The German Crisis* (New York: Farrar and Rinehart, Inc., 1932).

17. The Hitler depicted in the *Secret Conversations* is a completely different person than the well-mannered reichschancellor depicted by von Rheinbaben, a man trained in the Hohenzollern court. See Werner Freiherr von Rheinbaben, *Viermal Deutschland* (Berlin: Argon Verlag, 1954), pp. 325–33.

18. It is worth noting, for example, that in the "Hossbach Conference" of November 5, 1937, Hitler treated his military commanders to a supposedly cold-blooded analysis of the world situation in which the Jewish question was not once mentioned. Presumably he realized that these gentlemen would not be impressed by such considerations. International Military Tribunal, *Trial of the Major German War Criminals* (Nuremberg, 1947), XXV, Document 386 ps., 402–13.

19. Karl Wahl, . . . *es ist das deutsche Herz* (Augsburg: In Selbstverlag Karl Wahl, 1954), p. 391.

20. Heinz Guderian, *Panzer Leader* (New York: E. P. Dutton and Co., 1952), Chapter 11.

21. Sir Nevile Henderson, *Failure of a Mission* (New York: G. P. Putnam's Sons, 1940), p. 149.

22. The examples used here are drawn from the 1938 rally. See Nationalsozialistische Deutsche Arbeiterpartei, *Erster Parteitag Grossdeutschlands* (Munich: Franz Eher nachf., 1938).

23. *Ibid.*, p. 79.

II

THE GERMAN REVOLUTION

I

The discussion of recent German history has produced in the past several years two major points of view concerning the determining characteristics of that history. The one viewpoint, held most frequently by non-German historians, contends that because of a variety of defects inherent in her national life Germany has failed conspicuously in the twentieth century to adjust to the demands of democratic, industrialized society. The revolution of 1918 is viewed as either incomplete or inconsequential or as subverted by the various reactionary tendencies in German public life.[1]

The viewpoint held by a large number of Germans emphasizes the *discontinuous* nature of her recent history. The outbreak of World War I, the revolution of 1918, the advent of the Hitler regime, and the collapse of 1945 are each seen as constituting a break with the past so violent as to leave chasms between the periods. (1945, for example, is referred to, with some good reason, as the "Year Zero.") The reasons given for this series of disasters depend to a considerable extent upon the outlook of the various historians. The more nationalistic ones tend to blame outside factors, such as the jealousy of other powers, for Germany's troubles. Others, especially the Left-liberal writers, tend to agree with the non-German writers on the culpability of the conservative forces in German society without, however, condemning the German people as a whole.[2]

There are major difficulties with both of these points of view. The first approach, in attempting to answer the question of "why Germans are that way," has tended to treat as uniquely German things which are not. This is true whether the subject is German political apathy, German nationalism, the authoritarian German home, or the Evangelical church of Germany. By isolating the German problem in such a fashion, sight is lost of the fact that the Germans faced the same problems as the rest of Western society and that many of their solutions to these problems paralleled those used in other states. Secondly, the interpretation favored by so many of the non-German writers tends to gloze over the very real difficulties faced by the German people.

On the other hand, the second approach (that favored by the German writers) tends to raise these difficulties to apocalyptic dimensions. The disasters are treated as being so great as to have destroyed any real continuity between the past and the present. Again, the tendency of these writers, like the non-Germans, is to treat these events as though Germany were an isolated case. Yet it is becoming more obvious every year that the problems cannot be treated in isolation. The fate of Germany and that of Central Europe are closely tied together and perhaps could be considered a special case within the larger framework of Western society.

"What was wrong with Germany" was the same thing that was "wrong" with the rest of Western society. Beginning at slightly different times and proceeding at varying rates of speed, all of the states in this society were becoming industrialized. The impact of this event upon the political possibilities, the military policies, and the social structures of the various states was immense. Among other things, industrialization made the large nation-states of Europe powerful units and then, with the development of ever more powerful and wider-ranging technical devices, robbed these states of their power. The growth of industry certainly does not explain everything—why World War I should occur, why Hitler had certain character traits— but it served to set the stage for the particular events and did much to determine their course.

For Germany it meant that a society which had been largely rural changed in the space of two generations (1871– 1910) to one which was predominantly urban and industrial. The problems occasioned by this change have led many liberal commentators to question whether the Second Empire could have survived even if war had not broken out. Briefly, it is argued that the rising power of the working class was but poorly reflected in the institutions of government. The nobility and the upper middle class dominated the armed forces and the civil ministries while the Reichstag was merely a bit of democratic window-dressing which in actual practice faithfully followed the dictates of this ruling class. The one truly representative party, the Social Democratic party, was steadfastly denied any effective place in government or the armed forces. Given such a situation, it is argued, the probability of revolution grew as the gap between the feudal rulers and the people widened, so that by 1914 probably nothing could have saved the German Empire from the eventual wrath of the populace.[3]

The plausibility of such an argument is considerably less than its popularity in historical circles would lead one to believe. For one thing, it assumes that the conservative classes of Germany were so unbending that they could only break under the strain of change. Yet the evidence of social reform at the national and urban levels under conservative leadership indicates that this class did recognize the problems of change and did adjust to altered conditions. Thus the social insurance legislation of the 1880's and the urban planning and public services of the German cities provided models for reformers throughout the rest of European society.[4]

The political climate of Germany cannot be called "democratic" in this period, but it can only be termed "feudal" by ignoring rather obvious facts. The Reichstag did not have the same powers as the English Parliament, but it did have powers. For example, though the Chancellor was not responsible to the Reichstag he could not, under the Constitution, mistreat it with impunity. Majorities in the Reichstag were carefully cultivated. Important and controversial legislation was carried through that deliberative body only by the exercise of the most skillful politicking as in the case of the Navy bills.[5] It is well to remember that in a number of other "democratic" states of Western society, conservative control was also much in evidence. The power of the English House of Lords was not curtailed until 1911; in France the strength of the conservative groups was well illustrated in the hard-fought Dreyfus affair at the turn of the century. Germany lagged behind these states in the matter of democratic controls, but the lag was one of years, not centuries or even decades.

Finally, it should be noted that a great number of the really astute politicians of the Weimar era came from the ranks of the prewar "conservatives." Rathenau, Erzberger, and, above all, Stresemann, showed qualities of leadership and dedication to the Republic and to democracy clearly as great as that of any of the Social-Democratic politicians and much superior to that of the erstwhile Social Democrat Walter Ulbricht. Even

Hindenburg lent his prestige to the new Republic with apparent sincerity, though perhaps with misgivings. Many of the conservatives were intractable but, had the war not intervened, one may well wonder whether they might not have produced some leaders capable of solving by compromise the difficulties of the German state.

The most urgent problems of the German state and society (other than those of defense) were constitutional reforms in the direction of greater power for the popularly elected Reichstag, firmer control over the actions of the Kaiser, the opening up of governmental and military positions to eligible members of the non-privileged classes, the alteration of the Prussian three-class system of voting, an alteration of the voting districts to reflect the shift from rural to urban society, and legislation to insure a more equitable distribution of the social product. None of these would have been easy of accomplishment, but none of them was impossible through the normal processes of political development. A revolution was not necessary to gain these goals though it would have taken a good deal of hard politicking. At the end no one would have been completely satisfied nor would all of the goals have been completely realized. Class divisions would have remained, though less conspicuously than before. Inequalities of wealth would still have been obvious, though poverty would have been much less of a social problem than at the beginning of the century. We can say these things with some assurance because this is more or less what happened in other industrial states where revolutions did not occur.

If a revolution was not necessary, why did it nonetheless come to this? Such a question can never be fully answered and here it seems that the simplest answer is still in many ways the best. The war created the possibility for revolution, not only in Germany but in the other great states of Central and Eastern

Europe as well. Perhaps it is more correct to say the war *and* the losing of the war created the opportunity. Both seem to have been necessary to the outbreak of revolution: the war for its disruption of society, economic relations, and old certitudes of all sorts; the defeat for its discrediting of the responsible governments. The experience of the twentieth century seems to show that modern governments cannot withstand defeat; in both of the world wars the states which lost have, with some few exceptions, also changed their form of government. This was true in World War I of Germany, Russia, the Ottoman Empire, and Austria-Hungary. In World War II the same thing occurred in Germany, Italy, France, Poland, Hungary, Austria, Rumania, Slovakia, Yugoslavia, Albania, Bulgaria, and Japan. However, in World War II the governments of Norway, Denmark, Finland, The Netherlands, Belgium, Luxembourg, and Greece, almost all of them monarchies, managed to avoid such serious alterations. Apparently the nature of the war has a good deal to do with this rejection of government; in less general conflicts the governments of great states are able to face quite serious disruptions without being destroyed.

There is something very peculiar in all of this: when calculated over a reasonably long period of time (let us say from 1900 to 2000 A.D.) the losses and disruptions of both world wars would appear to be quite slight. In terms of population growth (especially world population), even the great losses of manpower are made to seem trivial. And what is true of manpower is even more true of production capacity. Far from destroying their ability to produce, the states of Europe and Western society stood on the threshhold of their greatest productive age. Yet the peoples of Europe after World War I did not realize this, nor perhaps could they. They had lost a considerable portion of their adult male populations, men in their most productive period of life. They saw many, sometimes all, of the fine but tenuous trade relations destroyed by the war and feared that they could never be reconstituted. The conceptual framework with which they faced the world did not permit them to envision any quick recovery, or possibly any recovery at all. Thus they lashed out at what existed in the hope of creating something different and better. In the victor nations (but not all of them) the forces of stability and tradition were sufficient to contain this reaction. In the defeated nations these forces were undermined by the undesirable outcome of the conflict.

Contributing to this confusion attendant upon the end of World War I was the fact that the war completed the politicizing of the peoples of Western society which had begun with the French and American revolutions over a century previously. In a most drastic manner the war demonstrated to the average man that he had a stake in society, that stake consisting of nothing less than his life.

While it cannot be argued that industrialization was responsible for the democratization of society, it does seem clear that the advances in techniques of communications and political control accompanying that industrialization did make possible the growth of mass participation in the processes of government. Thus, in the twentieth century the opinion of the majority of the entire society, rather than the opinion of a small, politically significant segment, had become important. This is true whether the state in question is truly democratic or totalitarian. Thus Joseph Goebbels, who said that he wanted to see that his message was understood by the "lumberjack in Bad Aibling," was in a peculiar manner as much interested in grass roots politics as many a democratic statesman.[6]

But if the process of democratization was not instituted by industrial society, nevertheless it does appear to be characteristic of this type of society. Too much depends upon the individual for it to be otherwise. Both as producers and consumers the masses of men are necessary in a manner never before envisioned. Militarily, the mass armies of the twentieth century could only be built with the cooperation of the entire society. Even more significant, the entire society is now considered a legitimate target for attack. Such importance could scarcely fail to be registered politically, and in all states of Western society this is just what has occurred. For most of these states World War I proved to be of the greatest importance in this development; in Central and Eastern Europe the war brought revolution.

II

The character of World War I came as a surprise to most people and not least to the generals who directed the battles. Almost without exception those who prepared for the possibility of war expected the offensive to be superior to the defensive. The reasons why this belief was held, as well as why the opposite was true, need not concern us here except to note that the Germans, like the French, expected to win the war in one grand battle. The army leaders thought the war would be short and that it would be decided by the forces of the regular army and the ready reserves without too much dependence upon the masses of the population. The great battles of the fall of 1914 shattered these expectations and decimated the ranks of the regular army and the officer corps. Thus very early in the conflict the officer corps abandoned its pretensions to being the supreme defender of the German nation and called upon all classes of the German population to participate in the struggle.

This is perhaps the true significance of the battle of Langemarck; it demonstrated clearly that warfare in the modern age could not be the private preserve of one class. It also spelled the end of the *Burgfrieden* agreed upon by all parties at the beginning of the war. Under the terms of this "Fortress Peace," Germany was conceived of as a sort of Platonic Republic in which all groups did their part for the victory: the warrior class protected the state, while workers exercised temperance. The artificiality of this concept was made manifest by the sacrifice of the raw regiments in Belgium. It meant that from that time forward more and more units would be composed of laborers and members of the lower middle class, while the officer corps would be more and more an organization of temporary soldiers and wartime volunteers.

In a sense World War I had become a martial Estates General with all of the classes of society being called upon to vote, with their lives if necessary, for the support of the state. In such circumstances it is scarcely surprising that demands for betterment of the political situation should be raised. Even if the war had not broken out the liberal middle class and the Social Democratic working-class parties—which were increasing in size—would have sought greater recognition for some of their most cherished ideals. Pressure to end the Prussian three-class voting system and an alteration of the constitution so as to make the chancellor responsible to the Reichstag could have been expected. In a peaceful atmosphere, a gradualist solution would have been probable—a solution which, though not perfect, would have allowed Germany to complete the transition from an agricultural to an industrial society without the sacrifice of traditional institutions.

The exigencies of war, after the first flush of brotherly feeling between the classes had waned, heightened the tensions surrounding the question of political change. To the newly powerful groups the changes seemed more necessary than ever; to the privileged groups such change seemed to threaten the war effort itself. Since it is always easier to resist change than to implement it, the privileged groups were able to avoid the unpalatable until the last days of the war. In so doing, however, they mortgaged the future by making it dependent upon victory. It is ironic that as the costs of war mounted to the point where it should have been obvious that no victory could justify the losses, it seemed that nothing less than victory was acceptable. Thus in Germany, England, and France, 1916 and 1917, the years of Verdun, the Somme, and Paeschendaele, were also the years when governments pledged to victory assumed control.[7]

The war had generated a spirit of recklessness in the leadership of all the participating states, a spirit which in Germany assumed the form of intransigence towards political change. For Germany it meant that a whole system of government, that of the Second Empire, which had staked its existence on victory, was shattered when that victory could not be attained. The cost of the war called all institutions into doubt with the result that when revolution came in 1918, scarcely anyone was prepared to defend seriously the old regime.

Not all of the contributions to revolution were made by the German statesmen, however. The Allied states, in the prosecution of their war effort, had consciously stimulated revolt in Austria-Hungary and the Ottoman Empire by playing upon the nationalist aims of groups within those countries. In Germany, where such tactics were not feasible, a distinction was made between the people and the government, and between the spirit of Prussianism and Germany's better self.

Until the last days of the war this policy enjoyed no great success, but in October, 1918, when the need for peace was apparent to the German leadership, the policy began to bear fruit. During that month the government of the Second Empire dismantled its military dictatorship and established a constitutional monarchy with a chancellor responsible to the Reichstag. Five years before, this would have been considered a decisive step in the establishment of a democratically oriented government. But the significance of the change was overshadowed by the specter of defeat. Furthermore, the Allied governments, and particularly the United States, seemed bent upon imposing on the German people a republican form of rule. Certainly the apparent delaying tactics of the Wilson administration toward German peace feelers, coupled with Wilson's statements on the subject, can lead observers to this conclusion. Just as certainly, the concept of a German republic had much more support in the United States than it did in Germany where the idea had no wide currency.

Thus Germany entered the final phase of the war with a set of governmental institutions whose foundations had been undermined and found herself pushed (or drifting) towards a form of government which had little support in the popular mind. Skeptical of traditional values; discouraged and desperate at the prospect of defeat; confused, divided, and angry; the German people faced the end of the war. It had been hoped in August, 1914, that the war would unite the disparate elements of German society and solve its differences through action for a common purpose. Far from realizing that hope, the German people, except for their continuing nationalistic fervor, lost much of what unity they had had.

III

The revolution which Germany experienced in the closing days of World War I has so often been described as a failure, or at least incomplete, that it is sometimes the fashion to remark that Germany has never experienced a revolution at all. Such statements as these indicate a frivolous attitude both towards the very serious and deadly business of revolution and towards historical fact as well. If one compares the Germany of our day with the Germany of 1910 the fact of revolutionary change is obvious. The governmental system of 1910 has been destroyed; the aristocratic class so much in evidence in 1910 has been reduced in importance or even entirely disappeared. In the East, a self-proclaimed workers' government gives preferential treatment to the sons and daughters of workers in the universities and in the offices of government. In the West, the working-class share of the national product is greater than at any time in German history. Union members sit on the boards of coal companies, and a large number of leading political figures have working-class or lower-middle-class backgrounds. The fact of vast change is apparent, and it takes a rather special vision to hold that the "same old crowd" rules Germany in the "same old way."

There are a number of features of this change that should be noted. The first is that in West Germany, at least, the old leadership groups have not been eliminated. Thus in business and industry many of the old names remain and this wealthy and powerful upper middle class continues to exercise a great deal of influence. But it does share this control with the other classes of society and it conducts its affairs in a manner quite different from the business community of 1910. Secondly, the changes which are evident have not taken place since 1945 but have been occurring continuously since 1918. Thus the power of the nobility has been shattered by a series of actions which include the revolutionary overthrow of 1918, the purge of the conservative ranks following the July 20, 1944, revolt, and the destruction of the landed estates in the area east of the Elbe since 1945. Similarly, the changes in the economic structure of Germany are the result of a series of grave crises including the inflation of 1919–24, the depression of 1929–33, the economic policies of the Hitler era, the collapse of the spring of 1945, and the currency reform of 1948. It would seem that the changes apparent in today's Germany are the result of a continuing process which began with the revolution (or even before) and to which each subsequent period of German history has made its contribution. In other words, the entire course of German history since 1918 has been revolutionary.

But it is also obvious that not all of the changes have been due to German action. Some have been imposed by outside powers as in the case of the resettlement of German population after World War II, or in the establishment of the two German governments of the present day. Some of the other changes would probably have occurred whether a revolution had taken place or not, such as the new freedom of women, the altered family situation, the continuing transformation of the village, and the gradual disappearance of the family farm.

The unstable European international situation which resulted from World War I and the ensuing peace settlements also contributed to the changes taking place in Germany. The bitterness felt by Germans over the Treaty of Versailles as well as the problems presented by the Balkanization of Eastern Europe would have existed whether there had been a German revolution or not. Lastly, a whole group of changes is due to technical advances in industry and military science which have greatly reduced the importance of European nation-states either as economic or military units. Thus the German revolution has been complicated by revolutionary changes which have occurred throughout Central and Eastern Europe and by a more general set of changes which have affected all of industrial society.

One may object that this presentation confuses change with revolution and that in the German case there is no clear line of revolutionary development such as can be discerned in the

French or Russian revolutions. There is no one great revolutionary party to which one can point, nor has there been a triumph of revolutionary good over reactionary evil. Men have not been dramatically freed from the chains of the past; no goddess of liberty led the Germans to the barricades. In other words, this may have been a revolution but it doesn't look like one. To the romantic worshippers of revolution the German revolution will be forever unsatisfactory, a revolt in which the railroad stations remained uncaptured because the revolutionists did not have their entry tickets.

The unsatisfactory quality of the German revolution leads us back to the question of what revolution is. In its most general sense revolution represents a breakdown in societal consensus. Thus it cannot be sharply distinguished from civil war, although revolution tends to alter society far more fundamentally. This consensus is simply the broad agreement within society upon ends and means. It does not mean that there cannot also be disagreement, or that there cannot be disaffected elements. It does mean that the disagreement will be kept within limits defined by the social order and that the disaffected elements will remain weak enough so as not to disturb the operation of the community. When the consensus breaks down, the society is dissolved into a greater or lesser number of contending elements that must eventually create a new consensus. The process of creating this new consensus may involve a large number of political, economic, and social changes within the society. It may also involve the partial or total destruction of some groups within the society. In striving for the new consensus it may appear to have been achieved only to have it break down again. This is normal, and one might say that the population is experimenting with solutions to its dilemma. It should be noted that the contending factions do not divide themselves neatly into two major groups, the Right and the

Left, as so many studies would have it (so much so, in fact, that the terminology is firmly fixed in our vocabulary of revolutionary analysis). Rather, it is probable that the majority of the contending elements are revolutionary in that they do not want to return to the old *status quo*. They may differ violently about their goals, but the conflict is not a simple two-dimensional one. It may also be assumed that the sum total of these contending elements represents a minority of the population. It is struggling to gain a firm majority to establish a new consensus which will enable the society to function reasonably well even in periods of crisis. To establish such a consensus may take years, even decades, and may involve experimentation with several forms of government along the way.

The end result of all this struggle may be nothing very spectacular; that is, as much might have been accomplished without a revolution. But, just as in the case of war between sovereign states, a great deal of struggle may have to take place in order to gain even the most rudimentary kind of agreement. The re-establishment of a consensus also establishes norms of what is and is not politically, economically, and socially legitimate. Until a consensus is regained the norms are either much broader or nonexistent. To try to label as illegitimate certain groups or points of view in a revolutionary period is usually to assume a set of rules which actually have not been agreed upon.

In the German case, the revolution which broke out in November of 1918 ended the old consensus of German society but certainly did not immediately create a new one. The ease with which the Kaiserreich was tumbled shows the lack of deep popular support for that institution by 1918, and after that date there was no great support for its return. But similarly, the Weimar Republic established in 1919 must be said to have been an experiment, one which was finally rejected. It was not undermined or betrayed because it was never firmly established. It was one of a number of solutions to the breakdown of consensus which struggled for acceptance and which failed in that struggle. This is not to say that the motives of the men of Weimar were not praiseworthy or that the Weimar Republic contributed nothing to the political development of German society. Many of the changes wrought by the Republic have continued in effect, and certainly the years of Weimar fixed the determination of the German people not to return to a monarchy. But when the Weimar Republic was ended through the actions of the Hitler regime, the change did not arouse any great storm of disapproval.

This failure does not show that the Germans lacked "training in democracy." On the contrary, the fourteen years of Weimar and, to a lesser extent, the forty-seven years of the Second Empire had given two generations of Germans a very considerable training in democratic processes. What it does show is that the Germans were not willing to support forever a regime that seemed incapable of solving economic crises or of restoring Germany to a pre-eminent position in the international realm. The Germans may have been wrong in their estimate of the Weimar Republic and were certainly wrong in their evaluation of the Hitler regime, but one can at least understand how a people might develop a distaste for disaster after repeated exposure to it.

The entire history of the Weimar Republic seemed to be one of disaster and disruption. The Armistice, the Treaty of Versailles, the Kapp *Putsch*, the occupation of the Ruhr, the inflation of 1923, and the depression of 1929 all came in too quick a succession to allow the Republic to gain any firm foundation in German national life. To many, the dismal history since 1918 seemed to indicate that the liberal democratic approach offered little hope of solving Germany's difficulties. The election results of the early 1930's, when almost half of the population voted either National Socialist or Communist, indicates how little faith the Germans had by then in the liberal approach. Nor were the Germans by any means unique in this loss of faith, for everywhere in Central and Eastern Europe democratic government, or the semblance of democratic government, was giving way before the demand for strong centralized rule. Even in the firmly established democratic states of the West the 1930's saw a marked trend towards the growth of stronger centralized administrations in an attempt to solve, in a politically acceptable manner, the industrial society's crises.

The Hitler regime presents a most difficult historical problem. Should it be viewed as an essentially counter-revolutionary force or was it the logical culmination of several centuries of German history? Or yet again, should it be viewed as a monstrous aberration, a twelve-year hole in German history? All of these viewpoints have been expressed, but none is especially convincing. The picture of Nazism as counter-revolutionary not only fails to find support in National Socialist statements of intention but also is unsupported by the record of measures taken during the Hitler reign. It is certainly true that the NSDAP was not interested in the same sort of revolution as were the Communists or Social Democrats, but neither was it interested in restoration. In fact, the actions taken during the years 1942–45 in the field of economic controls indicated that it had become, if anything, more radical than ever.[8] During the same period the assaults upon the conservative class, culminating in the reprisals which followed the July 20th revolt, showed little concern for bringing back the good old days. About the other two interpretations little need be said. To place Hitlerism in a sort of historical quarantine by maintaining that it represented a break in German history is simply unacceptable. Hitler did not happen while the Germans were out to lunch. On the other hand, the contention that Nazism was the logical culmination of German development has the same firm foundations as Hitler's view of Jewish history.

This leaves unanswered the question of how an intelligent and usually sober people like the Germans could allow Hitler to come to power. There is implicit in such a question the assumption that no reasonable person could accept the National Socialist regime unless motivated by unworthy intentions. However, such an assumption makes an understanding of the Hitlerian period almost impossible. In order to make any kind of sense of this period it must first be seen that Nazism did seem to present one feasible solution to Germany's difficulties and that during its early years it did bring work and hope to the German people. It is important to remember this because the problems of unemployment and national weakness were uppermost in people's minds. The forbidding qualities of National Socialism could be regarded as aberrations to be overcome rather than integral features of the movement. As to the losses of personal liberty which ensued, it should at least be remembered that in the 1920's and 1930's intellectuals of both the Right and the Left were telling the people of all countries in Western society that these liberties were a sham and that the day of the triumphant individual was past. All too often the only defenders of personal and political liberties were also defenders of what seemed to be a bankrupt political and economic system.

National Socialism did eventually get the enthusiastic support of the majority of the German population, whether or not this was true in 1933. It is doubtful that these supporters approved of all of Hitler's actions, just as it is doubtful that all of the Americans who voted for Roosevelt approved without reservation of the New Deal. The Germans voted (in the plebiscites) for employment, for the recovery of national power, some for the anti-Semitic laws. Perhaps most approval was given the apparent re-establishment of the national community. For a time at least, it seemed that Hitler had re-created the consensus which had disappeared at the end of the war, a task at which the Weimar Republic had failed.

There are a number of indications that the National Socialist regime was a revolutionary one. For one thing, it is quite clear that the leaders had no intention of restoring the Second Empire but wished rather to build a new type of government based upon the leadership of the non-aristocratic classes. In this they were in at least broad agreement with the parties of the Left. They did bring a new class to power: the leadership at the national and regional levels was made up of men from the lower middle class and to some extent the lower class of German society. To call these men outcasts or scum serves only to obscure their origin without admitting the reality of the change that occurred.

Beyond this the National Socialists also carried out a series of attacks, especially during the war years, upon the autonomy of the officer corps. This autonomy, which had been deeply disturbed by the revolution of 1918, was completely shattered by the egalitarianism of the National Socialists and the necessities of World War II. Hitler's hatred for the General Staff certainly contributed much to this movement, as did the reprisals following the July 20th revolt. But the rapid expansion of the Army, the institution of the Waffen-SS, and the rise in prominence of the untraditional Luftwaffe also aided in the downgrading of the Army officer corps.

In a similar manner the power of heavy industry was challenged, first to a minor degree by the establishment of the German Labor Front which at least brought industry under national surveillance, but more importantly by the setting up of the Speer ministry in 1942. Speer, in the process of coordinating production for the war effort, also robbed German industry of its freedom of decision. The history of the Speer ministry is the history of increased planning and the triumph (temporary) of technocrats over businessmen. Whether such arrangements could have survived the war had Germany won is problematical. That they occurred at all is at least an indication of the revolutionary trend in the National Socialist movement.

In several areas the National Socialists continued the revolutionary trend begun in 1918, though in apparent opposition to the movement. They continued to work for the displacement of the old ruling classes in civil and military life. They completed the process (for a time) of breaking down the semi-autonomous positions of the provinces (a process probably begun with Bismarck's creation of the Second Empire). They brought the economy under greater national control than it had ever known. Finally, they were almost successful in the attempt to create a new consensus.

The other accomplishments of the National Socialist regime are, of course, more memorable, and some of them are infinitely despicable. They did prove, in a most drastic manner, that the national states of Europe were no longer viable political and military entities. Hitler found, at an early stage of the war, that he could no longer solve his problems on a national but only on a continental basis. One of the most important results of his effort is that he did shatter those pretensions to international prominence which had lingered in the European states after World War I. He also showed how barbarous modern states can be. Unfortunately, his method of demonstration was so singular as to obscure the fact that other states were also capable of great barbarity, that in fact this barbarity might be an integral part of modern civilization.

So Hitlerism collapsed and with it, for a time, the German state. But the temporary dissolution did not bring the German revolution to an end. During the pause that followed the defeat, a number of Germans addressed themselves to the task of reassessing the position of Germany and of carrying forward the revolution. Perhaps misled by the completeness of the collapse, they tended to act and to speak as though all routes were open to them.[9] For several reasons, this was not the case. The influence of the occupying powers could scarcely be avoided, and it became evident by 1947 that Germany was being torn apart by the cold war. Furthermore, it was also becoming evident that the collapse had not been so complete as to wipe out the various groupings of German society. Thus old political parties, old companies, and old classes rose again as the Germans gradually regained their footing. In the East, the Socialist revolution triumphed with the heavy-handed aid of the Russian occupying armies. The nationalization of industry and the collectivization of farming were begun with loud fanfare and somewhat less impressive results. In the West, an economy based on private enterprise and backed by American encouragement and investment achieved amazing results, though public welfare and other civic programs tended to receive short shrift.[10]

Thus at the present time the German revolution has become polarized into two camps: one that is totalitarian and socialist, and the other democratic and conservative. Both represent a very considerable change from the Germany of 1910, yet neither satisfies all of the aspirations of the German people. This is particularly and acutely the case in regard to German national feeling; yet, given the international situation, it seems unlikely that either the Bundesrepublik or the D.D.R. can do much to solve the problem. In some ways the development of the two sections of Germany has been quite similar—a fact obscured by the ideological differences between them. The mechanization of agriculture and the disappearance of the small farmer is being accomplished on both sides of the Elbe. The authoritarian home has been replaced by a more democratic family complete with working mothers. Presumably something approaching the mass consumption pattern of West Germany will one day appear in the East, though it does not exist at the present time. In other words, the specifically German revolution has become merged with the more general change in industrial society. This is, in fact, so much the case that German problems can no longer be solved on a national basis but only on a Europe-wide basis. The German leadership in the Common Market, the pressure for a European political union—all indicate that this is the conclusion of many, though not all, West German leaders.

What had been implicit since before World War I has now become manifest: the day of the European nation-state is past. For military and industrial reasons it is no longer a feasible unit, though politically it commands more emotional response than any other sovereign form. The German revolution can be seen as an attempt to solve within this no longer feasible framework the problems of industrial society. In the process the Hitlerian rule became a European reign of terror and demonstrated clearly the weakness of all these states. This at least can be said of Hitler: he cleared the way for larger political groupings by turning the German revolution into a European one.

NOTES

1. The best summary of the literature and the various arguments is contained in Andrew G. Whiteside, "The Nature and Origins of National Socialism," *Journal of Central European Affairs*, April, 1957, pp. 48–73. Also of interest are such works as Edmond Vermeil, *L'Allemagne Contemporaine* (Paris: Aubier, 1953) ; Hermann Mau and Helmut Krausnick, *Deutsche Geschichte der juengsten Vergangenheit. 1933–1945* (Stuttgart: J. B. Metzlersche Verlags-

buchhandlung, 1953) ; Golo Mann, *Deutsche Geschichte des Neunzehnten und Zwanzigsten Jahrhunderts* (Frankfurt/M.: S. Fischer Verlag, 1958) ; Friedrich Meinecke, *The German Catastrophe* (Cambridge: Harvard University Press, 1950) ; and William L. Shirer, *The Rise and Fall of the Third Reich* (New York: Simon and Schuster, 1961).

2. See, for instance, Michael Freund, "Geschichte ohne Distanz," *Deutscher Geist zwischen Gestern und Morgen* (Stuttgart: Deutsches Verlags Anstalt, 1954), p. 315.; Werner Freiherr von Rheinbaben, *Viermal Deutschland* (Berlin: Argon Verlag, 1954) ; Erich Eyck, *Geschichte der Weimarer Republik* (Stuttgart: Eugen Rentsch Verlag, 1954).

3. See Carl Schorske, *German Social Democracy* (Cambridge: Harvard University Press, 1955) ; Rudolf Coper, *Failure of a Revolution* (Cambridge: At the University Press, 1955).

4. Frederick C. Howe, *European Cities at Work* (New York: Charles Scribner's Sons, 1913) ; ———, *Socialized Germany* (New York: Charles Scribner's Sons, 1915).

5. Admiral von Tirpitz, *My Memoirs* (New York: Dodd, Mead and Co., 1919).

6. To a cultivated Rhinelander, resident in Berlin, Bad Aibling (a town located close to the Bavarian Alps) had about the same connotations as Dogpatch has for Americans.

7. In England, the government of Lloyd George; in France, that of Clemenceau; in Germany, the military dictatorship of Hindenburg and Ludendorff.

8. There was a marked tendency for the Speer ministry to take control of industry away from the hands of the individual owners and managers and to place whole industries under the direction of state officials for the purpose of achieving maximum production. Many of these changes are traced in the various reports published by

the United States Strategic Bombing Survey. An excellent short study of the development of the German economy during these years (based largely upon the Strategic Bombing Survey) is to be found in Sir Charles Webster and Noble Frankland, *The Strategic Air Offensive Against Germany, 1939–1945* (London: Her Majesty's Stationery Office, 1961), I, 271–83, 473–92; II, 224–43; III, 207–82.

9. See, for instance, the selection of articles taken from the newspaper *Der Ruf* published in 1946–47 under American Occupation Authority in: Hans Schwab-Felisch (ed.), *Der Ruf. Eine deutsche Nachkriegszeitschrift* (Munich: Deutscher Taschenbuch Verlag, 1962).

10. See Hans Werner Richter (ed.), *Bestandsaufnahme* (Munich: Kurt Desch Verlag, 1962). Section III, "Wirtschaftliche und Soziale Wandlungen."

III

WARRIOR AND WORKER

I • POLITICAL STEREOTYPES

It is a difficult thing for a man to be himself. The pressures of society and his own desires drive him to assume poses and to play roles which he finds not always agreeable, and even when they are agreeable these poses may be only tenuously connected with the individual's innermost character. This situation is perhaps lamentable, but it does have the advantage of enabling us to orient ourselves in society. One would scarcely know how to react, for instance, if confronted by a funeral director with the boisterous mannerisms of a carnival barker. We move from place to place in our daily affairs, acting various roles, submerging various aspects of our personalities, meeting others who are doing the same thing, and somehow society operates a bit more smoothly thanks to the saving grace of small hypocrisies.

While a man assumes different roles, he will find that to some extent his actions are stereotyped. Administrators act like administrators, students like students, professors like professors, and soldiers like soldiers. At the same time, within the limits of the major role which a man plays there is room for variation according to personal taste and the audience for which he is playing.

The roles created by society are greatly useful, of course. They establish norms of action which aid men in their daily affairs. One might even doubt that society could operate without them. Furthermore, the roles in a relatively stable society mesh with one another to form a more or less unified whole. Since this is the case, it must be recognized that no society can allow an infinite number of stereotypes to be generated (otherwise they would not be stereotypes), for not all are useful or even endurable to a given society. Secondly, as society changes, the sterotypes will also undergo either gross or subtle changes. One could study the alterations in the figure of the American pioneer as the United States has moved from the old to the new frontier. Lastly, no two societies possess exactly the same set of stereotypes even though broad similarities may be noted.

Usefulness, however, does not mean that the stereotypes correspond only to existing roles within the society, for we are all aware of a number of stereotypes which exist only as societal dreams. In the United States at the present time, the plethora of TV frontier marshals and the screen persona of many a Hollywood star could be included in this category. The meaning of the cowboy may be difficult to assess, but the many "fast-draw clubs" and the not inconsiderable number of injuries resulting from this form of exercise attest to the importance of this figure.

Another form of the dream stereotype is that which is politically useful. The sturdy, independent yeoman farmer, backbone of democracy and sword and shield of the Republic, has existed for some time now only in the rhetoric of politicians. The "average man," John Q. Public, is another such figure, sympathetic though not particularly heroic. Such figures express certain longings of society: longings to be beautiful and loved, to be brave and true, to take the correct and decisive action, to be feared and listened to. If Matt Dillon expresses the quixotic hope of American men for romantic, self-expressive action, then John Q. Public is a latter-day Sancho Panza speaking home truths to the great or would-be great. That, as depicted in the newspapers, he more often rides an elephant than a donkey is a matter of minor importance.

Rooted in the society which generates them, these dream stereotypes live through the identification made with them by society's members. If the roles which men must play can be considered a sort of elaborate masquerade, then the dream stereotypes constitute a secret swindle of society in which a prosaic outward appearance masks a Lone Ranger, a Robin Hood, a Cyrano, or a Goetz von Berlichingen. That it is also a swindle of the self is certainly true and is even humorously recognized by the acclaim accorded to such figures as Walter Mitty or that ever-popular character, the confidence man.

The dream stereotype has at times assumed great political importance. Usually this occurs when a sufficiently large number of members of the society have participated in a venture which has about it the trappings of heroism. Veterans' organizations are an outstanding example of this phenomenon. Established to keep alive memories of some past conflict and to serve liquor in otherwise dry counties, these clubs aid in building a standardized view of what the war was about and what the men were like who fought in it. The veterans' groups in both the North and the South after the American Civil War had immense political power and, especially in the South, built a romantic myth of the nature of the struggle.

If, in a stable society, the dream stereotypes serve as an escape hatch or as a vehicle for certain interest groups, their function in a disrupted society is even more important. In societies which have been overturned, the ordinary roles may be discarded or fall into disrepute and room is left open for the dream stereotypes to come to the surface and to play a dominant role in public affairs. Thus, in the aftermath of successful revolutions, one may find a great many people playing revolutionary roles while the ordinary work of society is neglected. This was the case in the French, the Russian, and, most recently, the Cuban revolutions. During such a period, society's structure is being readjusted to the fact of revolution and the necessary roles are being re-created in the revolutionary image. The heroic figure of the revolutionary, the triumphant figure of the worker, and the new institutions which have been created all strive to make their impression upon society permanent and, in so doing, build a new society.

In Germany, following the revolution of 1918, no figures were more important than the soldier and the working man. Both had their heroic and tragic elements. Both, through the events of world war and revolution, had been freed from their prosaic and subordinate roles in society and had become apotheosized in the figures of the Warrior and the Worker. As idealized types, larger than life, they dominated the thinking of postwar Germany and, when captured by a political party, as they were by the National Socialists, they proved to be attractive to large numbers of citizens.

The stereotypes of the warrior and the worker as they appeared in 1918 were not yet completely usable for the purposes of the National Socialists. The figure of the warrior was still raw and unformed. The figure of the worker had for too long been a prop of the Marxist parties. In 1918 they were images of anger and rebellion; by the 1930's they had become useful and attractive fictions for the cause of Adolf Hitler. This work of transformation was carried out by a number of persons and groups, many of them without connection to the National Socialist party.

II • THE WARRIOR

The political importance of the figure of the warrior to the Third Reich is undeniable. Both the SA and the SS played heavily on the fact that they were the successors to the frontline fighter of the war, and much of the pageantry at Nuremberg revolved about this figure of the veteran. Hitler too lost no opportunity to remind his listeners that he was one of these millions of veterans. As an implement for evoking popular emotions, this figure was probably unsurpassed. His experience seemed unique, yet millions of men had shared it, and millions of others would share it vicariously in books and movies. The warrior was also a tragic figure—he alone of all the actors in the tragedy of the Second Reich remained truly heroic. Thus, while generals and statesmen were quietly forgotten, the figure of the *Frontkaempfer* was held constantly before the public eye in speeches, books, and monuments to the dead. In time, the figure would have lost its painful immediacy as the memories of the war receded, but the outbreak of the Second World War brought a revival of the figure, a cheapened version which in the manner of bad movies might be called "The Son of *Frontkaempfer.*"

The figure of the front-line fighter did not exist in 1914 when the war began, and only gradually did it assume the characteristics which would later become so familiar. In fact, it was not until well into the 1920's that the stereotype was finally completed. The figure owes something, although not a great deal, to German military tradition. If the writers who built the stereotype praised Prussian steadfastness, they were less than ecstatic about parade-ground discipline, and the concept of unswerving obedience to the will of the Emperor was almost never mentioned.

The image of the warrior owes much more to certain strands of prewar middle-class attitudes and to the perception of the impact of technology upon modern life. The romanticism and idealism of the German youth movement seem to have had a great influence upon the emerging stereotype, as did the prewar dream of a community not torn by internal divisions. In the *Frontkaempfer* the old nature romanticism, the distrust of rationalism, the rebelliousness of youth, and the hope for an idyllic community were melted together with the concept of the technologically competent barbarian to create a wholly new figure. The *Frontkaemper* did not have two souls in his breast, but the unity which he represented was the destructive unity of the oak and the powersaw.

The full development of the image of the front-line fighter required three stages: (1) the first great attacks, (2) the period of trench warfare, and (3) the homeward march of 1918.[1] In each of these phases, a part of the complete stereotype was established and each succeeding phase tended to modify the characteristics previously worked out. The completed stereotype was a tragic and angry figure capable of molding the future. Beginning in 1915, it took almost fifteen years to complete this process, after which, for the next fifteen years, the stereotype did yeoman work in the service of National Socialism, although in the process it became trivialized and lost most of the finer qualities it had once possessed.[2]

Phase 1 • THE OPENING BATTLES

In his excellent short story, "Wir fordern Reims zur Übergabe auf," Rudolf Binding tells of a small group of men under the leadership of a Prussian captain detailed to demand the surrender of the fortress of Reims. The story captures the flavor of high-spirited adventure, and even haphazardness, of the early days of the war with its mixture of modern techniques and outworn attitudes. Through a series of misadventures, the men remain in French hands for a month and only return after the battle of the Marne. But by then the war has changed so much in character that it scarcely seems possible that they could actually have demanded the surrender of so mighty a city as Reims.[3] In miniature, Binding has outlined the entire experience of the opening battles in which the high purposes of the first days were drowned in the bitter engagements which finally led to a stabilization of the front. The memories of this vast welling up of national enthusiasm remained, as a reminder of the bright world which perished in the flames of war, long after the enthusiasm itself was gone.

It is scarcely possible for us, living in a world which has given terrible meaning to such names as Verdun, Auschwitz, and Hiroshima, to understand the joy and idealism with which the people of Europe greeted the outbreak of World War I. Yet even such a sober historian as Friedrich Meinecke harks back to the August days as "one of the most precious memories . . . of the highest sort."

> All of the rifts which had hitherto existed in the German people, both within the bourgeoisie and between the bourgeoisie and the working classes, were suddenly closed in the face of the common danger which snatched us out of the security of the material prosperity that we had been enjoying. And more than that, one perceived in all camps that it was not a matter merely of the unity of a gain-seeking partnership, but that an inner renovation of our whole state and culture was needed. We generally believed . . . that this had already commenced and would progress further in the common experiences of the war. . . .[4]

To the Germans, the French, and the English, it seemed as though an opportunity had been given them to make a new beginning, to enjoy a rebirth through the cleansing experience of war. It may well be, as Jules Romains holds, that boredom with the circumscribed life in bourgeois society played a large part in the enthusiastic reception accorded to the outbreak of the war.[5] It was boredom with a life in which all of the courses seemed to have been charted, in which, from birth to death, all of the steps in a man's life were carefully laid out for him.[6] But with boredom were mingled rebelliousness and actual hatred towards the prewar society. These attitudes were, of course, prominent in the working-class movements of the prewar era with their emphasis on class warfare and the dream of the general strike. But hatred and rebellion were expressed by other groups as well. Much of the pre-1914 artistic endeavor could well be considered an art of hatred and even destruction. To be sure, it was a work of demolition aimed at clearing the way for new forms of expression; but it was destructive as well as creative. The attitude of the *Wandervogel* movement also reflects this spirit of dissatisfaction so prevalent in prewar Europe.

> The German Youth Movement erupted like a great phenomenon of nature. Out of unsuspected depths leapt forth defiance, hate, yearning, love, all the hopes and fears that for decades had been repressed, denied, forcibly sublimated. The movement was spontaneous, translating sentiment directly into action, with thought as a kind of intermittent and subordinate guide.[7]

Beginning in the late 1890's in the Berlin suburb of Steglitz, the movement spread rapidly to other large cities in the first decade of the twentieth century.[8] It was predominantly an urban movement and specifically a movement of *Gymnasium* and, to a lesser extent, *Realschule* students. Thus, at no time can it be said that the *Wandervogel* encompassed anything like a majority of the German youth.[9] Its point of departure was a rebellion against the classical German educational system which, it insisted, fettered the mind and body of youth. "The professor is the German national disease. . . . The present German educational system is nothing less than a slaughter of the innocents," Julius Langbehn had written in 1890, and his book, *Rembrandt als Erzieher*, became a sort of manual for the early *Wandervogel* movement.[10]

What the youth movement wanted was a closer contact with nature, not in the sense of scientific study but rather in the form of a mystical group experience. It was felt that this could be achieved by the organization of small groups of youths dedicated to exploring the natural beauties of the countryside in journeys which often lasted for weeks. In their wanderings through the forests of Germany, at their great communal fires, in the comradeship of the group, in their freedom from parental and official supervision, boys from the great cities felt that they were discovering their own souls and the "German Soul." Great emphasis was placed upon the collection of folk songs, the cult of the naked body, and abstinence from alcohol. All of these were considered as natural and untainted by the artificialities of Wilhelminian society. The friendships formed in the light of the great fire seemed somehow deeper, even transcending the bounds of mere fellowship into a union, called by Hans Blueher, *Freundesliebe*.[11]

Blueher, the early historian of the movement, says that the typical member of the *Wandervogel* was a mixture of German student, medieval wandering scholar, and thief.[12] The groups seem to have been patterned after the bands of wandering scholars, as the original name of the group leader, "Bachant," indicates.[13] The identification with the thief, at least to the extent of adopting the slovenly dress of thieves and employing their argot,[14] is of interest since it parallels a fascination shown by so much of European society in the twentieth century for these outcasts.[15] Thus the freedom desired by the members of the German youth movement was defined by its opposition to the values of middle-class industrial society. This does not mean that the boys severed their relations with that society, but rather that they were laying the foundations for its redefinition.

A number of the concepts of the movement were carried into the German army by the generation that fought the war. Among the most important of these was the concept of leadership by "personalities," the concept of *Freundesliebe* as the closest of all bonds, and the concept of the antithesis between nature and the artificiality of civilization. None of these ideas was originated by the German youth movement but all were intensified and made more general by that experience. The four years of warfare served to further intensify and alter these concepts so that in the end the figure of the wandering student-scholar-thief became subsumed in the new figure of the *Front-kaempfer*. The "personality" who leads by force of character appears first as a "Bachant," later as a storm troop leader in the war, and finally in the figure of Adolf Hitler.[16] *Freundesliebe* was translated into the *Kameradschaft* of the war and National Socialist eras, while the antithesis between nature and civilization was reconciled in the figure of the technically competent modern barbarian.

Wracked by internal quarrels and charges of homosexuality, the *Wandervogel* managed, nevertheless, to spread its influence widely before the war. In doing so, it may have lost some of its original spontaneity as its leadership was taken over more and more by the very professors against whom the rebellion had been launched.[17] But in spite of its many problems and failings, there was much that was undeniably attractive about this prewar movement. The independence shown by the German youth stands in marked contrast to the youth movements of many other countries. Nor can the mystical sensitivity towards nature or the inflated idealism of the movement be wholly condemned because of the later perversion of these attitudes. The simple fact is that at a crucial stage in the development from boyhood to manhood the *Wandervogel* movement provided a largely healthy outlet for youthful instincts.

The war was seen not so much as a drastic interruption in the normal affairs of men but as a release from the burdens of ordinary life. Young men in each of the warring nations crowded eagerly around the recruiting stations; they did march away decked with flowers, and they did sing happily as their troop trains rolled towards the front. All of this seems incredible to us, and it even seemed incredible to them at a later date in the war. Yet incredible or not, it was treasured and remembered as an age of innocence by the survivors. It was redolent of an enthusiastic idealism which was proof against cynicism. The student regiments at Langemarck rushing forward against enemy bullets "with the *Deutschlandlied* on their lips" remained a precious memory in later years, and for the stereotype of the *Frontkaempfer*, the vision of these regiments became one of the foundation stones.[18] The warrior had to learn how to handle himself in the presence of machine-gun and artillery fire; he might never sing, and the *Deutschlandlied* might change to an animalistic growl, but the spirit of the students at Langemarck remained. It was, of course, not only the students who fought and died, but since they were the articulate ones, they were more often remembered.[19]

The image of the pure young idealist was finally fixed by Walter Flex in the person of Ernst Wurche, the hero of his *Der Wanderer zwischen beiden Welten*.[20] Wurche was the archetypal *Wandervogel* in field gray. An officer, a student of theology, he carried copies of Goethe's poems, *Zarathustra*, and the New Testament in his knapsack, retained his sunny disposition under all difficulties, was beloved by all, and died secure in his idealism.[21] We are to understand that Wurche is the ideal type of leader, one who understands his men and who has the depth of character necessary to win their respect.[22] Wurche has firm ideas about leadership and feels that it is necessary to know more than how to die in order to be a leader of soldiers.[23] By the end of the book, Wurche, though dead, has emerged as that old *Wandervogel* ideal of the "personality" as leader.

Flex's vision is essentially adolescent. The purity of which he speaks is of a type and simplicity which commends itself to YMCA leaders; the idealism was the narrow idealism of nationalism and the even older aristocratic ideal of "wearing the king's coat." There is more than a faint aroma of boys' magazine literature about the *Wanderer*, and one may even detect the literary equivalent of locker-room fanny slapping. Nevertheless, there is an undeniable charm about Flex's writing in that he was able to preserve unsullied this adolescent approach even after three years of fighting. It is a refreshing change from the pseudo-toughness and cynicism of more recent war novels. As he said in a letter shortly before his death in 1917, "I believe that the German spirit in August, 1914, reached a height such as no other people has ever seen before. Happy is he who stood on this peak and has not found it necessary to descend." [24]

One of the most notable features of *Der Wanderer* is the fascination which Flex shows for nature. There was nothing specifically new in this nature romanticism, and Flex's relationship with the prewar *Wandervogel* certainly predisposed him in this direction. Perhaps it sounds odd to the modern ear that in a book devoted to war experiences the author should spend so much time eliciting the joys of the natural world. The "wandering army of wild geese" inspired him to write a poem in which he equates the grey army of wild geese with the Kaiser's grey army moving relentlessly towards its goal.[25] The world is filled with color, light and shadow, golden sandy shores of lakes, and dark green mysterious forests; red and blue flowers, untrammeled by war, bloom before the trenches.[26] The relationship with nature which the warrior felt was already present in the writings of Flex, although it was not yet as intimate as it would become, nor had the natural setting as yet become distorted by the actions of war.

The book is an elegy written with the tenderness of love and marks the carrying over of the *Wandervogel* concept of *Freundesliebe* into the war situation. The relationship between Wurche and Flex points towards the developing ideal of *Kameradschaft* but is both less utilitarian and less communal than the later friendship pattern. Flex's attitude toward Wurche is essentially based upon the character of Wurche and not upon the situation in which they find themselves. The fact that they are at the front does not obliterate for them the existence of the rest of German society or their ties to it. Nor do the units of which they are a member play more than an auxiliary role; the friendship is essentially a private one based on common background, though it marks a transition from friend to comrade.

There are several characteristics of the image of the *Frontkaempfer* which emerge during this first period of the war. He is a national and cultural idealist concerned for the preservation of both his fatherland and Western culture. As such, he goes into battle singing the national anthem and carrying copies of Goethe's poetry in his *Tornister*. Because he is an idealist he is also a volunteer. The *Kriegsfreiwillige* appears again and again among the leading figures of the war writings; conscription is scarcely mentioned. Often he is an officer or an officer-aspirant.[27]

Thus the major figures in this war literature do not stem from a wide range of backgrounds but are, almost to a man, from the professional and business classes. They have *Gymna-*

sium or even university training and are normally of urban origin. The figure of the *Frontkaempfer*, as developed in the German war literature, is then largely a result of the educated and articulate minority writing about itself. Members of the other classes appear on stage but largely for the purpose of adding a colorful Bavarian accent, bucolic steadiness, or mechanical proficiency to the scene. In these dramas of war the masses are largely relegated to walk-on parts.[28]

The experience of the war enhanced the urban soldier's already considerable appreciation for nature. The attitude expressed towards nature is almost mystical, and this relationship between man and nature remained one of the most important elements in the image of the front-line fighter, though the character of that relationship changed profoundly as the war progressed.

The ties between man and man, the comradeship of brothers-in-arms are present although they do not yet have the overwhelming importance that they assume at a later period of the war. That is, ties between comrades have not yet become more important than ties with other individuals, or with family, homeland, or the army command. Thus a whole network of relationships scarcely visible later in the war are still prominent in the early stages of the conflict.

Phase 2 • TRENCH WARFARE

In the West, the war of movement came to an end in November, 1914, when the opposing armies reached the English channel and found themselves with no room left for maneuver. No one expected the position warfare which ensued to be more than a temporary situation. That it should last three years and assume the characteristics of a siege was unthinkable. The nations did realize that the tremendous expenditure of men and materials in the earlier battles necessitated an effort of much greater dimensions than had been contemplated, and it was seen that war between industrialized states might be a very different thing than the traditional modes of warfare. At the front, life in the trenches became an orderly routine while the trenches themselves were extended and elaborated. Positions were stamped with names reminiscent of home as men accustomed themselves to the fact that the war was going to last much longer than they had expected in August. Later, this first period of trench warfare (December, 1914–spring, 1916) was looked back upon with a feeling akin to nostalgia: "The struggle had not yet taken on that grim and mathematical aspect which cast over its landscapes a deeper and deeper gloom." [29] But this was also the period in which it was seen with growing clarity that the war was turning into one of attrition. The Allied failures at Loos and in the Champagne were but preludes to the gigantic slaughters of 1916.

One gathers the impression that the trench system which clamped an iron hand on strategic possibilities also established itself among the soldiers as a way of life with all of the routine inherent in daily living. The men soon accustomed themselves to its pace—the placing of morning outposts, repair of trench areas destroyed by the previous day's shell fire, tours of guard, and, in the fetid dugouts, the interminable letter writing and card games; at night, listening patrols, wire repair, and sleep. Fear and boredom, the *lares* and *penates* of the battlefield, fixed the bounds of this existence still connected by innumerable strands to that other life of the rear areas, of the time of peace.

But as the war progressed, as the intensity of the artillery preparations increased and the battles became more insane in their savageness and waste, the conflict seemed to assume new dimensions. *Vernichtungskrieg* or *Materialschlacht* are the appellations assigned by the German writers to this later stage of the struggle. The battles of Verdun and the Somme mark the turning point. At the height of these great battles the trench systems broke down and the front lines became merely a series of shell holes held by isolated groups of men. A new world was created, a world of lunar landscapes.[30] Under the impact of the drum fire the old connections with civilian life were severed. Loyalty to comrades replaced love of homeland as a sustaining force in soldierly life; the values of civilization gave way to the utilitarian values of the zone of war. Even hatred failed; fatalism and an understanding of the common destiny of soldiers were its heirs.

Quite understandably, men being crushed under the weight of unprecedented bombardments and living in constant danger from one or another machine of modern warfare were impressed by the importance of technology. It seemed, in the static conditions prevailing on the Western Front, that technology had taken precedence over strategy. The machine gun, barbed wire, the howitzer, and the modern rifle had all helped to make offensive strategy ineffective. Cavalry was shattered by modern weapons and the only alternative seemed to be the employment of masses of infantry and artillery in an attempt to smash the enemy front. For three years this method proved disastrously inadequate. At Loos, in 1915, General French's army was broken; in the Champagne, the French lost eighty thousand men in each of two offensives. In 1916, German losses at Verdun and British losses on the Somme approached the half million mark, with the defenders in each case losing as many men. In 1917, the British lost another three hundred and seventy thousand men at Paeschendaele under conditions which, even for the Western Front, were incredible. Weaponry had robbed the generals of any freedom, with the result that they could only try to solve their problems by increasing the number of men and machines employed at any given point. Finally, abandoning hope for a breakthrough, many of them began to think in terms of attrition, that is, of forcing the enemy to sacrifice more men and more equipment than he could afford. In the American Civil War the Army of the Potomac had used this tactic against Lee; now both the German and the Allied commanders found themselves apparently forced to resort to its use.[31]

From the point of view of many a postwar observer the war had reached a stage where it had become a process over which the commanders had no real control. Jules Romains presents us with a picture of generals who were able to predict accurately the average costs of the struggle and to adjust their demands for men and materiel accordingly, but who were able neither to stop the process nor really to control its outcome.[32] A German writer stated simply, "War was no longer led, it was administered." [33]

The Western Front became a world unlike anything else that existed. Its landscape, formed by the machines of war, was a poisonous waste of denuded forests, polluted streams, and fields torn by innumerable shellings. Strewn across its surface was the wreckage of war—dead villages, dead machines, dead animals, and, everywhere, dead men. Yet the realm of war was peopled by millions of men living in intricate cities located just below the surface of the earth. Barbed wire bounded two contesting communities and the moon world of no-man's-land lay in between. This six-hundred-mile battlefield was in a sense isolated from the rest of the human community, a "monastery with walls of flame," [34] and men entering it severed their relations with the world from which they had come.

> The communications between the troops and the staff, between the artillery and the liaison officers were utterly crippled by the terrific fire. Dispatch carriers failed to get through the hail of metal, and telephone wires were no sooner laid than they were shot into pieces. Even light signalling was put out of action by

the clouds of smoke . . . that hung over the field of battle. There was a zone of a kilometer behind the front where explosives held absolute sway.[35]

Yet for all of its strangeness, terror, and isolation, there was something oddly familiar about the front. This world was a machine, a factory—the darkest and most satanic mill that the world had ever seen. It was truly an exact reflection of twentieth-century industrial civilization. Later writers treated the powers acting upon the soldiers as mechanical, often showing little regard for the actual constitution of these powers. Erich Maria Remarque says, "The front is a cage . . . we lie under a network of arching shells." [36] Ernst Juenger speaks of "the rolling mill of war." [37] Others speak of the war as a "murder machine," [38] or compare the labor of war to factory work [39] and speak of men vastly overshadowed by materiel.[40] Juenger sums it up in one longer passage:

> The modern battlefield is like a huge sleeping machine with innumerable eyes and ears and arms lying hidden and inactive, ambushed for the one moment upon which all depends. Then from some hole in the ground a single red light ascends in a fiery prelude. A thousand guns roar out on the instant and at a touch, driven by innumerable levers, the work of annihilation goes pounding on its way.
> Orders fly like sparks and flashes over a closed network, spurring on to heightened destruction in front and bringing . . . a steady stream of fresh men and fresh materials to fling into the flames. Everyone feels that he is caught in a vortex which drags him on with unrelenting precision over the brink of death.[41]

To the generation which fought the war the battlefield may well have seemed like a machine, though the present-day observer is probably more impressed by the relative scarcity and primitive quality of the machines employed. It is well to remember that the writers were not reporting exactly what they saw but were creating a vision of the front which was integrally related to their vision of twentieth-century civilization and constituted a devastating critique of that civilization. The images which emerged of both the battlefield and men were artistic creations that became fixed in the minds of the members of postwar German society. Of these writers, the two most important were Ernst Juenger and Erich Maria Remarque. Juenger especially, during the twenties, grappled with the problems of the war experience in a series of books and long essays that may well be the best works to emerge from the First World War. His *Storm of Steel* and his *Der Kampf als inneres Erlebnis* seem to have been particularly influential. Remarque's best work, *All Quiet on the Western Front*, appeared at the end of that decade and immediately received acclaim. Curiously, though the two writers were almost diametrically opposed in their view of war, their metaphors and images of the battlefield and the soldier are almost identical. Both were concerned to establish the relationship of the soldier to technology, although this is only made explicit in Juenger's work, and both also explored the relationship between the soldier and nature. Nature, as we have seen, was also treated by Walter Flex; but both Juenger and Remarque deal with a nature transformed by war and technology which Flex did not know. The other writers quoted here seem to follow the lead of Juenger in these matters, and it is of special interest to note how often Adolf Hitler deals with parallel themes in *Mein Kampf*.

A crucial question was how men could adjust to the inhuman regimen of the front. Did they have to be driven insane, as was the narrator of *Trommelfeuer* who as his artillery battery is pounded into the earth has a vision of an enormous Christ coming down off the cross and stamping his creatures to death? [42] Most men, of course, did not become insane, but the writers, in attempting to explain how men endured, did conclude that a number of radical changes occurred in their personalities. To some extent men fitted themselves to life in this death factory by becoming machines themselves. "There are no men here, only a totality, a wonderful, self-operating, self-contained machine" writes the author of *Wir von der Somme*.[43] Friedrich Georg Juenger speaks of the collapse of individualism,[44] while Erich Maria Remarque presents us with the following picture:

> The column marches on, straight ahead, the figures resolve themselves into a block, individuals are no longer recognizable, the dark wedge presses onward, fantastically topped by heads and weapons floating off on a milky pool. A column—not men at all.[45]

The Italian Futurist poet Marinetti was even more explicit than his German contemporaries:

> War has a beauty of its own because it brings forth the mechanical man who is perfected by the gas mask, the terrorizing loud-speaker and the flame thrower, or is enshrined in the armored car which stabilizes man's mastery over the machine. War has a beauty of its own because it starts the metalization of the human body.[46]

But the transformation of men into machines is not only a basically uninteresting project for novelists, it is also unjustified. Men may become machine-like but they can never be totally transformed from the organic into the mechanical. Yet if men do retain their human qualities under the stress of modern war, one must still ask what their condition is. Most of the writers dealing with this later period of the war were convinced that the ideals and views of humanity with which Germany had entered the war were inadequate to the task of enduring the sufferings of the later years. In two passages Remarque passes judgment upon the preparation of German youth for the conflict.

> In the *Wandervogel* of those days was all the fresh romance and enthusiasm of youth, that afterwards still lingered on in the trenches for a short while, only to collapse at last in 1917 under the awful horrors of the battle of machines.[47]

And again:

> . . . we saw that the classical conception of the Fatherland held by our teachers resolved itself here into a renunciation of personality such as one would not ask of the meanest servant.[48]

Actually the second criticism echoes that which the *Wandervogel* movement had voiced before the war. One may also doubt that the romanticism of the German youth movement died, as Remarque says, in the horror of battle. Instead it seems more likely that it was transformed from a "soft" to a "hard" romanticism while still retaining many of its prewar characteristics.

The writers were convinced that a real change did occur. Wilhelm von Schramm sounds very much like Remarque when he says that the

> . . . later stages of the war went against every precept of reason. Through its blind mechanism it destroyed all weak idealism and at best made fatalistic sufferers of fighting men, who, in the midst of a world of accident, destruction, and putrification created their own inner world which enabled them to carry on.[49]

This is again reminiscent of the attempt by the German youth movement to create a new society of the wandering horde with its own *Weltanschauung.* The conditions of war again offered the possibility of doing this.

It was not only "weak idealism" which had to be discarded but much of the cherished German intellectual tradition as well. Men entering the wilderness to build a new life must travel light. One soldier wrote in his diary:

> 7 July (1916) . . . While packing I made a painful discovery: Faust and Zarathustra no longer fit in the knapsack, they have to make room for a pair of shoes . . .[50]

Predictably, in his travail, the figure of the German soldier being developed by these writers turned again to nature for support. But it was no longer the magically lighted and mysterious nature of Flex and German romanticism but rather the hard, demanding, yet sustaining nature of nineteenth-century Darwinian science. Some of the older nature mysticism remained but was robbed of its theological import.

For some, the antithesis between nature and civilization seemed complete. Nature gave life and civilization killed. Opting for life, artilleryman Michael Anders in Ernst Wiechert's "Die Flucht ins Ewige" deserts the army because he feels an irresistible urge to farm again. We are to recognize this as the imperative call of nature against a murderous civilization. The Flemish woman Charlot, whose farm he works on, asks him, "Do you plow because you don't want to die?" He answers, "I am a farmer; I don't want to die because I must plow. . . . It is not the same thing." [51] Later Charlot expresses her wish for ". . . the grain to grow and the clouds to move, the animals to play with one another and the children to laugh in the fields. And I believe that the earth has the same purposes." [52]

As appealing as Wiechert's little myth might be in certain of its aspects, it finds hardly any parallel among the other German war writers. Desertion did not interest them as a literary topic nor were they really interested in resurrecting the cult of the beauties of agriculture. The nature which most of them dealt with was the natural world of strife. Even as they turned men into machines in their metaphor, so they also transformed the mechanical elements of the battlefield into natural forces. The battle became a "storm of steel," the shells, birds or beasts of prey diving and screaming at their victims. Shells roared like "rutting stags" and reminded one narrator of "flocks of wild geese." [53]

In this man-made jungle appeared a new type of natural man who through his blood and instinctual reactions bore a close relationship to his ancestors in the jungle swamp. He was a man who could find joy, a savage ecstasy, in the thirst for blood. Against the throbbing of distant centuries which one felt in the veins, the temples, the lungs and throat, what mattered the feeble sheathing of a few generations of modern culture? On the battlefields of Europe the man of the Ice Age crawled out of his cave, grenade in hand.[54] The idealist of 1914 has become "hard, suspicious, . . . vicious, tough . . . ," [55] a wild animal who sprang remorselessly upon his enemies.[56]

The thinking of the German writers did not end, however, with the reduction of war to an insane machinery and the reduction of men to bestiality. Perhaps spurred on by the hope of finding some reason in the war which had robbed them of so much, they embraced it as an experience and found in it a mystical, world-historical quality. In life at the front they discovered new meanings and depths both in the relationship between man and nature and between man and technology. Man at the front lived in a close symbiosis with nature.

> From the earth, from the air, sustaining forces pour into us—mostly from the earth. To no man does the earth mean so much as to the soldier. . . she shelters him and gives him a new lease of ten seconds of life, receives him again and often forever.[57]

In a much longer passage Remarque transforms one of his protagonists momentarily into earth and then returns him to his human condition spiritually reborn.[58]

But man also lived in the closest unison with technology. Perhaps this relationship was best expressed in the attention paid by the writers to the steel helmet. The helmet and the stern face beneath it became a symbol of the modern age of warfare. "I could see beneath his helmet Schrader's strong face, as like a machine he loaded and fired, loaded and fired," writes Ernst Juenger.[59] This vision of the face of the German soldier outlined by the rim of the steel helmet appears again and again in the postwar writings; it is the same face that could be seen on the stone guards at the forbidding circle of the Tannenburg memorial:

> . . . in his features were chiseled the lines of an energy stretched to the utmost pitch.[60]
> . . . his face appeared unforgettable, formed and moved by powerful spiritual concussion, shock, agitation . . .[61]
> Then out of the veil of the past, the iron front of the grey steel helmet will become visible, not wavering and not retreating, a monument to immortality.[62]

In truth, the face of the man became one with the steel frame of the helmet, the heavy coat, and the rifle, as solid and immovable as stone.[63]

The man who emerged from the great battles of 1916 and 1917 was presented as a barbarian with a complete command of modern technology. His barbarism was the expression of his humanity unfettered by the superficialities, the formalities, and the false conventions of bourgeois life.

> In the depths of the craters the war gained a meaning which no calculating art [was] able to [discount] . . . disgust with the old

values was wrapped up with the unconscious yearning for a new life.[64]

This new warrior was both a destroyer and a creator, smashing the old forms of society and building new and more humane ones in their place:

> If the German has brought forth a type as well born as any historical form, it is that of the front-line soldier. He is the symbol of the modern worker and fighter, the carrier of a new departure in the world.[65]
>
> . . . This is the new man, the combat engineer, the choice of middle Europe; a wholly new race, smart, strong and willful. What he has demonstrated here in action will tomorrow be the axis about which life will whirl, faster and faster. Not forever will he be laying paths through mud, fire, and steel. But the steady pace with which those are done here will remain the same. The glowing sunset of a dying era is also the dawn in which they arm themselves for newer, harder struggles. Far back await the great cities, the armies of machines, the empires whose inner solidarity will be ripped apart by the deeds of these audacious, battle-trained, heedless, [men]. This war is not the end, rather it is the jump-off point of violence. It is the forge in which the world will be hammered into new boundaries and communities.[66]

Yet even before these men applied themselves to the task of building new communities at home, they had already created one in the trenches. This front-line community was viewed as a classless society based on comradeship founded in common suffering. The leaders of this community, the sergeants and company officers, at least as they were portrayed in the literature, commanded because of their strength of character. Those who did not have this quality rapidly lost the respect of the men. Furthermore, these officers had more in common with their men than with the officers of the staff.[67] Ties with the homeland were weakened by long years at the front and the estrangement between combat soldiers and civilians was commented on by all of the writers; furloughs left the men uneasy and anxious to get back to the front.[68]

Comradeship broke down the old class barriers as university student and laborer or farmer found how much they had in common. It was no longer the friendship between men of similar intellectual background as was the case with Walter Flex and Ernst Wurche. Nor did this comradeship have the patronizing quality of the officer being a good fellow towards the "other ranks." It was rather the deep-felt bond of interdependence and trust forged under conditions of great danger, such as the friendship which Remarque depicts between Paul Bäumer and Sergeant Katczinsky.[69] Comradeship was the logical successor to a number of attitudes current in German thought at the beginning of the war. There was, of course, the old soldierly ideal of the comrade, but the millions who knew by heart the words of "Ich hatt' einen Kameraden" had scarcely any idea, until the war engulfed them, of what comradeship could mean. Nor, one might add, did the professional soldiers, for spirit of comradeship was in many ways antithetical to the spirit of military organization and bred a sense of conflict between front and staff.

Comradeship was also a vindication and continuation of the spirit of the August days. The sense of national unity which gradually disappeared at home retained some of its original intensity at the front, though a good deal of the optimism was gone. Lastly, those who experienced the intense friendships of the *Wandervogel* movement rediscovered that spirit at the front, and the spirit was passed on through their writings.

The sense of comradeship was essentially communal, and

it was usually a group that was dealt with in the depiction of comradeship rather than a relationship restricted to two persons. Adolf Hitler, who apparently had no close friends at the front, still had a lively sense of comradeship. Often, in attempting to show that the memory of the comrades lived on, it would be stated that they continued, even though dead, to march in the ranks of the living, implying that the dead somehow survived as long as the front community remained.

This sense of community extended even across no-man's-land to include the enemy. In this, the attitude of the *Frontkaempfer*, at least as it was consistently presented in the literature, was sharply distinguished from that of the civilian population, who retained for a considerably longer time the hypernationalistic attitudes of the prewar and early war period. "It was his fate that he had to fight; and like every fate it filled him with joy as with sadness, perhaps with grimness but with scarcely any poisonous hatred." [70] The enemy, the physical entity of the opposing infantryman, was a fact of life and, what is more, a pawn in the same fateful game, a participant in the great adventure from which civilians and staff were excluded. "The fighting opponent, the simple *Frontschwein*, the *cochon du Front* of the other side was nearer to him [than the population of his own land]. All cries of hatred . . . are weak. Only courage recognizes courage." [71] Thus Ernst Juenger. Remarque says much the same thing: "We would get along better with any Tommy, with any front-line Froggy, than with them." [72]

While many of the novels and memoirs deal to some extent with this "comradeship" of enemies, two novels, both printed in Germany during the Hitler period, are chiefly devoted to this non-nationalistic theme. Franz Franziss' *Wir von der Somme* (1936) attempts to recall the fury of the Somme battle from the point of view of three groups of soldiers, one

German, one French, and one English. The book, in which almost all of the principals die, is a plea for the necessity of peace. It is not a well-written book but it is interesting that it was done at all, given the nationalistic frenzy of the time. An even more interesting example of this line of thought is Sailler's *Brücke über das Niemandsland* (1938) which tells the story of the friendship between the German *Vicefeldwebel* Mack and the Frenchman, Sergeant Bouisson, two courageous and intelligent individuals who continue to encounter each other over the course of three years of war. The tale is in many ways contrived but the sentiment, something like Juenger's "only courage recognizes courage," is genuine. Like Franziss, Sailler is convinced that peace between France and Germany is a necessity, and he also emphasizes the lack of hatred towards the enemy.[73] He speaks of the creation of a new type of man on the battlefields and leaves no doubt that both Michael Mack and Marcel Bouisson are representatives of the new type.[74]

In the last years of the war the stereotyped figure of the warrior appeared, a denizen of a savage world of shell holes, barbed wire, trenches, machine guns, and terrifying artillery barrages. In this world the antithesis between nature and civilization was overcome by degrading nature to jungle and civilization to factory and then equating the one with the other. Rationalism and irrationalism were reconciled in the figure of the technologically competent barbarian who inhabited this world. The "soft" romanticism of the *Wandervogel* was changed into the "tough" romanticism of the battlefield, yet one could still detect vestiges of the wandering scholar and thief in this new figure of the *Frontkaempfer*.

The stereotype lacked only that touch of tragedy which translates excellence into greatness. Of personal tragedy there had been a surfeit. What was needed for greatness was a tragedy that towered above the personal level; that tragedy was provided by the defeat and revolution.

Phase 3 • THE RETURN HOME

For a brief moment in the spring of 1918 hope of victory returned to the German forces but then slowly ebbed away in the final punishing months of that year. And then the war ended. "It fizzled out," as one of the privates in Remarque's *The Road Back* put it. The march back under leaden skies, in thin ranks, sometimes drenched by late fall rains, established the mood, the point of view, from which the war would be measured.

> Roads stretch far through the landscape, the villages lie in a grey light; trees rustle, leaves are falling, falling.
> Along the road, step on step, in their faded dirty uniforms tramp the grey columns. The unshaved faces beneath the steel helmets are haggard, wasted with hunger and long peril, pinched and dwindled . . . by terror and courage and death. They trudge along in silence; silently, as they have now marched over so many a road, have sat in so many a truck, squatted in so many a dugout, crouched in so many a shell hole—without many words, so too now they trudge along this road back home into peace. Without many words. . . .
> And behind them, the army of the slain. Thus they tramp onward, step by step, sick, half starving, without ammunition, in thin companies, with eyes that still fail to comprehend it: escaped out of that underworld, on the road back to life.[75]

Germany in November, 1918, presented a strange sight indeed to the men who had no sympathy with the revolution of the Left. Red flags, Workers' and Soldiers' Councils, old leaders and institutions overthrown, roused no cries of gladness in their breasts.

Scornfully, silently, the Front Army marched back through this chaos. Marched back into a "homeland" in which the very word left a bitter taste. For this homeland was not the old one, ever cherished. It was now a strange and foreign one.[76]

This is, of course, a strongly partisan view of the events of the revolution, but it was the view held later on by the National Socialists, the men of the Right, and of many persons who served in the German army.

For these men the world had been turned upside down. A war which they had fought in self-defense had been transformed into an attempt by Germany to conquer the world. The class and caste systems, for better or worse, were disrupted and the economy was ruined. Starvation had followed the Armistice and a slow inflation followed the starving period. Land and colonies were lost; irregular troops roamed the highways while irregular governments held the capitals. The formerly solid bourgeois virtues became increasingly less realistic. One does not learn to save in a period of inflation nor gain in steadiness through chronic unemployment. Formerly respectable men were now dressed shabbily while fly-by-night opportunists wore the latest fashions. To many of these ex-soldiers the society had become a chaos.

The final depiction of the *Frontkaempfer* grew out of this postwar period. Benumbed by his experiences, gazing uncomprehendingly at this defeated Germany, the front-line fighter searched for a way in which he could come to grips with this reality. His old homeland had been spiritually destroyed by the war and revolution; his true homeland was now the battlefield.[77] Not liking what he saw, he still had not formulated any program or developed a method of facing this postwar world.

The comradeship of the battlefield could not stand the strain of return to a revolutionary Germany. There, the men had been united in a common purpose; here, they found themselves divided by a political situation in which their purposes were varied and often opposed. Only one group did not, could not, change its mind, and that was the army of the slain. These would always remain true to the "cause"—whatever cause their luckier comrades chose to support. Death insured the permanence of friendship; death was the fountain of youth, for the dead were forever young and in remembrance of them the veterans themselves became young once again. Comradeship, like the *Freundesliebe* of the *Wandervogel*, did not permit aging.

In a normal society, grief would have lost its edge, the memories of the war would have been stilled by the many concerns and opportunities of peace. But in Germany all things conspired to turn men's minds back towards the war. The harshness of the peace treaty, the enforced weakness of the state, the continuing vexation of reparations, all kept before the veterans the fact that their efforts had been in vain. It proved difficult under these conditions for many of them to grow out of the mood of 1918. Had it not been for the internal conditions of the country they might have stagnated into the condition of professional veterans so familiar in other lands— boring but relatively harmless. Instead, the instability of the Weimar Republic opened to them an avenue of salvation. The *Frontkaempfer* did not have to perish with the peace because the society itself was a battlefield.

> The street is empty and grey. It drags away into the distance. . . . "All one long fire-trench, Ernst." He indicates the houses: "Dugouts, every one—the war still goes on—but a dirty, low-down war—every man against his fellow— . . ." [78]

> The spirit of the trenches is no product of war, rather class, race, party, and nation, every community is its dwelling place, surrounded with ramparts and thickly wired—in the middle a wasteland. Deserters will be shot. [79]

Thus the front-line fighter survived, the stereotype was transferred from the military to the political realm, and the postwar world became the stage for a new type of warfare. The *Frontkaempfer* had found a moral equivalent for peace.

Epilogue • THE FATE OF THE *Frontkaempfer*

Erich Maria Remarque put the question: ". . . And so we shall march, our dead comrades beside us, the years at the Front behind us;—against whom, against whom." [80] The answer was given by the political parties, especially the parties of the Right which seized upon the image of the warrior and made him the symbol of all that was good and valuable in German life, the carrier of important political concepts and an ideal figure worthy of emulation.

For the National Socialists the steps in the warrior's career were obvious. The years at the front made him an ardent nationalist; upon returning from the war, one look at the German situation convinced him that he must join the *Freikorps*, and when these groups were dissolved his only hope of effecting the salvation of Germany lay in joining that band of fine young fellows, the SA.[81]

Throughout the 1920's and early 1930's the image of the *Frontkaempfer* continued to be effective and influence the actions of men. That is, while the image was still in the final stages of formation it lived in the minds of men. But with the triumph of National Socialism, the front-line fighter, like the SA, was left at loose ends, for Hitler took great pains to emphasize the unity of the new Germany.[82] The image continued to appear but in an ever more trivialized form. The human being was gradually erased, leaving only the tired lines of energy, the staring eyes, the tightly gripped rifle, and the steel helmet.[83]

But like the cheshire cat, the stereotype reappeared with the outbreak of the new war. The news stories used his image to evoke a ready response. It was not until the catastrophe of Stalingrad, however, that he really came into his own again. The announcements of the end of the battle prefaced by the opening bars of "Ich hatt' einen Kameraden" and the front page of the *Voelkischer Beobachter* showed the face of the *Frontkaempfer*, steel helmet, staring eyes, and determined mouth.[84] From time to time after that the stereotype could be found in news stories, illustrations, and photographs, but as the end neared he disappeared from view.

A survey of a few of the recent novels about the Second World War are, in a negative sense, very revealing. None of the ones which have come to this writer's attention show any tendency to mechanize the natural or to naturalize the mechanical. Nor does comradeship seem to be a prominent virtue; in fact, quite the opposite is the case, with strife between members of the group a predominating characteristic. The leading figures are more often either gross or weak than spiritually strong. Sergeant Steiner in Willi Heinrich's *The Cross of Iron* is possibly reminiscent of such figures as Katczinsky of *All Quiet on the Western Front* or Sailler's Sergeant Mack, but such parallels are relatively few in number. Even the steel helmet has lost its magical appeal as is indicated by the continual trouble which Gerhard Lorenz, in Hans Werner Richter's *Du sollst nicht töten*, has in keeping his helmet on straight. Finally, these men of the novels of the Second World War do not march back in decimated but steady ranks. They trickle back, solitary, pathetic survivors of a foolish and hideous catastrophe. We search in vain for the face of the warrior, the *Frontkaempfer*, but do not find him. He is missing and, we may presume, dead.[85]

III • THE WORKER

Of all the images of protest created during the past century and a half, none has been more often repeated or more important than the figure of the worker. Novelists from Zola to Steinbeck, artists as varied as Rivera and Köllwitz, have presented us with unforgettable glimpses of the life and visage of the archetypal working man. He is the foundation stone of a number of political and economic systems and, adored or feared, the subject of consideration by all of them. He may be depicted as the salt of the earth or as a brutalized creature but, hero or brute, he is the principal victim of our industrialized society. Poverty, anguish, and physical suffering are his lot, the creation of a new society his goal. Existing in a factory landscape of smoke-blackened walls and skylights, surrounded by the howling, monstrous machinery of modern technology, dehumanized by a demonic regimen of work, he hopes, contrary to all reason, for a better world.

Such at least was the picture of the worker in the first decade of this century. Its closeness to reality could not be denied even when it might be asserted that conditions were improving. When, in the second and third decades the governments of several European states were seized by workers' parties and when everywhere the workers' movement showed greater militancy, political parties found that they could ignore the worker only at their own peril. But for the parties and groups which did not consider themselves to be primarily workingmen's organizations the problem of defining their relationship to the worker was most difficult.

Several methods of approach, none of them altogether successful, had traditionally been resorted to in meeting the challenge of the worker. The time-honored method was that of simple repression, an approach which was satisfyingly direct and brutal but which suffered from the two undeniable difficulties: the workers were becoming too numerous to terrorize and working-class movements seemed to thrive under conditions of oppression. A less brutal, if no more logical, method of approach was that adopted by many middle-class theorists and legislators of the late nineteenth century. This approach assumed that there was really no such thing as a working class, but only a temporarily disaffected element of the society. The problem was shifted from the area of police jurisdiction to that of discovering the causes for discontent and eradicating them. It was thought that better education, better wages, and better working conditions would eventually end the strife which seemed to be dividing society. When, contrary to middle-class theory, the workers accepted the changes and continued to assert their independent existence, more than one bourgeois theorist was driven to reassess any optimistic notions he may have held concerning the nature of man.

Actually, the various reform measures, beginning with those enacted in the 1880's, were notably successful in either wiping out or basically altering the working-class movements in Western society.[86] Today the large Socialist movements existing in the Western European states can scarcely be called "revolutionary," and such militancy has never really existed in the United States. But half a century ago this trend was nowhere clear, so it appeared to many that reform was both politically and intellectually bankrupt. This feeling was further reinforced by the experience of the First World War. Furthermore, the easy denial of a working class distinct from the other classes of society was bluntly contradicted by the wide currency of political beliefs based squarely upon the presumed existence of such a class. Anarchism, Syndicalism, Marxism, to a lesser extent the labor union movement, all were based upon the assumption that there existed in society a figure, the worker, who was as identifiable as the nobleman.

This figure was the discovery of the nineteenth century, a product of the industrial revolution. He was distinguished from the craftsman and apprentice of the medieval period by his more general lack of skill, by his ill-defined relationship to the rest of society, by his existence in a mass of other workers, and by the generally deprived conditions in which he lived and labored. All of these distinguishing characteristics are essentially negative; they tell us what the worker is not, but not what he is. The working-class parties and organizations of the nineteenth century firmly established these negative distinctions and then, having isolated their subject, began to attribute to the worker a number of positive characteristics. As a proletarian he was not only deprived of property, it was his style not to possess property. In this manner the negative distinctions were transformed into positive characteristics and apparent defects became actual virtues. This overturning of values was the *credo quia absurdum* of the working-class movement and upon this foundation was built the vast and sometimes brilliant literature of labor.

For the men of the middle-class parties who were concerned with this deep rift in modern society it was painfully clear that changes, perhaps drastic changes, would have to be made in their own assumptions about society. One could not go on forever casting workers to the police lions nor, apparently, could any large number of workingmen be tempted by promises of sharing in society's banquet.[87] Thus, from the turn of the century onward, a growing number of middle-class leaders sought to reorient their thinking to include the worker and to give to the term "worker" a positive but non-Marxian definition. In Germany the events of the war and revolution made this movement not only desirable but immediately imperative.

The process involved the redefinition of society so as to preserve what were conceived to be the most important of its characteristics while at the same time opening the way for the inclusion of the working class. It also involved the creation of a new image of the worker which was believable and acceptable not only to the other classes of society but to the working class as well. Most of the redefinition fell far short of such a goal and it can scarcely be said that any one of these middle-class theorists matched the achievement of Karl Marx.

The task of redefinition was far from pleasant because many of the most cherished ideals of the middle class had to be abandoned. The central problem appeared to be that of class conflict and the solution seemed to lie only partially in the alleviation of poverty. More important, however, was the question of the very concept of class. "Class" was viewed as a definition of economic status fostered by the French Revolution and by the "middle class," and its very nature tended to divide society. This concept was supported by bourgeois individualism and the belief in the equality of man. These "false" ideas undermined the integrity of society and laid the basis for the murderous conflicts of the twentieth century.

Thus, the first step in the process of redefinition consisted in the denial of these bourgeois ideals. Men were by nature unequal: some were leaders, others followers. In such a world there was no room for unlimited individualism. In place of the atomistic society based on free individuals there had to appear an integrated community of cooperating members led by "personalities." In such a community economic problems would be ancillary to the problem of reawakening the "natural" relationships between its members; it would have to become what it "really" was, an organic whole.

Yet this new community would not lack in articulation for it would divide itself naturally into estates (*Staende*) organically linked to one another. Since the style of this community would be one of cooperation, rather than individual competition, the economic form would have to be socialistic rather than capitalistic (though this socialism would not be the barren and unnatural type promulgated by the internationalistic Marxians). In such a community the position of the worker would be an honored one. Though opinion varied here, the more radical thinkers tended to accord the worker a paramount position in society and even to insist that basically all of the members of the community were workers.

What were the limits of such a "natural" community, and what made it natural? To these questions the answer was given that the community could not be international in scope because of the basic law of inequality. The community which suited the Germans was unsuitable for Russian conditions. Thus nationality provided the "organism" from which the community grew. But the natural quality of this organism was rooted in the blood relationships of the people so that nationalism tended to be converted into racialism. Blood, not language or custom, defined the national citizen.

Not all of the men to be dealt with in the following appraisal supported every one of these conclusions, but there would seem to be a logical connection (or possibly progression) from the more conservative to the more radical positions. In only a very limited sense could this constellation of ideas be considered conservative or even reactionary, for it was aimed at altering society and the ideal towards which it aimed had not previously existed. As put into practice by the National Socialists it resulted in rather vast alterations in German society. Some of these alterations were but logical extensions of changes introduced in the years following 1918. Others grew out of the concepts formulated specifically by the group of thinkers we shall deal with here. It should only be noted that in most cases these men were not true forerunners of Hitler but individuals following lines of thought which paralleled those of the *Fuehrer*. All of them contributed, however, to the task of redefining the society and building a non-Marxian image of the worker.

Some of these theorists, such as Oswald Spengler, Othmar Spann, and Arthur Moeller van den Bruck, were frankly conservative. Others, like Ernst Juenger, Otto and Gregor Strasser, and Adolf Hitler, could be classified as "right radical," a position quite far removed from that of the conservatives.[88] Still others, of whom August Winnig is perhaps the outstanding example, began as Marxian labor unionists and then moved away from that position. Generally speaking, the conservatives were the least successful in presenting a usable image of the worker though they did often speak eloquently of the building of a national community which was the common underpinning of the systems of all these men.

1 • THE CONSERVATIVES

Many of the concepts of this group of thinkers were already well-established ideas in German intellectual and scholarly circles. The idea of the organic community, the hierarchical society, and the necessity of nationalism had been current since the late eighteenth century. New was the emphasis placed upon the position of the worker, though here the conservatives, and especially Othmar Spann, were less adventurous than any of the other groups with which we shall be dealing. Of interest is the manner in which "Prussianism," under heavy attack in sectors of German society before the war, gained new appreciation in its moment of defeat. Both Spengler and Moeller van den Bruck dealt most favorably with this particular expression of the German character although neither was, in the strict sense of the word, a Prussian. Despite Spengler's great name and despite the prominence of Spann and the interest which Moeller's translation of Dostoevsky had aroused, it cannot be said that their political writings had any large effect.

Othmar Spann's *Der Wahre Staat* is rather typical of the type of conservative thought which developed an answer to the challenge of the German revolution. His handling of the worker question was largely unimaginative and could scarcely have won many plaudits outside of the privileged or formerly privileged classes.[89] Yet certain of the points he made were also features of the systems evolved by other, more important writers.

Spann first established the opposition between individualism based on the concept of equality and "universalism" which arises from the fundamental inequality of men. Individualism as a social and political reality results in the atomistic society, while universalism leads to the homogeneous community. The first type of society is made up of equal individuals striving after private ends; in such a society the whole is no greater than the sum of its parts. The homogeneous community, on the other hand, is made up of unequal individuals arranged in estates which are harmoniously linked to form the whole. This community is far more than the sum of its parts; it is, in fact, the "true state" of which Spann was talking.[90]

In Spann's vision of the state the worker's position is inferior and the worker knows his place. This is true whether he is a hand laborer or a "higher worker" (an artist). The higher estates of society are peopled by professional men, educators, and the leadership of the state and church.[91] Spann made no effort to conceal the fact that he considered the workers to be of inferior stuff and he definitely did not try, as other writers would, to translate all forms of societal endeavor into work and their practitioners into workers.

There is nothing very new in all of this, and much that is quite old, but still it is of interest since Spann delineates in clear form certain of the antitheses and identities employed by most of the theorists in the conservative and Right radical camps. Destructive individualism is opposed to constructive universalism, "artificial" society to "natural" community. Again class is an artificial construct while estate is natural. The term "worker" is slightly broadened so as to include groups not normally classified as workers, though it by no means embraces the entire society. Spann was no racist but his emphasis upon homogeneity was a step along the same path.[92] Finally, it should be noted that Spann, like many other conservatives, viewed individualism as always self-seeking. For him the self-sacrificing leader, the "personality," was the antithesis of the individual. The personality was a true leader because he was gifted, selfless, and irresistibly attractive. A society could have many individuals but very few personalities, and there is the clear implication that society can do without the former but must have the latter. This emphasis upon personality was taken up by later writers, and Adolf Hitler subsequently based his claim to rule upon the fact that he was a personality.[93]

If Spann's work had no great appeal, the same can scarcely be said for Moeller van den Bruck's. His book *Das dritte Reich* gave the name to Hitler's regime long before it was established, while his term "conservative revolutionary" and his suggestion that black was the proper color for Germany's flag found echo in the writings of Otto and Gregor Strasser. But Moeller had a talent for more than catchy phrases, and a number of his more important ideas found their way into the work of other writers of the period.[94]

For Moeller, the proletarian position of the worker was only one of a number of political positions struggling for acceptance in postwar Germany. Proletarianism is not a situation forced upon the worker by the action of fundamental laws of economics. In fact, the economy does not form the substructure in the Marxian sense, but rather it is a superstructure based on a fundament of Power, Law, Idea, and State.[95] Thus to be a proletarian is a matter of choice—"the proletarian is he who wishes to be a proletarian." [96] It is a conscious act of divorce from the society which, because it is based on false premises, can only lead to oblivion. The salvation for the worker lies in finding his way from Proletarianism to the worker's estate (*Arbeiterschaft*).[97] The destruction of Proletarianism would in turn pave the way for national unity.

Possibly more important than any conclusions which Moeller may have reached concerning the proletariat were his condemnations of liberalism and reason. Liberalism was written off as "self-seeking," while reason was seen as a barren exercise as compared with irrational "understanding." This distinction became standard for all of the Right radical theorists and proved a most valuable weapon for pushing aside all uncomfortable arguments as being the products of barren reason.[98]

In an earlier work, *Der preussische Stil*, Moeller found himself concerned with the relationship between Prussia and Germany. This work marks, according to Fritz Stern, "the literary expression of his conversion and of his passionate support for Germany; the esthete had turned Prussian and political." [99] The importance of the work lies in Moeller's praise of the Prussian virtues of soberness and devotion to duty which had been under attack before the war. These same virtues later became one of the foundations for Spengler's concept of the new Germany (*Preussentum und Sozialismus*), and eventually Ernst Juenger equated soldierly and worker virtues in his

Der Arbeiter (1932). Thus, what were two separate strands in the thought of Moeller van den Bruck were finally woven together during the 1920's, and in the 1930's the National Socialists continued to present the warrior and the worker as the two sides of the coin of German manhood.

Preussentum und Sozialismus (1919) perhaps gains its importance more from the fact that its author was enjoying great success with his *Decline of the West* than from anything which the pamphlet itself had to say. Spengler wrote this article in response to the socialist revolution and from the viewpoint of a man who did not sympathize with that upheaval and was interested in somehow preserving what he considered to be the valuable parts of the German heritage in this new age. Hence, he endeavors to show what contributions Prussianism can make to socialism and finds that its greatest contribution is the realization that freedom lies in obedience.[100] This essentially soldierly virtue has been transmitted to the entire German nation by the school of the army, an army dominated by Prussian attitudes. But the German who has been instructed in Prussian freedom is basically a worker. "Every true German is a worker. It belongs to his style of life." [101]

All Germans—officers, officials, farmers and miners—are workers, and the real distinction is not between rich and poor but between commanders and followers.[102] Spengler denies that socialist attitudes and socialist powers are the prerogatives of any class. Class is an English idea and does not properly belong in the German setting.[103] Specifically, Spengler objects to the superficial rational basis for socialism which had been supplied by Karl Marx. "We do not believe in the power of reason over life any more." [104] Socialism in Germany was to be grounded in the instincts and could thus be shared by the entire German nation.

Spengler's pamphlet is interesting in that the ideas which

he put forward were later to be a feature of most Right radical analyses, but in the manner in which he presented them they were largely unusable. It is true that he made the linkage between the soldier and the worker which would later be so popular. But the soldier was the prewar drill-ground figure, not the veteran of the trenches. In like manner his worker was more the goodhearted menial than the strange and even awesome product of factory life. Spengler saw that socialism and revolution had to be accepted; what he evidently did not see was that much of what he considered desirable and even essential would either have to be done away with or altered out of all recognition.

2 • THE RIGHT RADICALS

The Right radicals were distinguished from the conservatives not only by their greater willingness to resort to violent action but also by their less than reverent attitude toward the past and many of the hallowed institutions of German society. They shared with the conservatives a mistrust of reason, but with them irrational understanding became a more emotional experience perhaps best expressed in the phrase "thinking with the blood." Not all of the Right radicals were National Socialists by any means, though the NSDAP did have a great attraction for them. Many were connected with the movement for a time but later left; such was the case with Otto and Gregor Strasser, Hermann Rauschning, and Herbert Blank. Others, such as Joseph Goebbels, remained true to Adolf Hitler, while still others, such as Ernst Juenger and Ernst von Salomon, never were able to bring themselves to join the movement, though for a long while they did not express any disapproval. Most of the ideas of these men were quite similar, but in the case of Ernst Juenger there is sufficient individuality to warrant treatment in a separate section.

Of all the Right radicals, Otto Strasser was probably the most coherent and succinct in the presentation of his political views, and certainly he has enjoyed the longest political life of any of them. In his *Aufbau des Deutschen Sozialismus* (1932), written after his break with Hitler, he gives a brief but complete outline of his concept of the socialist state. Again the opposition to liberalism is made clear and is equated with the capitalist economic form. Conservatism is organic and expresses the "we-idea" as opposed to the "I-idea" of liberalism. Hence, conservatism is basically socialistic. The trinity of conservative socialism, nationalism, and idealism is opposed to the liberal trinity of capitalism, individualism, and materialism.[105]

Having thus neatly (and superficially) established this opposition Strasser proceeds to delineate the meaning of socialism. Like Moeller van den Bruck he believes that each nation has its own socialism, and like Spann he argues that the community is based on a homogeneous group which he identifies with the nation and race.[106] Marxism becomes a socialism alienated by its liberal origins, an argument used by all of the Right radicals. For German socialism the chief goals become (1) the ending of private ownership of land, mineral wealth, and the means of production, while at the same time (2) deproletarianizing the German people. The accomplishment of these apparently contradictory tasks is facilitated by a distinction between property (*Eigentum*) and possession (*Besitz*). Property may be dealt with as one wishes while possessions are to be used by the possessor under the direction of the actual owner, the community.[107] Strasser also hoped to forward the program of deproletarianization by encouraging a resettlement of workers from the city to country areas.[108]

All of this was to be accomplished without the creation of a stultifying state-socialism which would choke off natural impulses through the establishment of a "dead" bureaucracy.[109]

Instead, the "living" people's community was to be the instrument of direction and this direction was to be accomplished through the spontaneous creation and advancement of "true leaders." Strasser's system was conservative in that he was concerned to preserve many of the traditional forms of work even at the expense of technical competence.[110] But the amount of space devoted to questions of the position of the working man within the society (as compared with the space devoted to other classes) shows that Strasser had moved a considerable distance from the conservative camp. Actually, he was interested in establishing a position which was neither Marxian nor capitalist, nor yet a mere compromise between the two.

The final goal of this German socialist state was the "unification of all Germans of Middle Europe." Unfortunately this goal could be accomplished only through war. This, however, was but a small price to pay for the accomplishment of a true racial goal.[111] As with a number of other Right radicals there appeared in Strasser's work a close linkage between work and war. The old bourgeois world would have to be destroyed by war; the new socialist state would complete itself in an act of war for the sake of justice.

Strasser's work remains rather coldly abstract. Nowhere does one really see the faces of living men, and even where he deals with problems of labor he speaks in terms of classes and groups rather than presenting us with individuals. The most that can be said of the worker as he appears in Strasser's system is that he is a man who has been led astray by Marxian ideas but yet remains the best hope for the building of the new German community.

Where Otto Strasser was cold and abstract his brother Gregor was emotional and concrete. Gregor's anti-Semitism was as blunt as Hitler's, while his pictures of the workers resounded with words like "whipped" and "enslaved." It was crude, popular, and very effective. All of the ideas of the other Right radicals appeared but in a scattered and non-analytic form. Gregor Strasser believed in the basic inequality of men, in the clash between "natural" estate and "artificial" class, in the necessity of changing proletarians into true citizens of the socialist community. He was an anti-capitalist, a socialist, and a nationalist. Above all he was a master of forceful invective, though perhaps not the peer of either Hitler or Goebbels.[112]

In most particulars Adolf Hitler agreed with the majority of the other conservative and Right radical theorists of the 1920's, though his ideas were more crudely expressed and immensely more popular. The national community was being destroyed, he said, by the twin forces of international capitalism and international Marxism; both were instruments of the Jews employed to suck the lifeblood from healthy communities. The bourgeoisie was so wrapped up in the life of business and in their own higher culture that they could scarcely see what was happening in the rest of society. In particular they were blind towards the needs and hopes of the masses and hence were incapable of leading them. The masses, on the other hand, were sadly misled by the forces of international Marxism and were in danger of being lost altogether to the true community. Yet because they were not yet engulfed by the spirit of avaricious individualism, as was a large part of the middle class, there was hope for them and they in turn were the best hope for establishing a true community.

Hitler's attitude towards the worker is by turns contemptuous and loving. When he describes the way in which the construction workers threatened him in Vienna one can feel his loathing, and many a writer has used this passage as an example of Hitler's petty bourgeois attitude toward the "people." Yet, in the same chapter of *Mein Kampf*, Hitler is capable of describing in vivid detail and with a good deal of sympathy the plight of the poor in Vienna and the effect which poverty has in molding a man's life.[113] Furthermore, he recognized something that was not at all clearly seen by most of the middle class: their moral outlook and standards did not coincide with those of the population in general.[114]

The worker was instinctively capable of recognizing, given half a chance, the correct goals for the community and the measures which would have to be taken in order to reach those goals. But this chance would never arise if the workers were unrelentingly driven into the internationalist camp by the scourge of poverty. Thus, for Hitler, social justice was a necessary first step on the way towards winning the mass of the workers back to the community so that they could lend their invaluable help to the work of salvation.

If Hitler respected the basic instincts of the workers he certainly had no high regard for their mentality. His well-known statements about propaganda show great contempt for the thought processes of the majority of men. Propaganda must be simple, blatant, and repetitive in order to have any effect. The masses are a passive instrument waiting to be formed and led by a strong personality. From Hitler's point of view these masses were spiritually dead and had to be awakened to the true communal life by the evangelistic NSDAP. Yet the party could accomplish this reawakening only if it could present itself to the workers as a workingman's party. During the 1920's it was not able to do this to any large extent, but in the 1930's the party did succeed in winning the support of a large majority of the workers as was proved by the manner in which labor backed the war effort.[115] This adherence was gained not by threats and violence, although these were sometimes used, but by placing labor in an honored position and by providing work for the millions of men who were jobless.

Most of the men treated thus far share a somewhat common background in that they came from the middle class and were educated either in the *Gymnasium* or the *Realschule*. None of them, with the exception of Adolf Hitler, had any long experience with the working class or with the lower classes in general. One might suspect from this that the similarity of many of their ideas was to a considerable extent inspired by the fact of common origins. Yet we find examples of National Socialist leaders who did come from working-class families and examples of a number of persons who shifted from the Marxist to the National Socialist camp. It may be tempting to treat these persons as renegade Marxists and opportunists but the history of at least one man who rose in the ranks of the Social-Democratic party shows that it was possible to arrive at many of the conclusions reached by the middle-class theorists though starting with a different set of premises.

August Winnig (1878-1956) is of interest to us not so much for the originality of his thought but rather because he is a good and fairly rare example of the working man who became an intellectual. In his early years he was apprenticed as a bricklayer and for the next ten years, excluding one year in prison and two in the army, he earned his living at that trade. At the age of twenty-six, having attracted attention as a militant trade unionist, he was selected to act as a union organizer in the Ruhr and then joined the editorial staff of his union newspaper, *Der Grundstein.* He later became editor of this paper and still later a member of the three-man committee which formed his union's leadership. The latter appointment was probably in recognition of his contributions during the building workers' strike of 1910.

With the outbreak of the war Winnig re-entered the army,

but after a short period of barracks duty was released to take up the work of interpreting labor's relationship to the war effort. Besides helping to assure the cooperation of the building workers through his position as union leader, Winnig published several pamphlets defining the wartime attitude of German unions. At the end of the war he found himself in the Baltic region and there was named General Plenipotentiary of the Baltic National Committee by the revolutionary government in Berlin. Later, as *Oberregierungs Praesident* of East Prussia, he came under severe attack for his equivocal attitude during the Kapp *Putsch*. As a result Winnig finally left the Social Democratic party and took up work as an independent writer on labor affairs. Over the years he drew farther away from the Marxian position and for a time showed considerable sympathy for the National Socialist point of view, though his final position could probably be called Christian Socialist.[116]

This transition was accompanied by the gradual development of an independent approach to the worker problem which, at least in its formative stages, owed little to conservative thought. One may trace the growth of these ideas through the series of his publications extending from the early days of the war to the early 1930's. Interestingly enough, as Winnig changed his intellectual position his method of presentation also changed. The earlier writings are filled with the statistical data so much in fashion in Marxist circles while the later writings depend almost entirely upon proofs growing out of personal experience which became extended to general laws.[117] It is also worth noting that the anti-Semitism which is so prominent in his later works was not visible before the late 1920's though he may well have harbored such sentiments all his life.[118]

Winnig's point of departure from the Marxist camp was his growing conviction that the condition of the worker had improved over the course of the nineteenth century and that the improvement was intimately tied to the bettered position of German industry.[119] The idea is reminiscent of Bernstein's revisionism, though Winnig does not acknowledge any debt. It may also have been an outgrowth of unionist emphasis upon wage improvement, an attitude deemed reactionary by the party theorists.[120] The general unionist attitude led to a de-emphasis of class warfare; Winnig's concept was more radical—it led naturally to the repudiation of the whole idea of class conflict.[121]

The second major step in Winnig's break with Marxism was the growth of his German nationalist sentiments. Already present before the war, they were much enhanced by the patriotic outburst of 1914. The nationalistic fervor with which the war was pursued and the rancor of defeat could only serve to enlarge these sentiments and to divorce them from attachment to a particular form of government. Yet even in 1921, after his departure from the Social Democratic party, his patriotism had not yet taken on that mystical attachment to *das Volk* which was to appear in some of his later writings. It was in *Der Glaube an das Proletariat* (1924) that Winnig decisively reversed his line of thought. The seemingly scientific view of the universe based on statistical inference was now abandoned for an immediate, irrational perception of reality. New in Winnig's thought as presented in this work were a mystical concept of *das Volk* and the opposition of estate to class.[122] The worker, he contended, was not a middle-class man; the worker transcended class limits—he formed a new estate.[123] The problem with the worker was that because of bad leadership he had come to view himself as a proletarian, that is, a deprived member of the middle class. This view was the natural result of Marxism which is, said Winnig, a malformation of bourgeois thought.[124]

Much of this smacks of the extreme conservatism of Spann,

and Winnig was basically conservative.[125] Yet he was not content to leave the worker's estate in the subordinate position assigned to it by Spann. Instead he proposed an evolutionary development of estates (somewhat in the manner of Marxian classes) in which new estates came into existence and assumed leadership in society without destroying the old ones.[126] Thus the workers, the newest estate, were destined to rebuild society. The workers could only do this, however, by recognizing their connection with the rest of society. Belief in the existence of a proletariat with its soul-killing internationalism was not the solution to the problem. Rather, it was necessary for the worker to become aware of his attachment to "blood and soil." [127]

Thus the worker was cast for a historic role, but he could miss his hour if he listened to the false ideas of the Marxists. Such a mistake would, of course, be disastrous for the entire society. What must be done, said Winnig, was to change the proletariat into an *Arbeitertum* organically connected with the rest of the national community.[128]

Having abandoned the Marxist approach to the problem of the worker, Winnig now began to develop his own approach to the problem, an approach which was both historical and personal. The 1926 edition of *Der Glaube an das Proletariat* is replete with "world historical" examples of doubtful value. In *Vom Proletariat zum Arbeitertum (1930)*, Winnig traces the development of the working-class movement in Germany and its relationship to the growth of the Marxian Social Democratic party. The book repeats many of the ideas already put forward in his previous study of the proletariat but it adds the ingredient of anti-Semitism, and it is probably most valuable for its personal reminiscences of labor leaders and for its reflection of conservative unionist attitudes towards the actions of the Social Democratic intellectuals. The last step in this direction was the autobiographical *Der weite Weg* (1932), which traced Winnig's adult development from his years as a bricklayer to the end of the war. The book also presents a number of idealized images of the German worker, in particular a goodhearted man named Julius Birne.[129] He becomes almost lyrical when he speaks of the ideal work condition in which master and worker labor in close cooperation and friendship.[130] Winnig realizes, of course, that such situations are rare and he had already made a sharp distinction between the artisan of the craft guild and the modern worker,[131] but there is no doubt that he wishes relationships could be so simple.

It is this dream of harmonious relationships which made Winnig pin his hopes upon the establishment of a true national community made up of estates led by the workers' estate and freed from the destructive influence of the alien-blooded Jew. Thus the Labor Front of the Third Reich, with its apparent linkage of workers and management in a single fair organization, seemed to Winnig a rather close approximation, or at least a promising beginning, of the community which he envisioned. He says as much in a work published in 1934,[132] though later he seems more intrigued by the possibility of a specifically Christian and European community.[133]

In its fully developed form Winnig's view of the worker question may be summarized in the following manner. The breakdown of the medieval world, with its highly corporate structure, under the impact of the rise of the Third Estate produced a new, hitherto unknown figure: the wage earner, or worker. Half-educated at best, the victim of the ruthless exploitation of the early capitalists, the worker was easily influenced by the Jewish intellectuals of the Marxian socialist camp. Much of what they said was perfectly true, but the emphasis upon class conflict tended to obscure the interests which capital and labor held in common. Furthermore, this emphasis on conflict made impossible the re-creation of the "people's community" which had been lost with the rise of the bourgeois estate. The true view of the worker's situation was that he represented a new estate in society, one with ways as different from those of the middle class as their ways were from those of the nobility. It was the great task of this new estate to lead in the creation of a new community and to stamp it with worker characteristics. However, in order to do this, the worker had to recognize that economic problems were subordinate to the fundamental problems of race, nationality, soil, and religion.[134]

The worker was capable of making sacrifices and rendering services to the community in order to lead it back to itself. This sense of sacrifice and service was what made the worker a socialist and differentiated him from the self-seeking bourgeoisie and from the negativism of the Marxian intellectuals.[135] The figure of the communal-minded worker can be seen in the person of Julius Birne. He was sober, upstanding, provident, generous, committed to doing a good day's work and charging a fair price for his labor. He was patriotic and instinctively mistrusted intellectuals who were attempting to divide and destroy the community. Ready to fight for his own rights, he still respected the rights of others. At his best the worker was a truly noble figure engaged in the honorable task of manual labor.[136]

There is nothing in Winnig's work that is specifically new or different. Most of his ideas parallel those current in Right radical or conservative circles. Nor can it be shown that his ideas exercised any particular influence—certainly not on Hitler, whose concepts were formed well before Winnig published his *Der Glaube an das Proletariat*. What is of interest is that Winnig's ideas grew as a natural extension of ideas developed while he was a member of the working class movement. While he was not immune to the climate of right-wing opinion in the 1920's, his basic formulation had been born before World War I.

Such power and attraction as Winnig's work held grew out of its presentation in the form of personal experience. He commanded attention because he was a worker speaking about workers. Such is certainly not the case with Ernst Juenger. The personal experiences which he had leaned upon to build his concept of the warrior failed him in this new area of discussion. Rather, Juenger depended upon logical extensions of a world view developed in the trenches carried over into the realm of the factory. In so doing he created the most original of all the systems under discussion here.

Juenger, in his major work on the subject, *Der Arbeiter*,[137] accepts at least some of the criticism of liberal and Marxian thought which were common to the other theorists of the Right. He too denies that the worker is an economic expression and argues that the middle class, by viewing him as such, misses completely the significance of the worker.[138] But the worker cannot be viewed as a representative of the Fourth Estate, as Winnig and the others wished.[139] Rather, the definition hinges upon the relationship to the "elemental" in human life, the irrational basis and wellspring of human existence.[140] Middle-class man, with his emphasis upon reason, law, and order, lacks any concept of this elemental stratum of life or else considers it vaguely as evil. He lacks any real connection with this "elemental" and is therefore astounded and shaken when it bursts forth into everyday life as it did during the war. Civilization may paper over the fissures created by such an outburst, but it cannot abolish it from life.[141]

The worker does not shrink from the elemental or its consequences but embraces it and learns to live according to its imperative commands. In this the worker is more "natural" than middle-class man, but this naturalness is neither good nor evil—it is beyond such valuations. Juenger recognizes the quality of the demonic in the elemental and argues that it must be accepted.[142]

If the term "worker" is not defined by membership in a class or an estate, how is it defined? Juenger answers that the worker is a form (*Gestalt*) which transcends these limits of middle-class thought. The *Gestalt* is a "whole which includes more than the sum of its parts"; it is the "highest meaning-giving reality." [143] As a reality it *is*; it neither is born nor dies, and individuals gain reality to the extent that they partake in the *Gestalt*. Apparently, various forms dominate at various periods of history and affect all things during their period of dominance. In the period in which the form of the worker dominates there is nothing which is not conceivable as work. "Work is the tempo of the fist, the thoughts, the heart, the life by day and night, science, love, art, belief, worship, war." [144]

The form of the worker, then, cannot be bounded by any of the nineteenth-century middle-class constructions because it dominates all of life and brings it into a new relationship with the elemental.[145]

In this manner Juenger is able to extend the area covered by the term "worker" as the other Right radicals had done. But with Juenger it is not so much a matter of awarding more tasks the designation of "work" as it is one of describing the style of approach as "workmanlike." Thus he notes that there is a marked tendency for the modern journalist to carry out his tasks like a worker rather than as a member of the middle class.[146] In a similar manner he frequently equates the front-line soldier of the war with the worker, calling him in one place the "wage earner of the battlefield." [147]

The triumph of the *Gestalt* of the worker in the world is signalized by the appearance of a new form of mankind—the *type*. Juenger argues that one does not find worker types and middle-class types, but rather that the "type" defines men in the world controlled by the form of the worker just as the "individual" expressed the middle-class world and the "person" expressed the world of warriors, priests, and farmers. The identifying marks of the type are his close connection with numbers, his love for mathematical structures, the metallic cast of his features, his lack of spiritual differentiation, and the marked simplicity of his standard of living and home furnishings.[148] The type is not only different from the individual, it represents an attack upon individuality which we can see being carried through everywhere. The modern journalist is a worker, says Juenger, because his writings report facts and do not reflect his opinions. To this extent he is a type just as the nineteenth-century journalistic commentator was an individual.[149]

This new race is first concretized by the mobilization of the world through modern techniques. Juenger is distinguished from almost all of the other men discussed here by his fascination with machinery. While the others ignore or minimize the importance of machinery to the figure of the worker, for Juenger the machine is the indispensable and often demonic means by which the worker realizes himself. Whether in the factory or on the battlefield the worker is inseparable from the machine. It is through the machine that he gains contact with the elemental and releases that often devastating force into the world.[150]

The eventual goal of this mobilization of material through the *Gestalt* of the worker is the destruction of the bourgeois world and its replacement by a workers' state. Liberal democracy must give way to a workers' democracy which will probably be dictatorial in form (though certainly not a dictatorship of the proletariat). Even nationalism and socialism will have only transitional value in the movement from the middle-class world to the worker's world, for they are, according to Juenger, essentially middle-class forms.[151]

The figure of the worker in this strongly anarchistic construct is clearer than in the systems of any of the other writers with which we have dealt. He appears as an intelligent, ruthless being who rips apart the old world for his own purposes. He has transcended the categories of good and evil just as he has transcended the limits of present societal categories. He is the result of a man of extraordinary ability pursuing his assumptions to their uttermost limits.

5 • CONCLUSION

This body of thought developed by the men surveyed here, whether it be called conservative, conservative revolutionary, or Right radical, does show a high degree of consensus on the part of the theorists both as to premises and goals. All of them were convinced that some changes had to occur in the society in which they lived in order to alter it from what they conceived to be a jungle into a true community. They all agreed that analyses of societal problems offered by the liberals and the Marxists did not go to the heart of the matter. This was not a *reasoned* response to the problems of the 1920's but rather an expression of their deepest feelings. In abandoning the economic approach to social problems they did not conclude that economic reforms were unnecessary; indeed most of them favored sweeping economic changes in the direction of socialized control. Rather it seemed to them that the community had to be based upon some deeper motive than selfish pecuniary gain (for so they interpreted the liberal concepts of social organization). This deeper motivation had to spring from some fundamental source and they turned quite easily to the realm of the biological. It matters little that their grasp of biological problems was, to say the least, slight. They felt, and were able to convince others to feel, that it offered the key to the solution of social problems. Perhaps it is significant that the one man of this group who was trained in biology, Ernst Juenger, did not use the racist argument. His concept of the elemental was common to all of nature, and not to any particular racial group.

If their analysis of the ills of society was considerably more slipshod than that of the Marxists (though not necessarily more wrong-headed), their conception of the society which they wished to bring into being was much more detailed than anything which Marx had offered. Perhaps this was because these men were at least partially conservative and at least knew what they wanted to save. Again, it was Ernst Juenger, in so many ways the least conservative, who offered the sketchiest picture of the coming society.

Critics of the ideas of these men have been at pains to show their lack of scientific basis and have often written off these systems (especially Hitler's) as being a mere hodgepodge of ideas. No one now claims for them a scientific basis, but these systems are not the only ones which suffer from such a weakness. More serious is the charge that they are not systems at all but rather grab-bags of ideas. The charge is serious not because of its correctness, but because its widespread acceptance has blinded observers to the power of these ideas and has made the understanding of the Hitler era more difficult.

Finally we must see what image of the worker emerged from the systems of these men. He still retained some of the characteristics of his Marxian background. He was stalwart, intelligent, and fundamentally goodhearted. But instead of being oppressed he was now viewed as perhaps oppressed but certainly misled. Yet since he was not degenerate he represented the greatest hope for the salvation of society. Master of the world of machines, he had to be led back to an understanding of nature so that he could fulfill the task which destiny had laid on him—the building of the people's community. Lastly, it might be added that a larger and larger segment of the community was viewed as being part of the working class, so that when the National Socialists had the opportunity to put into practice their theories they could say, and really believe, that they had created a society of workers.

IV • POLITICAL STEREOTYPES: CONCLUSION

The warrior and worker were both political stereotypes of the greatest importance to the burgeoning National Socialist movement. Neither was an entirely realistic picture but both had roots in experience common to millions of Germans. Therefore these Germans were able to identify with the figures and find National Socialism more acceptable than otherwise might have been the case. Both of the figures had elements of nobility about them that were carefully played up by the Nazi orators in order to please their listeners and win their confidence. This was not actually a swindle because the National Socialists believed themselves to be the party of the warrior and worker; they were national *and* revolutionary. The more bizarre elements of the ideology were somewhat muted by the acceptability of these stereotypes.

The warrior and the worker stand as symbols of destruction and creation which apparently have a wide appeal and touch the deepest currents of man's being. By amalgamating these figures the impression was given that destructiveness was being used for creative purposes, an impression satisfying both to the brute instincts and the conscience of man. That destructiveness would win out over creativity was perhaps not readily apparent in the years of the rise of the NSDAP.

While the particular figures of the warrior and the worker might not evoke ready response everywhere, it would seem that effective stereotypes do very often stimulate the impulses towards destruction and creation, though their particular features may vary greatly. Thus, in the United States the frontiersman is not only a farmer building a new land but also a figure of violence destroying both man and nature to accomplish his purposes. The same is true of the figure of the bearded Castro revolutionist or the laborer-soldier of the Russian Revolution. These images serve to cloak with heroism and decency motives that are often neither heroic nor decent. But the political stereotypes also serve to spur men on to necessary action and help to sustain them through it. These powerful images testify both to the importance and the ambiguity of illusion in the affairs of men. It is obvious that illusions are often dangerous; what is less obvious is whether it is possible for society to operate without them at all.

NOTES

1. This division agrees with that of Dr. Kurt Kamp, *Die Haltung des Frontkaempfers* (Wurzburg: Konrad Triltsche Verlag, 1940). This work, which shows a considerable National Socialist influence, is not, however, very helpful. A much better study of the literature of the First World War is: William K. Pfeiler, *War and the German Mind* (New York: Columbia University Press, 1941).

2. There was a noticeable lag between the actual experience and its assimilation in literary form. This is especially true of the second phase when a valid exposition of the front situation might have been considered dangerous to morale. This at least seems to have been the case with Fritz von Unruh's *Opfergang* (Frankfurt/M.: Societaets Verlag, 1931). This was written in 1916 but suppressed. Instead, the public was offered such sickening confections as Walter Flex's *Die schwimmende Insel*, which managed to combine the worst elements of German romanticism, philistine religious sentiments, and crass patriotism. (Munich: C. H. Beck'sche Verlagsbuchhandlung, 1925). This play was first produced during the war.

3. Rudolf G. Binding, *Wir fordern Reims zur Uebergabe auf* (Frankfurt/M.: Ruetten und Loening Verlag, 1935).

4. Friedrich Meinecke, *The German Catastrophe* (Cambridge: Harvard University Press, 1950), p. 25.

5. Jules Romains, *Death of a World* (New York: Alfred Knopf, 1938), pp. 463–65.

6. See Otto Strasser, "Von Sinn des Krieges," *Die Gruenen Hefte der "N.S.-Briefe"* (Berlin: Kampf-verlag, 1930).

7. Fritz Stern, *The Politics of Cultural Despair* (Berkeley: University of California Press, 1961), p. 176.

8. *Ibid.*, p. 176. See also Hans Blueher, *Wandervogel: Geschichte einer Jugendbewegung* (Prien/Obb.: Anthropos Verlag, 1919), II, 137.

9. See Harry Pross, "Das Gift der blauen Blume." *Vor und Nach Hitler* (Freiburg: Walter-Verlag, 1962), pp. 106–7. Hans Blueher speaks of the failure of the movement to include boys from other classes of society (*Wandervogel*, II, 126). This failure is attested by the membership rolls of one group which includes 51 *Gymnasium* students, 4 *Realschule* students, and 1 merchant. See Richard Poppe, *Jungdeutschland* (Waldenburg-in-Schlesien: [n.p.] 1912), p. 15.

10. Julius Langbehn, *Rembrandt als Erzieher*, 37th ed. (Weimar: Alexander Dunker Verlag, 1922), p. 91. See also Stern, *op. cit.*, pp. 97–180; and Hans Blueher, *Wandervogel*, I.

11. Blueher, *Wandervogel*, II, 116.

12. *Ibid.*, I, 116.

13. According to Karl Fischer, the founder of the movement, the term "Bachant" was derived from the latin "Vagus," or wanderer.

14. Blueher, *Wandervogel*, I, 115.

15. Hannah Arendt comments on the widespread interest in crime and vice shown by Europeans at the turn of the century. Hannah Arendt, *The Origins of Totalitarianism* (New York: Harcourt, Brace and Co., 1951), pp. 80–81. At a later date Bertolt Brecht was also to play on this fascination.

16. Blueher's entire study shows the importance of the charismatic personality to the *Wandervogel* movement. He returned to this theme in a later work, *Fuehrer und Volk in der Jugendbewegung* (Jena: Eugen Diederichs, 1917). Ernst Juenger, in his *Der Kampf als inneres Erlebnis* (Berlin: E. S. Mittler und Sohn, 1929), dwells on the importance of the personality of the storm troop leader. See also Adolf Hitler's chapters on personality in *Mein Kampf*, (New York: Reynal and Hitchcock, 1940), pp. 660–72; 750–63.

17. Blueher, *Wandervogel*, II.

18. Adolf Hitler later had a picture of the charge at Langemarck in his office at the Brown House. Fridolin Solleder, in his *Vier Jahre Westfront* (Munich: Verlag Max Schick, 1932) has a somewhat more prosaic explanation of why the young volunteers of the List Regiment sang as they went forward. Instead of being issued the normal spiked helmet at the beginning of the war, they were given a peaked cap somewhat reminiscent of the later SA cap. Near Langemarck they were mistaken for the enemy by nervous troops and fired upon. Singing "Deutschland ueber Alles" seemed to them the best quick way to establish their true identity. Shortly after the battle they exchanged their caps for the more conventional spiked helmet.

19. Perhaps in a land which placed such high valuation on education this is scarcely surprising, but it is well to remember that *Gymnasium, Realschule,* and University men cannot have constituted more than a few hundred thousand soldiers. By contrast, German labor unions, during the first year, sent over one million men, or about 43% of their membership, into the armed forces, and by 1918, 58% of the union membership had been called into service. About 10% died there. See Max Schippel, *Die Gewerkschaften, der Krieg, und die*

Revolution (Berlin: Bund deutscher Gelehrter und Kuenstler [Buch-abteilung] 1919), pp. 6–8. One other conclusion arises from these figures: the majority of the German army was made up of groups other than students or organized laborers.

20. Walter Flex, *Der Wanderer zwischen beiden Welten* (Munich: C. H. Beck'sche Verlagsbuchhandlung, 1917).

21. *Ibid.*, pp. 9, 40. "Rein bleiben—Reif werden" a slogan of the *Wandervogel*.

22. *Ibid.*, pp. 9–11, 31.

23. *Ibid.*, p. 9.

24. Walter Flex, *Gesammelte Werke*. Bd. I. (Munich: [n. p.] 1925), pp. xi-xii, quoted in Kamp, *op cit.*, p. 7.

25. —— *Der Wanderer . . .* , p. 2.

26. *Ibid.*, pp. 28 ff.

27. This was the case with Flex, Wurche, Juenger, Brandt, and Binding, to name but a few.

28. Certain important exceptions to this rule will be mentioned below.

29. Ernst Juenger, *The Storm of Steel* (London: Chatto and Windus, 1929), p. x; on this sense of nostalgia see also Siegfried Sassoon, *Memoirs of an Infantry Officer* (New York: Coward, Mc-Cann and Co., 1930), p. 116.

30. Ernst Juenger, *Storm of Steel*, p. 108.

31. It is possible that more imaginative men than Haig might have discovered a better and less expensive solution than the head-on attack by massed infantry. But it is also true that no general shone brilliantly on the Western Front. Even such men as Allenby and

Falkenhayn, who demonstrated much greater ability in Palestine and Rumania, were no better than average in the West. Falkenhayn is even credited with the classic proposition of the attrition theory though he may not have had this in mind at Verdun.

32. Jules Romains, *Verdun* (New York: Alfred Knopf, 1939), Chapter 1.

33. Wilhelm von Schramm, "Schoepferische Kritik des Krieges," *Krieg und Krieger* (Berlin: Junker und Duenhaupt, 1930).

34. The phrase is Jules Romains'.

35. Ernst Juenger, *Storm of Steel*, pp. 107–8.

36. Erich Maria Remarque, *All Quiet on the Western Front* (Boston: Little, Brown and Co., 1929, 1945), p. 99.

37. Ernst Juenger, *Der Kampf* . . . , p. 100.

38. Heinrich Brandt, *Trommelfeuer* (Hamburg: Fackelreiter Verlag, 1929), p. 179; Joachim von der Goltz, *Der Baum von Cléry* (Munich: Albert Langen, 1934), p. 52.

39. Solleder, *Vier Jahre Westfront*, p. 82.

40. Friedrich Sailler, *Bruecke ueber das Niemandsland* (Leipzig: Wilhelm Goldmann Verlag, 1938), p. 8.

41. Ernst Juenger, *Storm of Steel*, p. 118.

42. Brandt, *op. cit.*, pp. 187–202.

43. Franz Franziss, *Wir von der Somme* (Freiburg: Herder und Co., 1936), p. 20. Compare this with Juenger: "The Army, men, animals and machines, hammered into one weapon." *Der Kampf* . . . p. 111.

44. Friedrich Georg Juenger, "Krieg und Krieger," in *Krieg und Krieger*, p. 61.

45. Remarque, *All Quiet . . .* , p. 56.

46. Marinetti, "Il Poemo Africano," quoted in Henry M. Pachter, "National Socialist and Fascist Propaganda for the Conquest of Power," *The Third Reich* (London: Weidenfeld and Nicolson, 1955), p. 724.

47. Erich Maria Remarque, *The Road Back* (Boston: Little, Brown and Co., 1931), p. 337.

48. ———— *All Quiet . . .* , p. 23.

49. Von Schramm, *op. cit.*, p. 39.

50. Von der Goltz, *op. cit.*, p. 46.

51. Ernst Wiechert, "Die Flucht ins Ewige," *Die Novellen und Erzaehlungen* (Munich: Verlag Kurt Desch, 1962), p. 134. This story was first published in 1927.

52. *Ibid.*, p. 135.

53. The terms appear in the writings of many authors. "Storm of steel" is, of course, Ernst Juenger's. Shells as "birds of prey" appear in Franziss, *op. cit.*, pp. 15, 47; Brandt, *op. cit.*, p. 173; shells as animals appear in Juenger, *Der Kampf . . .* , p. 79; Brandt, *op. cit.*, p. 166. The last two figures are from Remarque, *All Quiet . . .* , p. 58.

54. See Ernst Juenger, *Der Kampf . . .* , pp. 6–10.

55. Remarque, *All Quiet . . .* , p. 25.

56. Brandt, *op. cit.*, p. 194.

57. Remarque, *All Quiet . . .* , p. 44. In a longer passage in *The Road Back*, pp. 308–10, Remarque is even more explicit and more mystical about the closeness of this union.

58. ———— *The Road Back*, pp. 308–10.

59. Ernst Juenger, *The Storm of Steel*, p. 309.

60. *Ibid.*, p. 109.

61. Friedrich Georg Juenger "Krieg und Krieger," p. 65.

62. Hitler, *Mein Kampf*, pp. 212–13.

63. Other similar references include: ". . . the face thrust forward, the screaming mouth open, wild hot eyes under the rim of the steel helmet . . . " Sailler, *op. cit.*, p. 9; ". . . deeply earnest manly faces under the black rim of the steel helmet . . ." Franziss, *op. cit.*, p. 188; "Yet the exhausted eyes of the man, under the filthy rim of the steel helmet continued to search." Wiechert, *op. cit.*, p. 127. The best visual representation of this figure can be found in the paintings of the National Socialist-approved Elk Eber.

64. Ernst Juenger, "Totale Mobilmachung," *Krieg und Krieger*, p. 29.

65. ——— "Vorwärts," *Der Kampf um das Reich* (Essen: Wilhelm Kamp, 1932), p. 6.

66. ——— *Der Kampf als inneres Erlebnis*, pp. 76–77.

67. This estrangement grew, of course, out of the bitterness felt by the men who had to endure the life of the trenches toward those who were able to live well in headquarters located safely out of battle range. To a greater extent than in previous wars, staff officers were absent from the battlefield. The necessity for this situation can be understood, but the unfairness of the arrangement, coupled with the advantages of the position sometimes taken by the staff officers, did not endear them to the front line. One might almost say that the solidarity felt by the officers and men in the trenches foreshadowed the rejection of the ruling class which occurred in the postwar revolutions.

68. Remarque, *All Quiet* . . . , pp. 155–88.

69. *Ibid., passim.*

70. Von Schramm, *op. cit.,* p. 40.

71. Ernst Juenger, *Der Kampf als inneres Erlebnis,* p. 53.

72. Remarque, *The Road Back,* p. 117.

73. Sailler, *op. cit.,* pp. 152, 196.

74. *Ibid.,* p. 160.

75. Remarque, *The Road Back,* p. 25.

76. Edgar Schmidt-Pauli, *Geschichte der Freikorps. 1918–1924* (Stuttgart: Robert Lutz nachf. Otto Schramm, 1936), p. 23.

77. Kamp, *op. cit.,* p. 93.

78. Remarque, *The Road Back,* p. 216.

79. Ernst Juenger, *Der Kampf als inneres Erlebnis.* p. 88.

80. Remarque, *All Quiet . . . ,* p. 43. In a somewhat similar vein Sailler writes, "The living comrade has not forgotten his dead brothers." *Op. cit.,* p. 395.

81. This pattern is repeated in the National Socialist tales of the period. See, for example, Walter Wuelfing, *Peter Krafts Kampf* (Reutlingen: Enslin und Laiblins Verlagsbuchhandlung, 1936); and Hans Zoeberlein, *Der Befehl des Gewissens* (Munich: Franz Eher nachf., 1937).

82. The concentration camps were one means of burying any signs of opposition.

83. He was ritually invoked at the annual Nuremburg Rally, of course. See Nationalsozialistische Deutsche Arbeiterpartei, *Erster Parteitag Grossdeutschlands.* (Munich: Franz Eher nachf., 1938).

84. Curt Riess, *Joseph Goebbels* (London: Hollis and Carter, 1949), pp. 314–15; ——— *Voelkischer Beobachter.* (North German ed.) Feb. 4, 5, 1943.

85. This statement is based upon a reading of what might be called the "naturalistic school" of German war novel as represented by such authors as Willi Heinrich, or Wolfgang Ott, *Sharks and Little Fish,* trans. Ralph Mannheim (New York: Pantheon Books, 1958). The best of the works on World War II are not at all naturalistic and thus are difficult to compare with those of World War I. See, for example, Günter Grass, *Die Blechtrommel* (Darmstadt: H. Luchterhand, 1960), or Heinrich Böll, *Wo warst du Adam* (Opladen: F. Middelhauve, 1951). Another immensely popular genre of war literature is that which appears in such magazines as *Der Landser* and is roughly akin to the "dime novel" of yesteryear. The author has made no attempt to survey this literature.

86. Thus many supposedly militant Social-Democratic parties before 1914 acted in a suspiciously "revisionist" manner. See Wm. A. Jenks, *Vienna and the Young Hitler* (New York: Columbia University Press, 1960).

87. In 1900 even the most progressive-minded citizens did not imagine that it would be possible to raise the majority of the population to a condition of comparative opulence. The hopes of most men centered on achieving a rather Spartan condition of decency.

88. Otto Strasser called himself a "conservative revolutionary" and both he and his brother showed some influence of Moeller van den Bruck.

89. Othmar Spann, *Der Wahre Staat,* 4th ed. (Jena: Verlag von Gustav Fischer, 1938). Spann was professor of political economy and society at the University of Vienna. The previous editions of the book are dated 1921, 1923, and 1931.

90. *Ibid.,* pp. 23–24, 47 ff., 154 ff., 158.

91. *Ibid.*, pp. 168–70.

92. For Spann's connections with Alfred Rosenberg's *Kampfbund fuer Deutsche Kultur*, see Hildegard Brenner, *Die Kunstpolitik des Nationalsozialismus* (Hamburg: Rowohlts deutsche Enzyklopaedie, 1963), pp. 7 ff.

93. Hitler, *Mein Kampf.* pp. 660–72.

94. See Stern, *op cit.*, for a good resumé of the work of Moeller van den Bruck.

95. Arthur Moeller van den Bruck, *Das dritte Reich*, 3rd ed. (Hamburg: Hanseatische Verlagsanstalt, 1932), p. 46.

96. *Ibid.*, p. 147.

97. *Ibid.*, pp. 125, 152.

98. *Ibid.*, chapter "Liberal" pp. 69 ff.

99. Stern, *op. cit.*, p. 211.

100. Oswald Spengler, *Preussentum und Sozialismus* (Munich: C. H. Beck'sche Verlagsbuchhandlung, 1934), p. 30 (1st ed. 1919).

101. *Ibid.*, p. 8.

102. *Ibid.*, p. 68.

103. *Ibid.*, pp. 13–14.

104. *Ibid.*, p. 43.

105. Otto Strasser, *Aufbau des deutschen Sozialismus* (Leipzig: Wolfgang Richard Lindner Verlag, 1932), pp. 19–21.

106. *Ibid.*, pp. 15 ff.

107. *Ibid.*, pp. 34–36.

108. *Ibid.*, pp. 39–40.

109. *Ibid.*, pp. 37 ff.

110. *Ibid.*, p. 40.

111. *Ibid.*, pp. 77–78.

112. Gregor Strasser, *Freiheit und Brot* (Berlin: Kampf Verlag, 1928). On the various topics see: inequality, p. 61; estate and class, p. 15; proletarians, p. 56; anti-capitalism, pp. 28, 33–36; socialism and nationalism, *passim.*

113. Hitler, *Mein Kampf*, pp. 42–44.

114. *Ibid.*, p. 41.

115. It was a favorite myth of the 1930's that the German workers were prepared to rise in revolt against their Nazi enslavers. Actually there was no working-class revolt. Those that stayed in the factories during the war produced to the best of their abilities. Those that entered the armed services performed their tasks with only the normal amount of complaint. The workers may have accepted the National Socialist revolution with reservations, but accept it they did.

116. Most of this biographical material is contained in: August Winnig, *Der Weite Weg*, 2nd ed. (Hamburg: Hanseatische Verlags-anstalt, 1932). For his statements about the Kapp *Putsch* episode see August Winnig, *Volkspolitik und Parteipolitik* (Berlin: Verlag fuer praktische Politik und geistige Erneuerung, 1921) ; for his later views see August Winnig, *Europa* (Berlin: Eckart Verlag, 1952).

117. For comparison, Ernst Juenger's most usual method of presentation is the diary. Hitler's *Mein Kampf* is another good example of the style.

118. The first appearance of this strand of his thought is found in: August Winnig, *Vom Proletariat zum Arbeitertum* (Hamburg:

Hanseatische Verlagsanstalt, 1930). It is really the only major addition to the ideas he had already developed in *Der Glaube an das Proletariat*, neue Fassung (Munich: Milavida-Verlag, 1926).

119. The idea is put forward in: August Winnig, *Der Weltkrieg vom Standpunkt des deutschen Arbeiters* (Hamburg: Verlag Deutscher Bauarbeiterverband, 1915), pp. 25 ff. The idea was enlarged upon with statistical data in: August Winnig, *Der englische Wirtschaftskrieg und das werktaetige Volk Deutschlands* (Berlin: Verlag Reimar Hobbing, 1917), pp. 17–22. Later Winnig would trace the origins of this idea back to his early days on the editorial staff of *Der Grundstein*. See Winnig, *Der Weite Weg.* pp. 192–99.

120. Carl Schorske, *German Social Democracy 1905–1917* (Cambridge: Harvard University Press, 1955).

121. That this repudiation did not occur immediately is indicated by Winnig's continued membership in the Social Democratic Party and by his continued use of Marxian terminology, such as the concept of "surplus value." See *Der Weltkrieg . . .*, p. 8. Even as late as 1921 he still thought in class terms. See *Volkspolitik . . .*, pp. 4, 5, *passim*.

122. Winnig, *Der Glaube . . .*, pp. 3, 5.

123. *Ibid.*, p. 30.

124. *Ibid.*, p. 34.

125. Hannah Vogt, *Der Arbeiter*, 2nd ed. (Groene-Goettingen: August Schoenhuette und Soehne, 1947), p. 16.

126. Winnig, *Der Glaube . . .*, p. 5.

127. *Ibid.*, p. 7.

128. *Ibid.*, p. 39.

129. Winnig, *Der Weite Weg*, pp. 17 ff.

130. *Ibid.*, pp. 101–21.

131. Winnig, *Vom Proletariat* . . . , pp. 47–63.

132. August Winnig, *Der Arbeiter im dritten Reich* (Berlin: Buchholz und Weisswange Verlagsbuchhandlung, 1934).

133. August Winnig, *Europa* (Berlin: Eckart Verlag, 1938).

134. Winnig, *Vom Proletariat* . . . , pp. 35–38.

135. *Ibid.*, p. 96.

136. For a fuller resumé of Winnig's ideas, see Vogt, *op. cit.*, pp. 37–52.

137. Ernst Juenger, *Der Arbeiter* (Hamburg: Hanseatische Verlagsanstalt, 1932).

138. *Ibid.*, pp. 26 ff.

139. *Ibid.*, pp. 17, 64.

140. *Ibid.*, pp. 19–20.

141. *Ibid.*, pp. 42, 46–47, 50, 253–54.

142. *Ibid.*, pp. 19, 47–48, 50.

143. *Ibid.*, pp. 31, 295.

144. *Ibid.*, p. 65.

145. Vogt, *op. cit.*, p. 59. This excellent survey of Juenger's ideas has been used as a guide through much of this section.

146. Ernst Juenger, *Der Arbeiter*, p. 263.

147. *Ibid.*, pp. 106, 107–9, 142–44.

148. *Ibid.*, p. 218; Vogt, op. cit., p. 62.

149. Ernst Juenger, *Der Arbeiter*, pp. 261–62.

150. *Ibid.*, pp. 34, 72, 124, 161, 149–94.

151. Vogt, *op. cit.*, p. 67; Ernst Juenger, *Der Arbeiter*, pp. 78, 237–38.

IV

THE IDEOLOGIST

I • INTRODUCTION

The twenty years which have passed since the end of the Second World War have not served either to dull the shock of German atrocities or to increase greatly our understanding of the type of mentality capable of committing such acts. We quite easily assume that there was something uniquely German about the establishment of annihilation centers and wonder uneasily whether they may "try it again." As we forge the weapons for the destruction of Russian cities and steel our minds to accept the death of tens of millions of Americans we still find it difficult to believe that men could have so cold-bloodedly planned and carried through the wholesale murder of innocent people.

There will probably always remain some mystery as to how men move from bloody thought to monstrous deed. Obviously, constant repetition does help to transform the once unthinkable into the immediately feasible. Opportunity is also necessary; "kill the Jews" is not a conceivable program unless an incredibly favorable situation such as continental domination exists. When the proper situation and climate exist, then and then only does the road open to what is ordinarily out of bounds.

But why kill the Jews in the first place, and why so many of them; why not just the leaders? The answers to such questions are neither neat nor simple. They involve not only the hopes, fears, and ideas of the few men ultimately responsible for the planning of the "final solution," but also the private fantasies of the thousands of men who carried out the project, and beyond them the attitudes of the entire German people and indeed the attitudes of their victims. In other words, there can be no final answer to the questions posed; we can only hope to understand broadly what happened and why it happened.

In any such study some attention should be paid to the stated beliefs of the leaders. For whether they seem plausible or not, the chance at least exists that the leadership will not only justify its actions in accordance with its beliefs but may even view the world through the framework provided by its ideology. The amount of casuistry employed to explain the apparent contradictions of the official ideology indicates the value which these men place upon consistency. Even if we perceive more deep-seated motivations—whether they be urges for raw power or corrupted sexual desires—these will appear at the conscious level of action in the form of a more or less consistent ideology.

The ideology of National Socialism has diverse roots and not all men who called themselves National Socialists believed precisely the same things. The old division between the Strasser and Hitler wings of the party was to some extent a split between those who emphasized the socialist and those who emphasized the nationalist aspects of the ideology. Heinrich Himmler and the SS were deeply concerned with racial questions, and to a much lesser degree with economic problems. Judging from his wartime diaries, the reverse was true of Joseph Goebbels. Alfred Rosenberg, the official party philosopher, was seldom in a position to implement his ideas or even to guide the actions of more important party members.

Thus it is by no means entirely clear what the National Socialist ideology was. Our knowledge of the party structure and power relationships, however, gives us good reason to believe that the personal beliefs of Adolf Hitler formed the central body of doctrine and certainly had the most influence upon decisions made by the Nazi regime. The major statement of these beliefs is contained in Hitler's most famous work, *Mein Kampf*, and particularly in Volume I. These ideas have been roundly condemned as being superficial, based upon false premises, unoriginal, and crude. All of these charges are true but scarcely to the point, because though the ideas in question were defective they had great effect. It is unfortunate but true that mediocre and even bad ideas have perhaps more impact upon the affairs of men than do great ideas. Therefore it behooves us to review once more the idea world of Adolf Hitler.

II • THE MIND OF THE FUEHRER

There are a number of features of Adolf Hitler's mentality with which the world is all too painfully familiar: his ability to conceive and pursue monstrous projects, his brutal crudity, his willingness to lie. All of these have been repeatedly remarked upon and do not necessitate discussion here. There are other qualities of his mind, however, which have been less often noted and which do seem worthy of more attention: Hitler's intellectualism, his logicality, the rigidity of certain of his idea patterns, and his artistic attitude.

We so often study National Socialism as an anti-intellectual movement that we lose sight of the fact that Hitler himself was an intellectual. He built his movement upon ideas and was a purveyor of ideas for a good part of his adult life.[1] Evidence from various periods of his life indicates that he read widely, if haphazardly, and was extremely retentive. He had many fields of interest: military works from the Franco-Prussian War and other works on military and naval technique; Karl May; Ibsen; Goethe; the librettos of Wagner's operas; Roman, Greek, and Germanic history; Nordic mythology; books on art and architecture; and the philosophical works of Schopenhauer and Nietzsche.[2] He tended to gather together a great number of books on one subject, go through them all, and retain a good deal of what he had read. Sometimes he astounded his aides by his grasp of the particulars of their field of specialization. During the war he entertained his secretaries by reciting from memory entire pages of Schopenhauer and other works.[3]

Of this reading Hitler said,

> [It is necessary] to distinguish in a book that which is of value and that which is of no value . . .; to keep the one in mind forever, and to overlook, if possible, the other. . . . Reading, furthermore, is not a purpose in itself, but a means to an end. It should serve, first of all, to fill in the frame which is formed by the talents and abilities of the individual . . . [4]

To this statement his biographer, Alan Bullock, replies,

> This is the picture of a man with a closed mind, reading only to confirm what he already believes, ignoring what does not fit in with his preconceived system.[5]

This is perfectly true, but compare Hitler's attitude with that of Gandhi, who

> ". . . frequently read into texts what he wanted them to say. A creative reader, he coauthored the impression a book made upon

him. He put things into it and took them back with interest. "It was a habit with me" he once wrote, "to forget what I did not like and to carry out in practice what I liked." [6]

It can be seen that one should not underestimate the power of the closed mind—it can alter the course of history.

The evidence of Hitler's intellectualism can be seen not only in his reading habits but also in his willingness to live by ideas and their consequences. That his ideas were bad or based on faulty premises does not make them any the less ideas, and there was about them an amazing internal consistency. This consistency extended also to his activities which were, to a striking degree, consonant with his view of the nature of the universe.

Hannah Arendt has long remarked upon the "ice cold logic" of Hitler.[7] The term at first sounds peculiar since we are not given to considering Hitler as a logical person. We cannot extend this idea of logicality to the premises upon which he based his system, since he was willing to accept the flimsiest grounds for his contentions. Rather, the logic appears in the consequences which he drew from his premises: culture was the only protection of the human race against the forces of nature; the Jews were culture destroyers; therefore the Jews were the enemy of the human race. Hitler always believed that he who says A must say B, and thus derived the conclusion that he who loves the human race must destroy the Jews. From insane premises to monstrous conclusions Hitler was relentlessly logical. There are evidences that he was not able to bring himself immediately to the decision that the Jewish population had to be murdered. That is, he seems for a time to have hoped that they could be "eliminated from public life" or "stripped of their power." But subsequently he felt that these were evasions of responsibility. Even when he did make his decision the brutal reality was masked by the understatement of the term "final solution." Yet reluctant or not, Hitler did face his responsibilities as an intellectual and acted in a manner fully consistent with his principles.

More curious than his consistency was the rigidity of certain patterns of his thought. August Kubizek, Hitler's companion in Linz and Vienna, had very early noted that Hitler had a series of phrases each of which was a shorthand notation for some political concept which he carried in his mind's eye. "One phrase was linked to another. It began with 'the storm of Revolution' and went through countless political and social slogans to the 'Holy Reich of all the Germans.' " [8] This same tight linkage appears again in his recorded conversations from the years 1940–44. Here it is interesting to note that the connections are often voiced spontaneously and in an apparently unconscious manner. Mention of the northern Germanic countries such as Norway or Holland calls to his mind the Swiss, the Austrians, or the Bavarians.[9] An even more consistent association is that between England-India and Russia.[10] Now it is true that not every mention of one of the members of the pair calls to mind the other member, but it does occur often enough to lead one to suspect that Hitler tended to think in terms of geographic and qualitative polarities. Such a polarity of thought has been mentioned by Alfred Rosenberg.[11] Norway and Austria were the two poles of the territory of the Third Reich and they also represented the two poles of the Germanic race. More often than not Hitler spoke of the southern Germanic groups in terms of apparent distaste, perhaps occasioned by their inferior state of "racial purity." England's empire in India paralleled Germany's empire in Russia, and one suspects that Hitler envisioned a future dominated by Germany in partnership with England which then would control Eurasia. The two "culture creating" races could between them protect Europe from the ravages of the "degenerate" French, the "cultureless" Americans, and the "culture destroying" Jew. Not enough is known about Hitler's mind to be very definite about this matter but it seems possible that it might provide some help in establishing the final boundaries of the Reich as envisioned by Hitler.

Lastly, in considering the mind of Adolf Hitler it is well always to remember that he considered himself an artist. The importance of this lies not in any artistic works which he may have produced (for these were negligible) but rather for the attitude which he often exhibited towards the world in general and towards political problems in particular. Architecture, with its mingling of artistic and social considerations, had always held an appeal for Hitler—in his youth he spent some time feverishly planning the reconstruction of Vienna.[12] When he rose to power he frequently caused his lieutenants great anxiety by dawdling over plans for new buildings when he should have been attending to more serious political matters. One may hazard the guess that some idea of what Hitler had in mind when he spoke of the Third Reich can be gained from a study of the plans for the rebuilding of Berlin as the new capital "Germania"; the plans for the party congress hall and rally area at Nuremberg; and from the Autobahn system which tied Germany together with broad bands of concrete.[13] The buildings and the road were to remain as a gigantic memorial to the efforts of Hitler and also were to serve to bring into existence that "Holy Reich of all the Germans," with its capital in Brandenburg, its great annual circus at Nuremberg, the tomb of its martyrs at Munich, and highways linking all parts of the system.

The architectural monuments served not only as memorials and concretizations of the idea of the Reich, but also as a magnificent stage from which Hitler could play his dramatic role before the world. Perhaps Hitler's greatest talent as an artist lay in the area of acting. The care which he gave to the staging of his speeches, the suspense which he deliberately created, were all carefully calculated to achieve the greatest effect. Even hostile observers were moved by the overpowering impact of the Nuremberg Rally proceedings. It needs only to be noted that these rallies were apparently also necessary to Hitler. Like many a good actor he fed on applause and needed the constant assurance that this world which he had created was real. One may even suspect that he hoped to broaden its reality by widening the stage.

Hitler's view of the Reich was to an important degree architectural and dramatic, artistic qualities which were given intensity by his merciless logic and strengthened by the rigidity of his idea patterns. These qualities of mind, unencumbered by moral sense or humaneness, were to make possible the planning of a disaster of tremendous proportions.

III • THE IDEOLOGY

Because of Hitler's strong sense of the dramatic he did not present his ideology as a rigorously constructed thesis but rather let it appear in bits and pieces scattered through his narration. Although it suffuses the whole of his speeches and writings it is seldom wholly distinct; but from his *Secret Conversations,* from his speeches, and especially from *Mein Kampf,* one may put together an outline of the ideology that is sufficiently detailed to cast some light on Hitler's policies.

Of his writings, *Mein Kampf* is undoubtedly the best and certainly the most widely known. Somewhere, long ago, someone described the prose of this work as "turgid." Now, every person writing in English who discusses the book seems impelled to use that epithet. Unfortunately, while there is some reason for such a description, it tends to blind one to the dramatic qualities inherent in the narrative which is the story of the education of the young Hitler. Commentators are at great pains to demonstrate the falsity of many of the statements made—a necessary task, but a demonstration which should not be confused with proof that the book is valueless. *Mein Kampf* is a compound of mendacity, nonsense, good sense, and shrewd observation. It is an immoral book which is highly moralistic. Though the narrative often drags, it is essentially dramatic and in some chapters, such as "The Revolution," it provides a brilliant presentation of the National Socialist view of the German upheaval. To borrow from Coleridge, it should be read with "the willing suspension of disbelief." When approached in this manner one is able, through *Mein Kampf*, to make contact with the mind and world of Adolf Hitler.

National Socialist ideology has been described as a "crude Darwinism," and certainly it contains much of the popular late-nineteenth-century spillover of Darwin's theories. The naked struggle for existence is present but not quite in the form that Darwin or his popularizers depicted it. Essentially, Hitler found two sets of laws of nature, or even two natures—the organic and the inorganic. The inorganic forces of nature are at war against the organic, and because of their great power they threaten to destroy organic nature and mankind in particular. The basic law of relationship between the two natures is one of conflict. Mankind, facing this implacable foe, can only survive through a constant, heroic effort of resistance.[14] By contrast, the basic law *within* the realm of organic nature is one not of conflict but of cooperation. Only by cooperative endeavor can mankind create the one sure defense against the forces of inorganic nature: culture. Only by bowing to the laws of organic nature—cooperative laws—can man survive.[15]

Hitler never did define what he meant by "culture." It was certainly something less than the sum total of man's achievements—since many of those achievements he despised. It seems to have been the product of "true people's communities" (of which more later) and included both technological and aesthetic creations. In the early twentieth century culture was considered by him to be in a state of stagnation and degeneration, but exactly what parts were still healthy is not really clear from a survey of Hitler's statements. Suffice it to say that culture represented for Hitler a real, though mystical, entity which was in dire danger of destruction, and it was against these forces of destruction that he took up his prophetic mission.[16]

If he was indefinite about the nature of culture, Hitler was most explicit about the relationship of man to this culture. Mankind is divided into a number of races which can be ranked according to their cultural abilities. There is no scientific basis for this assertion but it has nonetheless, in one form or another, gained considerable adherence in the modern world. White supremacists, Black Muslims, advocates of *Apartheid*, and supporters of the British Raj have all been eager to sanctify their prejudices with the patina of scientific respectability, no matter how specious the premises may be. Our predilection for scientific objectivity has forced hatred to don the white coat of the laboratory. Cultural creativity, then, became for Hitler the touchstone of racial differentiation. One race, the Aryan, is creative; many races—the Mongoloid, the Negroid, the Malaysian—are capable of carrying a culture for a time after it has been created for them by the Aryans; some groups, such as the Americans, are cultureless; and one race, the Jewish, is destructive of culture.[17] At various periods of history different groups within the Aryan race have borne the heavy burden of creation. In the ancient world it was the task of the Greeks and the Romans. In medieval Europe the Germanic tribes led the way. In the modern world, wracked by degeneration and internationalism, no Aryan group was really pure, but probably more "racially healthy" persons were to be found among the

Germans than in any other Aryan society. Thus the hand of fate itself lay on the shoulder of the German nation. It was commanded to save mankind from destruction by the forces of inorganic nature.[18]

The quality differentiating the culture-creating race from the other races is not, as one might have expected, an intellectual one. Hitler is quite explicit in affirming that the Germans are not more intelligent than the culture-carrying or culture-destroying races; he even refers to the "blockheaded" Germans.[19] The key point is, rather, the degree of selflessness imbedded in the character of the various races. The self-sacrificing Aryan can build a community; the highly individualistic Jew can never do so.[20] This difference is carried in the blood and hence all Jews, no matter how worthy may be their lives, are basically dangerous to communal life. For the Jew cannot survive except as a parasite feeding upon and eventually destroying healthy communities.[21] It is interesting to note that Hitler characteristically speaks of "the Jew" as though he were dealing with a single entity. It is a technique of personification which focuses the mind of a people on a single enemy in the fashion that the "Hate Sessions" of Orwell's *1984* were directed against the "sinister" figure of Goldstein.

The crisis of our age, as seen by Adolf Hitler, involved the breakdown of the healthy Aryan communities of Europe. If the process were to continue, human life would be impossible within a matter of centuries. There were at least three methods by which the Jew accomplished his nefarious scheme of devouring the healthy communities. The first, symbolized for Hitler by Vienna, was mongrelization. Through this process healthy German blood was polluted by intermixture with the lesser races or by union with the unspeakable Jew. His long diatribes on this score (and that of syphilis) show a perhaps pathological fascination with sexuality which forms a curious counterweight to his public puritanism.[22] Persons thus mongrelized were lost to the race and to the racial struggle.

A second manner in which the healthy national communities could be debauched was through the action of international finance (a Jewish scheme, naturally) which removed healthy national industries from Aryan control and placed them and the population at the mercy of the international financiers.[23] A concomitance to this process was the tendency of the bourgeoisie, debilitated by the heady wine of international speculation, to adopt liberal attitudes. This "inner Judaization" turned racially pure Aryans into spiritual Jews by giving them a selfish sense of individuality. Prewar Munich was a good example, Hitler said, of the insidious way in which a good German city could be ruined.[24]

Where the machinations of international finance could not corrupt, as for instance among the ranks of the workers, the international socialist movement took its place—directed, of course, by Jews. Hitler did not deny that these movements addressed themselves to real evils, evils brought on by the operation of the international capitalist system. He only objected to the internationalist solution offered which blinded the workers to their national obligations and interests. International socialism had made dupes of the workers and had left them terribly exposed when the war broke out, but it had not as yet corrupted the workers in the same manner that international capitalism had corrupted the bourgeoisie.[25]

For a man who believed implicitly that the Jews were plotting against the Aryan world, what was most impressive was the devilish cleverness of the whole plot. International capitalism drained the healthy national communities of their monies and resources while the natural results of this process, economic chaos and poverty, drove the workers into the net of international socialism. It was being carried out on such a grand scale and was so beautifully masked by the liberal Jewish press that only the most acute observer would realize that a plot existed.

Seen in this light, the events of the First World War and the revolution were the logical results of the long internal demoralization of the German state. Hitler, adopting the tones of an Old Testament prophet, argued that this collapse was a just retribution for the Germans' sin of forgetting their racial mission. Only one group, the front army, did not deserve to share this fate, but it too was caught up in the disaster. To the veterans of the front army fell the task of leading the Germans back to their true selves, of capturing the imagination of the workers and the masses of the German populace. It was to this task that the party of the soldiers and the workers, the NSDAP, was dedicated.[26]

The stakes were high in this battle because it was one of cosmic proportions. From the National Socialist point of view, if the Jew succeeded culture would inevitably be destroyed and man would again descend into the chaos of bestial life and final extinction. Because Hitler took this view of the situation he could claim that history would not record the manner in which the victory was sought but only whether it had been obtained.[27] He was not thinking in terms of decades, or even centuries, but of interglacial epochs.

Since the struggle was one of cosmic proportions it was necessary to bring into action the hero, here viewed as the warrior-worker-leader.[28] Hitler emphasized again and again the necessity of responsible personalities. "With the destruction of the personality and the race in this world, there vanishes the essential obstacle for the domination of the inferior: . . . the Jew." [29]

Leadership (responsible personality) was necessary for carrying out the fight. Democracy was the abandonment of responsibility to a weak majority rule, to compromise and half measures; it was the first step on the road to Marxism. "His [the Jew's] final goal in this State, however, is the victory of 'democracy' or as he understands it: because it eliminates the personality—and in its place puts the majority of stupidity, incapacity, and last, but not least, cowardice." [30]

The greater portion of these leaders could not be drawn from the old leadership classes, the nobility and the bourgeoisie. Those groups had compromised themselves through cowardice, cupidity, and blindness. The only group which remained that could possibly be effective was the great mass of the workers.[31] But, unfortunately, it was this group which had been most thoroughly alienated from the racial community through the process of proletarianization. Therefore, any party which hoped to struggle successfully against degeneration had to be socialist in order to win troops; but, on the other hand, it could not strive for a proletarian state for this would involve the destruction of the racial community.

In the Nazi cosmology it was impossible for the warrior-worker-hero to remain unattached from his race and the *Volk*-community. In Hitler's mind the dissolution of the community had gone so far because industrialization had created a large property-less mass of city dwellers who had lost their attachments to the soil and the community and had been drawn into the internationalist web.[32] In order to re-establish the community it was necessary to revivify the spirit of disinterestedness in the self and to re-emphasize racial and communal ties. The agency for this revivification was the mystical concept of *Blut und Boden*, blood and soil, in which the German community would be welded together not only by blood relationships but also by the mysterious relationship of organic to inorganic nature.

Just as German "idealism" was expressed by the mystical

nexus of blood and soil so "Jewish materialism" was expressed by the crass internationalist nexus of the stock exchange and Marxism. Here again we can see Hitler's tendency to establish polarities and parallelisms. The "natural" German community was opposed to the "artificial" Jewish group. Hitler's predilection for the natural goes back to his assumption that the great forces of inorganic nature cannot essentially be overcome, that only by cooperation can progress be obtained.[33] Thus, even the basic conflict between organic and inorganic nature resolves itself into a contest in which the organic can only hope to survive by cooperation. Only the natural people's community has the ability to cooperate with rather than coerce nature. History for the National Socialists was the story of consecutive attempts on the part of man to establish a working symbiosis with nature.

The National Socialist concept of time presented a curious picture, for the state of nature represented not only the background but the future of the race. The past was merged with the future in the identity of the barbarian, Germanic warrior with the barbaric German soldier. The First and the Third Reichs were identified with each other in one eternal Reich.

In reading various of Hitler's statements, especially those contained in his *Secret Conversations*, one becomes aware of the fact that he is speaking in two different dimensions of time. The one, which may be called "racial time," is the continuum in which such concepts as race or *Reich* are dealt with. It is in this dimension that the cosmic battle takes place. The dimension which might be called "historical time" is discontinuous and is contingent upon events occurring in "racial time." Hence the First World War and its immediate causes exist in the second dimension, but these events were determined by the increasing success of the Jew, a process taking place in the first time dimension.

Hitler's ideas on "space" were even more confusing. He

apparently saw the world divided into cultural "living spaces" —but their boundaries were blurred. "Nature does not know political frontiers." [34] It seems fair to say, however, that the idea of cultural living spaces tended to limit the area which any one society might dominate. It is true that Hitler was thinking in terms of middle European or European domination, but still the idea of limitation did exist. [35] The limiting factor was the community, the *Volksgemeinschaft*. It should not be expanded to the point where it would break up from lack of inner cohesion. On the other hand it must not be crowded to the point where the individual members would lose contact with the soil. There is no doubt that Hitler envisioned an expansion into Eastern Europe but it is not clear how far he intended to carry this expansion. [36] Perhaps the revelation of what could be done with road systems, fast trains, and airplanes extended his horizons. [37]

A number of terms constantly used by Hitler and the other National Socialists—*Volk*, *Reich*, *Blut und Boden*, and *Freiheit* —deserve special consideration. The *Volk* is the German people as an organic unit which passes beyond the ideas of citizenry; it places the individual not in a legal relationship to the other members of the state but in a blood relationship to the other members of the people's community. This is a relationship not only of present members of the community, but also of all past and future members as well. This mystical community, extended in time and space, is expressed politically and historically by the concept of the *Reich*.

The *Reich* is a limited space-time continuum which encloses the soil and is the field of action for the natural forces of race and blood. Since the *Reich* is a political ideal, it is not always realized by the form and the extent of the German state. (This was the case during the period of the Weimar Republic.) As a political concept the *Reich* is intimately connected with the

Roman imperial ideal, and through the Romans to Hellenism.[38] It is important to bear in mind Moeller van den Bruck's dictum that there is but one *Reich*, the *Reich* of the Germans.[39] Other states may become empires but the mystical grounding is absent. In any case it is well to remember that Hitler's Thousand Year *Reich* extended not only one thousand years into the future but a thousand years into the past as well, and beyond that to the Roman empire.[40]

The concept of *Blut und Boden* (blood and soil) is the reduction of the ideas *Volk* and *Reich* to their essential mystical character and might well be considered the mystical center of the National Socialist ideology. From this nexus a number of symbols of extraordinary power were drawn: the "blood flag" and the "Order of the Blood," the shovel and grain symbols, and the recurring red and black colors of Nazi pageantry. This concept was not arrived at by any rational method but rather by "thinking with the blood"—a process which was not only permitted but demanded by the ideology.

Just as the *Reich* was presented as an ideal state towards which the Germans should strive, so the ideal type of the warrior-worker was held up for emulation by all German men. Through the achievement of this ideal type of personality the individual best served the community and the Reich. The idea of the worker leads directly to the question of the socialistic content of National Socialism. It was long charged that Hitler employed socialism merely as a snare for the workers and that he actually delivered the state into the hands of the "bosses." [41] This attitude shows a basic misunderstanding of Hitler's socialist ideas. The first distinction which must be made is that for the National Socialists economic relationships did not form the substructure of the society—racial relationships occupied that position. Consequently, economic relationships were merely the reflection of the racial struggle. As Hitler analyzed the problem, industrialization had resulted in the removal of large numbers of workers from their connections with the community and the soil to the "soulless" cities where they became the ready targets for Marxism.[42]

Hitler did not agree that "the Jew" was primarily responsible for industrialization; "the Jew" had merely added to this process the idea of democracy which by destroying responsibility weakens the community.[43] This whole process by which the community weakens itself he termed "inner Judaization." Yet, though these masses had been lost to the community they had not been compromised as had the bourgeois politicians, nor had their minds been poisoned by Jewish rationalism as had those of the intellectuals, nor yet again had they become so thoroughly enmeshed in the toils of Jewish international finance as had the industrialists and the financiers.[44] Therefore they could be won back to the community and could create a fighting force capable of strengthening the society—but only through the agency of National Socialism and social justice.[45] The goal was not a dictatorship of the proletariat but a people's community of workers in which work, both of the hand and of the brain, was honored.[46] True communal balance rather than proletarian dominance was to be sought after. Thus, for Hitler, the appeal to the worker was not a fraud; it was one of the basic necessities of National Socialism.

But these goals could not be achieved while Germany acceded to the shameful conditions of the Versailles Treaty. The chains had to be broken—*Freiheit* (national freedom and honor) had to be regained. Freedom, for Hitler, was not an individual achievement. The freedoms of the Weimar Republic were a sham so long as the nation was enslaved.[47] Freedom was not only a state of existence, it was also a striving. Men marching in columns through the streets expressed this striving for freedom, and the National Socialist party was the best expression of all, for the NSDAP was the physical embodiment of the will to national power.

In its own terms the party was nothing short of an instrument of struggle against the forces of cosmic degeneration—the nineteenth-century state and the Jew. The party was the energy center of National Socialism ("Every German is a National Socialist, only the best National Socialists are party members"), and it was organized on the basis of responsibility, that is, on the leadership principle. But leadership worked not only from the top towards the bottom, it also implied that the leader drew inspiration from his followers. This was especially the case at the public meetings where the speaker drew his strength and ideas at least in part from the crowd.[48] This interplay between leader and follower, between speaker and listener, is difficult to describe except as a symbiosis in which each side supplemented the other. It was the great advantage of the Nazis that they understood this relationship. Not only was this true of Hitler and Goebbels, but of the minor party leaders as well.[49]

The Nazis also enjoyed other advantages. Many men recognized that postwar Germany was a battlefield, but only the National Socialists evolved the tactics proper to this battlefield. It was one of Hitler's contributions to the art of politics that he was able to define the tactics of the political soldier. Alan Bullock holds that Hitler did not want to stage a *Putsch* in 1923 against the power of the army and that the attempt of November 8th and 9th of that year failed because the basic prerequisites had not been fulfilled.[50] This may well be true, and it is certain that after 1925 the SA was never intended by Hitler to be an instrument for capturing the government by force.[51] No matter how many members of the *Freikorps* entered the SA and no matter what their intentions may have been, Hitler kept a tight rein on their ambitions and used them for his own purposes in his own way.[52] He transformed (or recognized the transformation of) each street into a battlefield. The right to march on these streets was symbolic of a victory. It is true that actual battles were fought but these only augmented the atmosphere of combat—if a fist had never been swung in anger the effect would still have been achieved. It is worth noting that in these marches the SA men often carried packs. This was not ordinary parade equipment; packs are worn by troops moving into the line of battle. This was the effect desired: these men were not parading for a victory already secured but rather were marching towards future battles. The psychological effect of the weight of the pack and ammunition belts upon the veteran must have been a considerable one.

If the streets were symbolic battlefields this was even more true of the meeting halls, for here the speakers fought for men's minds—fought to hold those already in their camp and fought to win new ones. Goebbels has said that the important phases of these battles were won before the speaker had even opened his mouth. The timing, at the end of the day's work when minds were tired and receptive, the flags and the bunting, the lights and the singing, this was the psychological artillery barrage which paved the way for the "infantry attack" of the speakers' words.[53] To the outside world this whole panoply of power appeared as a threat staged for the benefit or intimidation of the other parties. It is true that it acted in this manner but, more importantly, these demonstrations grew out of the inner needs of the party and were closely linked to the warlike vocabulary of the ideology. These demonstrations were far more necessary for the party members and for the unattached bystanders than they were for beating down the opposition. In fact, it is the contention of this author that internal considerations of both a party and national character always outweighed external considerations in the formulation of Hitler's policies.

The Nazis succeeded in 1933 because they had a coherent policy (again, insane but logical), because they had a determined membership that knew what it wanted and was not inhibited by considerations of proper conduct, and because they gave a great deal of attention to even the smallest details. That they succeeded was largely due to the energy, will power, and mental capacities of one man: Adolf Hitler. His ideas, seen at this distance and with the infinitely bitter experience of the annihilation centers behind us, seem unspeakably repulsive. To the generation which brought him to power this was not the case. Hitler's talk of a true people's community, his romantic visions of renewed ties with the soil, and his promise to restore national vigor all held their attraction for the German of that day. For those who recoiled from the racial hatred of his program—including many German Jews—it was always possible to take refuge in the old saw that the soup is never served as hot as it is cooked. They might better have taken counsel with another culinary proverb: "Don't read the menu; find out who is in the kitchen."

NOTES

1. See Alan Bullock, "The Political Ideas of Adolf Hitler" (International Council for Philosophy and Humanistic Studies *The Third Reich.*) (London: Weidenfeld and Nicolson, 1955), p. 351.

2. Reading interests: Franco-Prussian War, Adolf Hitler, *Mein Kampf* (New York: Reynal and Hitchcock, 1940), p. 8; Karl May, Kurt Luedecke, *I Knew Hitler* (London: Jarrolds, 1938), Chapter 27; Ibsen, Wagner, Goethe, etc., August Kubizek, *The Young Hitler I Knew*, (London: Alan Wingate, 1954), p. 135.

3. A. Zoller (ed.), *Hitler Privat* (Duesseldorf: Droste Verlag, 1949), p. 81.

4. Hitler, Mein Kampf, pp. 46–47.

5. Alan Bullock, *Hitler, A Study in Tyranny* (New York: Harper and Bros., 1952), p. 43. Kubizek also agrees with this judgment. See Kubizek, *op. cit.*, p. 136.

6. Louis Fischer, *Gandi: His Life and Message for the World* (New York: Signet Key Books, 1954), p. 30.

7. Hannah Arendt, "Ideologie und Terror," *Offener Horizont. Festschrift fuer Karl Jaspers* (Munich: R. Piper and Co., 1953), p. 244.

8. Kubizek, *op. cit.* p. 173.

9. Adolf Hitler, *Hitler's Secret Conversations. 1941–1944* (New York: Farrar, Straus and Young, 1953), pp. 14–15, 19, 21, 23, 24, 28, 39, 66, 105.

10. *Ibid.*, pp. 13, 15, 17, 20, 22, 24, 35, 39, 76, 170, 201.

11. Alfred Rosenberg, *Memoirs of Alfred Rosenberg* (Chicago: Ziff-Davis Publishing Co., 1953), p. 248.

12. Kubizek, *op. cit.*, pp. 118–23.

13. The plans for the *Autobahnen* did not originate with Hitler, but since he actually put them into effect he could reasonably claim credit for their creation.

14. Hitler, *Mein Kampf*, pp. 396–97.

15. *Ibid.*, p. 393.

16. *Mein Kampf* has, ironically enough, a good deal of Old Testament fervor about it. Hitler is telling the chosen people, in this case the Germans, that they deserve their fate because they have worshipped false idols. It was his purpose to transform them into true idolaters.

17. Hitler, *Mein Kampf*, pp. 407–25.

18. *Ibid.*, pp. 593–94.

19. *Ibid.*, p. 784.

20. *Ibid.*, pp. 412–16.

21. Hitler, *Secret Conversations*, pp. 115, 256.; *Mein Kampf*, p. 589.

22. Hitler, *Mein Kampf*, pp. 388 ff.

23. *Ibid.*, pp. 316–21.

24. *Ibid.*, pp. 200–3.

25. *Ibid.*, pp. 302–88.

26. *Ibid.*, pp. 267–69, 384, 510, 620–23.

27. *Der Hitler Prozess vor dem Volksgericht in Muenchen* (Munich: Knorr und Hirth, 1924). II, 262–69.

28. Peter Viereck, *Metapolitics: From Romanticism to Hitler* (New York: Alfred Knopf, 1941), Chapters 5 and 6.

29. Hitler, *Mein Kampf*, p. 441.

30. *Ibid.*, pp. 435–36.

31. *Ibid.*, p. 680.

32. *Ibid.*, Vol. I, Chapter 2.

33. *Ibid.*, p. 393.

34. *Ibid.*, p. 174.

35. *Ibid.*, pp. 174–81.

36. *Ibid.*, Vol. II, Chapter 14.

37. Hitler, *Secret Conversations*, pp. 4, 13.

38. Dr. Werner Rittich, *New German Architecture* (Berlin: Terramare, 1941), pp. 38–39; German Library of Information, *A Nation Builds* (New York: German Library of Information, 1940), p. 15.

39. Arthur Moeller van den Bruck, *Germany's Third Empire* (London: George Allen and Unwin Ltd., 1934), p. 263.

40. Hans Frank notes that the NSDAP of the party standards is to be equated with the SPQR on the standards of the Roman legions. Hans Frank, *Im Angesicht des Galgens* (Munich: Friedrich Alfred Beck Verlag, 1953), p. 102.

41. See especially Franz Neumann, *Behemoth* (New York: Oxford University Press, 1942).

42. Hitler, *Mein Kampf*, pp. 67–68, 360–64, 438–47.

43. *Ibid.*, p. 438.

44. *Ibid.*, pp. 452–54.

45. *Ibid.*, pp. 464–70.

46. "Germany Has Today Become the Land of Labor." Speech by Hermann Goering to the German Labor Front, Sept. 10, 1938. NSDAP, *Erster Parteitag Grossdeutschlands* (Munich: Franz Eher nachf., 1938), p. 241.

47. See Hitler's speech of April 12, 1922, in Adolf Hitler, *My New Order* (New York: Reynal and Hitchcock, 1941), pp. 11-27.

48. Bullock, *Hitler* . . . , p. 347.

49. See Karl Wahl, . . . *es ist das deutsche Herz* (Augsburg: Im Selbstverlag Karl Wahl, 1954); Ernst von Salomon, *Fragebogen* (New York: Doubleday and Co., 1955), pp. 235–36.

50. Bullock, *Hitler* . . . , pp. 102–3.

51. Frank, *op. cit.*, p. 103; *Mein Kampf*, Vol. II, Chapter 9.

52. For the entry of the *Freikorps* men into the SA, see R.G.L. Waite, *Vanguard of Nazism* (Cambridge: Harvard University Press, 1952); for the revolutionary ideals of the SA, see Ernst Roehm, *Die Geschichte eines Hochverraeters*, 2nd ed. (Munich: Franz Eher nachf., 1930), and Hermann Mau, "Die 'Zweite Revolution'—Der 30. Juni 1934," *Vierteljahrshefte fuer Zeitgeschichte*, April, 1953, pp. 119–37.

53. Curt Riess, *Joseph Goebbels* (London: Hollis and Carter, 1949).

V

THE SUICIDE

I

At about three-thirty on the afternoon of Monday, April 30, 1945, Adolf Hitler, having finished his lunch and shaken hands with his staff for the last time, retired to his apartment within the Reichschancellery bunker and shot himself. With him died his wife of one day, Eva, through a self-administered dose of cyanide. Although neither body has since been produced, the circumstantial evidence and the testimony of a variety of witnesses all serve to corroborate this conclusion.[1]

Perhaps never in recent history has a man's death been so widely applauded. Except for those who felt frustrated because he had cheated the gallows, men everywhere were relieved to know him dead. It is true that some believe him still to be alive and that sensational magazines occasionally print rumors of his appearances, but these doubts about his death have, with the passing of time, largely disappeared. One question remains unanswered, and almost unasked: why did Hitler commit suicide?

The apparent answer to this question is that he had no other alternative. He had lost a disastrous war and had instigated monstrous actions which left him universally scorned. He did not wish to be exhibited at a postwar trial, nor even to have his dead body put on display.[2] Finally, it did not seem possible that he could escape and, therefore, his game played out, he put an end to his life. Yet this explanation still raises questions. Could he not have done his cause more good by leading a last hopeless, yet potentially glorious, charge against the enemy? Or could he not have pleaded his case brilliantly in court as he had done in 1924 following the *Putsch?* Or was it not possible for him to reach safety as did so many lesser Nazis with the same difficult problem of escape facing them? The answer is that he could have chosen any of these alternatives but did not. He chose, instead, death by his own hand.

We have by and large accepted Hitler's own appraisal of the situation—that there was no real alternative to death—and have thus obscured the fact that his death was suicide. As is often the case with famous persons, we tend to view as singular what is actually not at all uncommon. Suicide is a recurring phenomenon which seems to have been accelerated by the industrialization and urbanization of society until now it is a frequent cause of death, particularly in the middle and younger age groups.[3] Of greatest interest is the fact that it does not strike at random; certain groups, certain types are more given to suicide than others. These characteristics are so pronounced that it is possible to predict when and where the incidence of suicide will be heaviest, and psychoanalysts are able to identify "suicidal" personalities, though they have been largely unable to prevent the occurrence of the act.

A comparison of the facts surrounding Hitler's suicide with the statistical information available on suicide in general is interesting in that it reveals how "typical" Hitler's death was.

Sex: Male.

Male suicides are three to four times as common as female suicides, though evidence from a number of sources indicates that the female rate is increasing while the male rate is declining slightly.[4]

Age at time of death: 56 years, 10 days.

Though suicides have been recorded at almost all ages (even childhood suicide is a problem), certain age groups appear to be more susceptible than others. There seems to be general agreement that the years around the fiftieth birthday mark a period of increasing frequency of suicide in Europe.[5]

Nationality: Born of German parents in Austria-Hungary. Acquired German citizenship in 1931.

The suicide rate in Austria is, surprisingly, the highest in the world for some years; in others it is second only to Japan's. In 1959 the number of suicides per 100,000 inhabitants ranged from Japan's 25.3 to Egypt's 0.2. Austria was second with 23.3, while the figure for Germany was 18.9. The United States stood well below these countries with 10.9. But Ireland, Nationalist China, and the countries of Latin America all had yearly averages of less than five suicides per hundred thousand persons. The figures for the top-ranked states, Japan and Austria, were 125 times that of the lowest-ranked state, Egypt.[6]

Religion: Raised a Roman Catholic but had no religious commitment at the time of death.

Roman Catholics seem less prone than Protestants to commit suicide, though this is certainly not true of heavily Catholic Austria. All authorities agree that, in Western society at least, the important factor is actually the intensity of religious feeling. Non-believers are more likely to kill themselves than believers.[7]

Class Status: Born into the lower middle class of Austrian society.

Suicide seems to be more a threat to the middle and upper classes of society than to the working classes. At least one author states flatly that, "the higher you rise in life the greater is the danger of suicide." [8] Others are less emphatic.[9]

Occupation: Artist, soldier, politician, head of government.

Artists have a high suicide rate.[10] The rate among soldiers is higher than among civilians.[11] No figures are available for the incidence of suicide among politicians or government officials, but it is not a rare occurrence.[12]

Urban–Rural Status: Born in Branau-am-Inn. Lived in Passau, Linz, Vienna, Munich, and Berlin.

Cities are the focal points of suicide activities, with rates often double or triple those of rural areas. Vienna and Berlin have long been suicide centers, and Berlin now has the highest rate of any place in the world.[13]

Marital Status: Wedded Eva Braun, April 29, 1945.

In general, marriage reduces the tendency to suicide. Children in marriage make suicide even less probable. But there does exist a whole class of marriages concluded for the purpose of committing double suicide. In Japan this is even institutionalized under the name *Shinju.*[14]

Age at Death of Parents: Father (January 3, 1903) 13 years, 8 months; Mother (December 21, 1907) 18 years, 8 months.

Though not much is known about this particular aspect of suicide, such studies as have been made indicate that the loss of one or both parents during childhood or adolescence is much more frequent among suicides than among the general poulation.[15]

Condition of Affairs: Disastrous.

Suicide rates rise during periods of economic depression and fall slightly in wartime. Yet a large number of suicides are occasioned by sudden success so that the relationship of suicide to disaster is by no means clear.[16]

Immediate Cause of the Suicide Decision: News of Himmler's defection.[17]

Most investigators have been struck by the apparently trivial reasons given for suicide by many persons. In the light of what was happening to the Third Reich at that moment, Himmler's attempt to contact the Western Allies seems of minor importance.[18]

Weapon: Pistol.

Although fashions change, shooting is often used. It is the method most often employed by American men and German soldiers. In Austria, excluding Vienna, it is second only to hanging among male suicides, though hanging (and, in Vienna, gas) is much more frequently employed.[19]

Date of Suicide: April 30, 1945.

April and May are the two peak months for suicide in Europe and most of the Western world. In Germany, May is the peak month.[20]

Day of the Week: Monday.

Male suicides occur more frequently on Monday than on any other day of the week.[21]

Time of Day: 3:30 P.M.

In Europe suicides occur more frequently in the morning and early afternoon than at any other time.[22]

Weather: Information not available.

Contrary to popular opinion, suicide is more likely to occur in good weather than in dismal weather. The fine clear days of spring, with alternating sun and shadow, a brisk wind, and a falling barometer, seem more likely to precipitate suicide than other types of weather.[23]

Previous Suicide Threats: At least nine during the days preceding his death.

Authorities on the subject are agreed that suicide threats are to be taken seriously and that most persons who intend to die make their intentions known, often by explicit statements which frequently go unheeded by their listeners. From the 22nd of April, 1945, until the time of his death nine days later, Hitler expressed either verbally or in writing his intention to kill himself. More interesting is the fact that upon at least five previous occasions, extending as far back as 1905, Hitler stated that he would kill himself, and twice he named a pistol as the weapon of destruction.[24]

Thus we find that in many particulars, Hitler's suicide

conforms to what is known about suicide in general. In fact, its most unusual characteristic is that it is very nearly that statistical freak, the *typical* suicide. This conformity suggests that the answer to the question of why Hitler killed himself is not to be found only by studying the situation at the time of his death, for if anything is certain about suicide it is that the causes of the act lie deep in the individual's past. We may never be able to establish the fundamental causes for Hitler's death, but it may be possible through a study of what is known about suicide in general to cast some light upon Hitler's particular problem and to note certain suicidal patterns in his life.

Sociological studies of suicide are interesting in that they show that suicide is not a random occurrence and for our purposes demonstrate how well Hitler's suicide fits known patterns. Yet the statistical approach cannot tell us why one person with these sociological characteristics kills himself and another does not. Thus far, the discipline which has dealt most fruitfully with the dynamics of suicide is psychoanalysis. This is not to say that psychoanalysis has been very effective in the prevention of suicide, for its successes have been quite limited.[25] But the psychoanalysts, by examining the case histories of patients with a record of suicide attempts and of those who have later committed suicide, do give us more information than is otherwise available on the *nature* of suicide and place it within the framework of a more general theory on the nature of human personality.

All students of the subject seem convinced of one thing: suicide is not the result of a momentary decision. Rather, the causes of this self-destructiveness are to be found in the early stages of the victim's development. Everyone, to a greater or lesser extent, harbors the self-destructive impulse. Karl Menninger has analyzed the components of this impulse as: (1) the wish to kill, (2) the wish to be killed, and (3) the wish to die.

The urge to kill, basic to all human beings, is an instinctive reaction to anything seen as a threat to one's existence, and is demonstrated even by infants in the rivalry with their brothers and sisters. In its rawest form, it is an urge to destroy that which threatens the self; however, in most human beings this primitive instinct is curbed and transformed by societal pressures and by the ameliorating effects of the creative sexual instinct. Thus the normal person directs towards external objects fused impulses of hate and love, or is both aggressive and loving towards others in a non-injurious manner. In certain persons whose emotional development has been arrested at an immature stage, this fusion is not complete, and they show a marked ambivalence of emotions towards these external objects.[26]

A phenomenon of importance equal to that of the destructive instinct is *introjection*. This manifestation of the primitive layers of the mind involves the ability of a person on the one hand to view his own body as an object and on the other hand to identify this body with some external person, particularly one that is loved, hated, or feared. In the suicidal person it is suggested that with the loss of the external object (through death or rejection) the impulses of love and hatred are turned inwards on the introjected object instead of being reinvested in some other external object. In some individuals the aggressive instinct, the primitive wish to kill, is thus turned against the self and may result in either immediate or attenuated suicide, which may be viewed as a "displaced murder."[27]

The second outstanding characteristic of suicide is the "wish to be killed": the victim wishes, for whatever reason, to be punished in the most severe manner for his transgressions. The psychiatric explanation of this phenomenon is that the conscience, or the superego (perhaps a product of the original aggressive instinct), demands of the ego retribution for externally directed destructiveness. It matters little whether this destructiveness was carried out or only desired—the superego does not recognize a difference between thought and deed. With some people the demands of the conscience are so imperious as to be satisfied only with physical suffering and possibly with death. This wish to submit to punishment is often ameliorated, just as is outward aggression, by the fusion with the creative instincts so as to be "eroticized." This results in the subject's deriving pleasure from pain, a particular feature of attenuated suicide.[28]

Menninger cites a third characteristic of suicide, "the wish to die." Since he states this only as a hypothesis, it may be well to note simply that he considers the "wish to die" as being active in cases of successful suicide but absent in most miscarried attempts.[29]

The suicidal act may be either fatal or unattenuated. In the latter form the forces working against self-destruction are strong enough to mitigate the aggression against the self, at least for a time. The solution is usually an unhappy one, but at least it is an avoidance of death. Many of these attenuated suicides do eventually kill themselves, however, often by suicide. The forms of attenuated suicide most familiar to us are alcoholism, neurotic invalidism, focal suicide (in which self-destruction concentrates upon a particular member of the body in a non-lethal manner), asceticism, and martyrdom. It may be somewhat surprising to see the last two mentioned as forms of suicide since asceticism is often practiced for reasons of health and martyrdom seems by definition to be passive. However, there are many instances of neurotic asceticism in which great privations are sought for no apparent reason and with no regard for health. In the case of martyrdom, there are numerous recorded instances in which the martyr actively sought death, and many of today's victims might well be termed "martyrs without a cause." [30] Chronic suicide is a condition which may last for years, even a lifetime, causing the subject great suffering but perhaps for that reason assuaging the conscience. In some cases, however, the payments become ever greater till finally only death seems to suffice.

Of the greatest interest to us in connection with the study of Hitler's suicide are asceticism and martyrdom. Asceticism involves the voluntary deprivation of the amenities and possibly the necessities of life or, and often in addition to, the voluntary punishment of one's body—sometimes to the extent of causing either serious or fatal injury. Suicidal martyrdom involves the active courting of situations which in one manner or another will cause injury to the subject. In a large number of cases of "chronic bad luck" there is good reason to believe that the situations are created by the sufferer.

In both asceticism and martyrdom the urge to punish the self is apparent. What is not so apparent is the aggressive quality attached to these forms of action. Yet the literature of both historical and clinical martyrs is filled with evidences of aggressiveness carried out by the martyr against his parents or other persons.[31] A third component is an erotic satisfaction often elaborately disguised.[32]

Closely allied to, but in a separate category from, suicide and chronic suicide is attempted suicide. The chief difference between attempted suicide and the other forms lies in its apparently non-serious nature. So many attempts are carried out with weapons of an often non-lethal type, or in circumstances which make the intervention of others possible or even probable, that more and more researchers are being led to the belief that the major purpose of the suicide attempt is not self-destruction but rather an appeal for help.

Stengel and Cook, who have made some of the most extensive studies of attempted suicide, argue that this type of aggression against the self may result in death if the appeal for help is not heeded. They also suggest that the victim may be subjecting himself to an "ordeal" in order to determine whether he has the right to live or not. Failure of the suicide attempt is usually accepted with equanimity and often the person's depression vanishes.[33]

Many of the persons who attempted suicide, according to Stengel and Cook, actually received needed medical care after being admitted to the hospital following the attempt. Others achieved some change in their environment which enabled them to reconcile themselves to life. Thus the attempt served purposes other than self-destruction and should not be viewed merely as an abortive suicide. There is strong suspicion, on the other hand, that many actual suicides are "bungled" attempts.

One may well ask how much of this information is useful with regard to Adolf Hitler. He is now beyond the reach of psychoanalysis and never submitted to it during his lifetime. Thus we can have no real knowledge of those motivating forces which may have precipitated his suicide. On the other hand, we do have a fair knowledge of his life history, and it is at least possible that this biographical material will yield symptoms of a self-destructive pattern long before he ended his life in the bunker. Thus if we cannot find all of the causes of his suicide, we may nevertheless be able to explain certain of his attitudes and actions in relation to a suicidal tendency, which in turn may further illuminate his public activities.

II

Information about Hitler's early years is scanty, and much of it is unreliable. For instance, his own account in *Mein Kampf* tells us something of his attitude towards the experiences of his youth, but often the facts are distorted to fit the picture he had constructed. Many of the memories of the early

Hitler by neighbors and schoolmates have proved upon investigation to be fictitious.* The few good sources for this period include Franz Jetzinger's study of the documentary material from the years before World War I,[34] Konrad Heiden's study of Hitler's school record,[35] and above all August Kubizek's considerably colored picture of his boyhood friend of the years from 1905 to 1908.[36] Josef Greiner's account [37] seems extremely unreliable, and Jetzinger expresses doubt whether Greiner ever knew Hitler at all.[38]

Of the little that we do know of Hitler during this early period, one outstanding trait is apparent and that is his tendency to fail in everything he attempted. He failed at school, he failed as an artist, and he failed in his relationships with other human beings. Furthermore, there is at least some reason to believe that these failures were self-induced.

The failure at school is particularly difficult to explain because Hitler did show in his early years definite promise as a student, and his later accomplishments indicate that his mental capacities were far from negligible. Nor was he "preternaturally lazy" as Jetzinger would have it,[39] or at least he was far from lazy in dealing with problems which interested him. But the evidence is there that he did fail and that his diligence was less than satisfactory.

Hitler began his formal education in the one-room country school at Fischlam in the spring of 1895 and attended that school until July of 1897. His teacher, Karl Mittelmaier, re-

---

*During the 1930's a number of people could remember the young Hitler playing in the streets and hills of Branau-am-Inn though he had left that city when he was three years old. It must also be noted that the people who knew Hitler have learned to trim their stories to the changing political winds.

membered him as "mentally alert, obedient, but lively," and Konrad Heiden states that he received grades of "excellent" in almost all of his subjects.[40] In 1897 Hitler began his third year of school at the *Volksschule* in Lambach and continued there apparently till the end of the year 1898. While in Lambach, he also received choral training from a Father Bernhard Grüner. Again, as at Fischlam, he was awarded "1's" (excellent) and was remembered as a leader at play.[41] The second semester of his fourth year and the entire fifth year (January, 1899 to July, 1900) were spent at the *Volksschule* of Leonding, a suburb of Linz. Again he apparently did well, especially in geography and history (according to Goerlitz and Quint), and Hitler himself states that school was ridiculously easy for him. He spent much time out of doors and was again the leader of a gang of boys.[42] Thus until the end of his fifth year of school Hitler did generally excellent work but showed some tendency towards unruliness.

In September, 1900, he entered the *Unterrealschule* at Linz (form I) and began the compulsory studies which Hitler says his father hoped would prepare him for the civil service. Jetzinger demonstrates that this must have been a distortion on the part of Hitler because one prepared for the Austrian civil service by attending the *Gymnasium,* not the *Realschule.*[43] In any case Hitler did so poorly (failing mathematics and natural history, and showing little diligence) that he had to repeat form I in the year 1901–02. In the second year his work was satisfactory, but then in his third year (form II, 1902–03) he again failed mathematics and his diligence was described as "variable." In September, 1903, he passed a re-examination in mathematics and was allowed to enter form III. However, he failed French and again his diligence was below normal. Because of this poor showing, he was passed only on the condition that he leave the Linz *Realschule* (1904). Hitler's last year in school (1904–05) was spent at the secondary school in Steyr about fifteen miles from his home. In this year his performance was even worse than before. He failed German, mathematics, and shorthand; received "4's" (5 was the lowest grade) in diligence, religious instruction, geography, history, and chemistry; and achieved a "3" in moral conduct and physics, a "2" in freehand drawing, and a "1" in gymnastics.[44] Jetzinger surmises that Hitler was asked to leave school.[45] Hitler himself says that a severe chest illness ended his schooling, but the implacable Jetzinger shows evidence which casts serious doubt as to whether this illness ever occurred.[46]

Why, we must ask, did Hitler fail so miserably in his secondary-school work? Jetzinger's suggestion that boys transferring from country schools often experienced difficulties certainly seems reasonable and may well account for Hitler's problems during his first year at Linz.[47] However, the explanation by Jetzinger and others, namely that he was "bone lazy," does not seem satisfactory. Hitler was often hesitant and indecisive, but not lazy. Hitler himself takes responsibility for his failure although he immediately blames his father for causing him to take the drastic course of neglecting his studies.[48] Whatever the precise reasons were, it must be admitted that he did create the situation which led to his failure at school. We might say that Hitler deliberately chose to create difficulties for himself through neglect and that at the same time he inflicted pain upon others, most notably his mother, by his lack of success.[49] It was a pattern that would be repeated in the ensuing years. Hitler assumed a position, in many ways detrimental to himself, which eventually led to a crisis. As we shall see, his standard reaction was to assume a position even more extreme than the one which had led to the crisis in the hope of ending it. In a sense, he never solved his problems; he only submerged them by assuming a new role.

Hitler's actions in the years before World War I in many ways resemble the pattern of neurotic martyrdom familiar to psychoanalysts. He punished both himself and others and took an almost masochistic delight in his sufferings. If, as is the case of many neurotic martyrs, the aggression against the self is the result of its redirection from some outside object, or an atonement for some injury supposed to have been inflicted upon another, we might well ask who this other could be.

During Hitler's school years his family suffered three losses which may have had some effect upon his attitude. In February, 1900, his six-year-old brother Edmund died of the measles. The next fall Hitler began his first year at the Linz *Unterrealschule*, a year which ended in failure. On January 3, 1903, his father died suddenly of a heart attack. The following July Adolf again failed, though he passed his re-examination in the fall. On September 14, 1903, Hitler's half-sister Angela married Leo Raubal, a man whom Hitler disliked intensely, and in the year following he performed so poorly that he was asked to leave the school. Whether there is any causal relation here we do not know. We do not know what Hitler thought of his younger brother Edmund; we know that he feared and probably hated his father; Angela has been variously reported as a favorite sister and as one whom Hitler disliked.[50] Yet one would expect that these losses would have at least some effect.

During the years in which the future dictator was failing at school, he was also undergoing a marked physical and mental change which caused comment and even concern among those who knew him. The earliest recollections of Hitler show him as a robust and even unruly child who was constantly out of doors and was the leader of the group of boys with whom he played. His outward appearance, at least until he was a student at Linz, was not such as to arouse any comment, but from 1900 to 1905 (that is, between the ages of ten and sixteen)

Hitler underwent a change which seems to have greatly altered his character. We may suppose that this change was of the type often seen in adolescence although it may have been somewhat more severe than is ordinarily the case. Whatever the reason, during these years the formerly gregarious boy became the solitary youth until by 1905 he could tolerate only one companion, August Kubizek, and often preferred to be entirely alone. Physically, he changed into a gaunt, sallow-faced young man with unusual eyes who gave more than one person the impression that he was consumptive.[51] Since the severe illness of which Hitler speaks did not occur until the end of this period and may not have occurred at all, we can safely say that the alteration must have had other causes.[52] Since these physical and social changes occurred during the same period that Hitler was failing at school, we may hazard the guess that there was some sort of interrelationship between the events, but what the nature of it was, we do not know.

In the year 1905 Hitler faced the first of the many crises in his life which forced him to make some sort of major decision. If he were to remain in school, he would have to alter drastically his habits of study and work, an unpleasant prospect to him at best. Kubizek, who says that he knew Hitler at this time, portrays the boy as being torn between following his own bent to become an artist (which seemed to him incompatible with schoolwork), and pleasing his mother, who wanted to fulfill her husband's wish that Adolf become a civil servant.[53] Jetzinger has shown that the road to the Austrian civil service led through the *Gymnasium* and not the *Realschule*, but the possibility exists that this was not understood by the mother or the son. In any case, failure at school could hardly have pleased Klara Hitler.

On the other hand, Hitler had already begun to develop the "artistic" personality which was to dominate the next phase of his life. At the time Kubizek met him in the fall of 1904, he was already a solitary person devoting the major amount of his interest to art.[54] Since as late as the spring of 1904 he was described as playing "red Indians" with a group of neighborhood boys after his confirmation, at least a part of the change must have occurred rather rapidly, and his solitary attitude may have been connected with his transfer from the school at Linz to that at Steyr.[55]

A word must be said about Hitler's artistic pursuits since his ability has been so often called into question. There can be no doubt that his qualities as a painter were limited, though they were undoubtedly better than those of most persons. His abilities in the field of music and literature were even more modest, though he showed an interest in these arts at the time. Nor did his qualifications for the study of architecture in any way match his interest in that subject. Nevertheless, his devotion to the artistic pose cannot be doubted. Nor was he entirely unsuccessful either in maintaining this pose or in transmitting his artistic enthusiasm to at least one other person. It is well to remember that due to his instigation and example August Kubizek left the upholsterer's trade to study music and eventually become a practicing musician and director.[56] We do not have to believe that Hitler's pose would have impressed a sophisticated audience. The key to the matter is that he was a provincial playing to provincials and creating the semblance of an artistic world for them and, more importantly, for himself.

Thus, at the time of his first grave crisis Hitler was already predisposed to choose only one of several alternatives open to him. These alternatives were (1) to continue on at some school until he had received his secondary diploma, (2) to enter some trade as an apprentice and thus assure himself of a livelihood, or (3) to carry on with his efforts to become an artist. Undoubtedly he chose the worst of the three alternatives. If he had continued in school, he would have laid the necessary foundation for later admission into the Academy for Architecture in Vienna (Hitler recognized in *Mein Kampf* that this failure to finish school had been a serious mistake). If he had chosen to enter a trade, he would have had the help of his guardian, Herr Mayrhofer, one of the most respected members of the community of Leonding, in selecting a good position. As an artist, he had no assurance of success and in fact only limited assurance of survival. He could, as he did, live for a time on his mother's indulgence and after that on his orphan's pension and modest inheritance.[57] But this would probably have been insufficient to support him during the long period of waiting for recognition (assuming that he ever would have been worthy of recognition).

Hitler chose the poorest of three major alternatives open to him, though we may feel that it was a better choice, on the basis of his interests, than entering a trade. But the intellectual arrogance which made it impossible for him to finish school was also the ground for his failure as an artist. A comparison between Hitler and his friend Kubizek makes this point clear. Both had artistic aspirations, but Kubizek applied himself seriously to the task of learning his art. He submitted himself to teachers, to long hours of practicing, and eventually attained his goal. Hitler applied himself fully, but not seriously, to his task. He would have nothing to do with teachers or with systematic self-study of the problems of painting or architecture.[58] Instead, he pursued a variety of projects—writing poetry, copying paintings, reading widely and haphazardly, planning public buildings for the city of Linz, and paying close attention (for perhaps the only time in his life) to his dress.[59]

Hitler showed more concern for the pose of the artist than he did for artistic work and in so doing he prepared the ground for the new crisis which would overtake him in 1908.

During these last two years in Linz and later, during the first year in Vienna, he was able to maintain his position as a "young gentleman of leisure" and as an artist-Bohemian. He was able to afford the rather fine clothes that he wore and the ivory-headed walking stick that he carried because his mother provided him with free room and board. Nor did he have any duties to distract him from his projects. Essentially this situation did not change for almost a year after the death of his mother in 1907 for even in Vienna he had no specific duties and continued to wear good clothes.[60]

During this period in Linz, Hitler, according to Kubizek, fell deeply and ineffectually in love with a young girl of a well-to-do family. Every evening in fine weather Hitler would go to watch Stephanie (as she is called by Kubizek) walk with her mother and perhaps some admirer from the local garrison. Apparently Hitler never tried to approach her, nor was Stephanie ever aware of his existence.* At one point in the spring of 1906 Hitler became so discouraged that he decided to "end it all" by leaping into the Danube.** He planned his suicide in great detail and even gave Stephanie a role in his little drama—she was to jump with him. The faithful Gustl was to explain things to Stephanie's mother.[61] One does not have to believe that there was anything immediately serious about this threat—it was all of a piece with his fantasy love for Stephanie—but it is of some interest to find that even at this

---

* Kubizek says that she was, but Jetzinger, who spoke to Stephanie, says not. Furthermore, he demonstrates that during the time Hitler was supposed to have been admiring her—1905 and 1906—she was actually in Geneva and Munich. In spite of this, Jetzinger believes the story of Hitler's infatuation is correct, though overdrawn.
** This according to Kubizek. The date must be wrong since Stephanie was not in Linz at the time.

early period of his life Hitler could dwell on the possibility of self-destruction.

Hitler's life during this time was not without its effect upon others. If he dominated Kubizek, he caused his mother a good deal of grief and pain. His failure at school and his refusal to seek a profitable occupation were sources of great worry to her.[62] After he had gone to Vienna there is some evidence that he did not even return home during her final illness. This is not certain, for the two accounts available of Klara Hitler's death are directly contradictory. Kubizek pictures the faithful son returning to his stricken mother during her final days, but a neighbor in the same building stated (in 1938) that Hitler had returned home only after his mother died (December 21, 1907) but in time for the funeral on the 23rd of December.[63] This rejection of his mother was to be followed in the next years by a severance of ties with all of his relatives and acquaintances.

The decision to move to Vienna in September, 1907, was recognized by Hitler and by all of the students of his career to be one of the most important steps of his life. It was here that almost all of the basic concepts which governed his future course were established or reinforced. The immediate effect of the move was, however, detrimental to his career. Having wasted two years' time in Linz which should have been devoted to learning the fundamentals of painting, he now sought admission to the Academy of Art in Vienna and, quite understandably, was denied entrance.[64] The effect of this first rejection was to turn Hitler even more violently than ever against the whole academic system. Kubizek mentions a number of diatribes possibly inspired by his own successful completion of the entrance exams to the Music Academy.[65]

During this first year, Hitler's interest in architecture assumed a central position in his thought. Whether it is true, as he says in *Mein Kampf*, that one of the examining professors said that his real talent as an artist lay in the field of architectural design we shall never know.[66] We do know that he had fancied himself an architect in Linz and that now in Vienna he devoted himself more fully than ever to its study. Characteristically, Hitler had but little time or patience with the fundamentals. Instead he spent weeks upon a grand design for rebuilding the city of Vienna. As described by his roommate, Kubizek, the plan seems to have been both audacious and ruthless, to have shown a concern for social justice mingled with a disregard for the desires of anyone but the designer and an equal disregard for cost.[67]

Whatever its importance for Hitler's future development, this devotion to architecture was immediately unfortunate. Without a secondary-school certificate, he could not begin studies in architecture, and he knew it.[68] But this left him only the alternative of taking the entrance exam for the Academy of Art, and to pass that he would have to improve during the year of his stay in Vienna. Yet, in his curious self-defeating manner, he refused to apply himself in an organized or diligent fashion to the study of painting and thus insured the second failure of September, 1908. We cannot say whether Hitler ever, even with diligent application, could have succeeded in passing the Academy examination, but we can say that he chose to act in the manner least likely to gain him success.

Thus, after a year in Vienna and two failures of the entrance examination, Hitler was again forced to salvage what he could from the wreckage of his career. He was almost at the end of his resources [69] and could no longer afford to live either as the young gentleman of leisure or as the artist-Bohemian. He had not made contact with any colony of struggling artists who might have helped him along, and in fact he now broke contact with his one remaining friend, August Kubizek.[70] It might also be added that any dreams which he may have entertained of winning fame as an artist and returning to claim Stephanie's hand were now much dimmed, if not entirely shattered. Yet, as in 1905, Hitler was not without alternatives. They were possibly not as good as they had been, but they still existed. Undoubtedly he could have asked his guardian, Mayrhofer, for help. The man had been a good friend of Hitler's father and might still have been willing to aid the son in finding an apprenticeship. Hitler's godparents were still living in Vienna at this time and might have been willing to help him as they had during his first visit to the city in 1906. His half-sister, Angela, and her husband, Leo Raubal, lived in Vienna, and though Hitler hated his brother-in-law, he might still have received help in finding work.[71] Finally, Hitler could have searched for unskilled work on his own, or he might even have volunteered for army service. Perhaps none of these alternatives would have helped, but, so far as we know, Hitler did not even explore them.

Instead, Hitler allowed himself to sink into a condition lower than which he could not go without coming into conflict with the police.[72] The few glimpses we have of him during this time reflect how complete was the change from his former condition. His good clothes, his walking stick, had now disappeared (probably pawned) and he was reduced to wearing cast-off clothing. He ate in soup-lines when he ate at all; he slept on park benches or possibly in some of the more sordid flop-houses which abounded in Vienna.[73] His regard for his personal appearance seems to have entirely disappeared. In short, he dropped the pose of being the young gentleman-artist and had become, instead, the derelict.

Undoubtedly the year 1908–09 was, for Hitler, his worst (with the possible exception of 1913–14). Although technically not destitute, for he still had his orphan's pension, he lived in such a manner as to suggest destitution. Furthermore, in the autumn of 1909, Hitler failed to report for military service, an action that was bound to get him into trouble with the police. In a country which practices universal military conscription and which posts notices everywhere concerning the duty to register, one does not simply forget to do so. In 1914, when the police finally investigated the matter, Hitler explained that while he had not reported in the fall of 1909, he did make good the omission in February, 1910.[74] He did this, he said, in Vienna rather than in Linz, and then for four years heard nothing more. Hitler explained his reason for the failure to report in a letter to the Linz Police:

> . . . And as far as appertains my sin of omission in the autumn of 1909, this was an infinitely bitter period for me. I was a young, inexperienced man without any financial support and too proud to accept it from no matter whom, let alone ask for it. Without any monetary help, cast on my own resources, the few Kronen often only Heller obtained through my work barely sufficed to give me somewhere to sleep. For two years I had no other friend but care and want, no other companion but ever-lasting insatiable hunger. I never learnt the meaning of that fine word Youth. Today after 5 years the tokens are still with me in the form of chilblains on fingers, hands and feet. And yet, now that I am over the worst, I cannot recall those days without a certain feeling of satisfaction. Despite the most utter penury, in the midst of . . . dubious surroundings, I have always preserved my good name, am untainted before the law and clean before my own conscience except for that one omission over the military report, which at the time was not even known to me. That is the only thing for which I feel responsible . . . [75]

Though this letter misrepresents his means of support and implies that he had had since childhood a much more miserable life than was actually the case ("I never learnt the meaning of that fine word Youth"), and though it seems scarcely credible that he could have been unaware of his duty to report, the letter does give an accurate picture of Hitler's view of the situation.

Assuming that Hitler was telling the truth when he said that he finally registered in February of 1910 (and his statement has, for once, the ring of truth), we may conclude that he drew back from this further flirtation with failure and chose to stabilize his life at the low level of the destitute painter. From 1910 to 1913 he kept body and soul together by painting postcards which were then sold by such business partners as the tramp, Hanisch. Though by no means lucrative, it sufficed to purchase Hitler continued lodging at the Meldemann Home for Men. It also allowed him to remain indefinitely in a position which punished him without destroying him, while at the same time serving as a reproach to those relatives who had all but lost contact with him.

In 1913, Hitler moved from Vienna to Munich where he continued to exist much as he had in the Austrian capital. For Hitler the transfer was important because he was at last living in a "truly" German city.[76] For his official record it was important because he had now compounded the original crime of failing to register by leaving the country without first clearing himself of his military obligation.[77] Whether Hitler realized this or not is open to question. If he did, it might mean that he was opening a new realm of punishment for himself. If not, it would probably mean only that he was continuing the old situation in a new environment. At any rate, when the police came pounding at the door in January of 1914 to inquire why he had failed to report for a physical examination, Hitler was able to present a good enough explanation and a pitiable enough figure so that he was both exempted from army service and excused from penalty for his dereliction.[78]

Between 1900 and 1914 Hitler acted in such a manner as to insure his continued failure. On at least two occasions during this period he was forced by self-created crises to make a rather drastic alteration in his mode of existence. In each of these crises, although a number of alternatives were again open to him, he chose that alternative which offered the least possibility of success. By 1914 this manner of action had reduced him to a point from which there was little likelihood of change. In fact the move from Vienna to Munich in 1913 may, if he was aware that this constituted a violation of the Austrian conscription act, have been unconsciously calculated to bring him into difficulties with the police. This is, of course, entirely uncertain, but the continued pattern of attenuated self-destruction makes it possible that at some time in the future Hitler might have gone to prison. It is also distinctly possible that he might have ended his life at an early age as an unknown suicide.

However, in 1914 the fate of nations intervened to offer Hitler a new and unexpected opportunity as a fighting man. One certainly does not have to assume that every man who volunteered had self-destructive tendencies, but it is certain that this new alternative fitted Hitler's predilections to a striking extent. It offered him a socially approved form of aggression coupled with an equally commendable form of self-punishment. It was the sort of ordeal to which Hitler could submit himself and accept with equanimity whatever decision fate made for him. Hitler served four years on the Western Front as a runner for the Bavarian Reserve Infantry Regiment 16. He participated in such major battles as the Somme and Paschendaele, was wounded twice, and was awarded the Iron Cross First Class, an unusual decoration for an enlisted man.[79]

Hitler may not have developed his belief in providence during this period, but the war can scarcely have weakened that belief. Again, the war may have held for him something of the "ordeal" character mentioned by Stengel and Cook (see above, p. 155), for in *Mein Kampf* he says:

> The time came when everyone had to fight between the instinct of self-preservation and the admonition of duty. I, too, was not spared this inner struggle. Whenever death was on the hunt, an indefinable something tried to revolt, tried to present itself to the weak body in the form of reason and was really nothing but cowardice which in this disguise tried to ensnare the individual. A strong pulling and warning set in and only the last remaining spark of conscience made the decision. But the more this voice tried to warn me to take heed, the louder and more urgently it lured, the sharper was my resistance, till finally after a long inner struggle my sense of duty triumphed. This struggle had already been decided for me during the winter of 1915–16. My will had finally become master. Whereas during the first days I was able to join exuberantly and laughingly in the storm, now I was quiet and determined. This was the most enduring. Only now could Fate set out for the last tests without tearing my nerves or my reason giving out.[80]

In October of 1918, Hitler was blinded during a mustard gas attack and the war ended while he was in the army hospital at Pasewalk. Depressed by the news of the loss of the war and by the revolution, he made the decision which was to alter the entire course of his life. He ". . . resolved now to become a politician." [81]

The importance of this decision for the recent history of Europe has certainly never been subject to underestimation, but it does raise some interesting problems. For one, it is amazing that a person who had failed so consistently in the endeavors of the first half of his life should be so astoundingly successful in the following years. It would be reasonable to assume that

Hitler abandoned the self-defeating habits of the earlier years and applied his truly extraordinary abilities to gaining the power which became his in the 1930's and 1940's. Yet the contrary seems to be actually the case. The mode of operation established by Hitler in his school years remained with him till his death. Crisis after crisis in his career rose simply because he failed to take action in time to prevent the occurrence, and in most cases he solved his problems by taking the most extreme and least promising of the alternatives open to him.

It will not be contended here that this is *the* fundamental factor in Hitler's political career, for such a mode of operation could not explain his astounding successes. Hitler did possess truly creative qualities which enabled him with the slenderest of resources to raise a gigantic political party, to build the Third Reich, and almost to conquer Europe. He was a visionary, though that vision was in so many ways terrible. He was also an opportunist able to take advantage of the chances thrown in his path. What interests us here, however, is that spirit of recklessness which so often supplemented his policies but finally undermined them—a recklessness with the fate of his party, his state, and Europe itself which was closely connected with the recklessness shown for his own life and career. It was a recklessness which passed the bounds of gambling, for Hitler seemed not to care whether he lost or not. He was equally prepared to win everything or to lose all. In fact, it will appear that he had a marked tendency to place himself in, or to allow himself to drift into, situations where no other alternatives were possible. The real mystery of Hitler's career is why, when faced with such situations, he so often succeeded.

If we turn to Hitler's initial steps in the political field, the quality of gambling becomes immediately apparent. His description of the circumstances connected with his joining the

"German Workers Party" indicates that he was aware of the odds against political success:

> Now I was faced by perhaps the most serious question of my life: was I to join or was I to refuse?
>
> My reason could only advise me to refuse, but my feeling would not let me find peace, and the more I tried to keep the absurdity of this entire club before my eyes, the more often did feeling speak in favor of it. . . . I had long since made up my mind to take up political activity; that this could only be in a new movement was also clear to me, so far only the instigation to action had not come. I do not belong to those who start something one day in order to end it again the next day or to change over, if possible, to another affair. But this very conviction was the chief reason, among others, why it was so difficult for me to make up my mind to form such a movement. I knew that for me this would mean a decision forever, where there would never be a "turn back." For me it was not a temporary game, but dead earnest. . . . Now Fate itself seemed to give me a hint. I should never have joined one of the existing parties, . . . for this reason, however, this ridiculously small foundation with its handful of members seemed to me to have the advantage that it had not yet hardened into an "organization," but seemed to offer to the individual the chance for real personal activity . . . here one would still be able to work, and the smaller the movement was, the easier it would be to bring it into the right shape. Here the contents, the goal, and the way could still be fixed, something that with the existing great parties was impossible from the beginning.[82]

Like the lottery ticket which he had once purchased, this insignificant political party promised vast success, but as with the lottery ticket, the chances of winning were slight.[83] One might well ask whether Hitler had any alternatives which were more promising of success. The army was weeding out large numbers of men so that he would very probably have had to become a civilian in any case. As an artist he had been a failure; he had no other trade and was probably too old (thirty) to learn one. His political attitudes made it impossible for him to join the ranks of the Socialist, Independent Socialist, or Communist parties, nor did the conservative parties offer much hope to this social outcast. Thus, short of remaining in the army where his prospects of advancement were slim, the choice of the obscure political party seems to have been a rational one, although it also indicates the extent to which Hitler had narrowed his chance of achieving any kind of success.

Though the probability of any single new party attaining success was rather slight, the unsettled conditions of Germany during the years following the war made it quite probable that some radical parties would enjoy great success. On the Left, the Communist party added steadily to its strength, and on the Right, the NSDAP began to absorb a number of its fellow parties of the Right until, by 1923, it had become a power to reckon with in Bavaria. Hitler's contribution to this success was great, just as his contribution to the failure of 1923 was also great. What is of interest to us here is not the reason for the party's success but rather the question of whether Hitler conducted the affairs of the party in such a fashion as to cause a crisis which forced him to take action under conditions where the possibilities of failure were enormous.

The major difficulty with the party policy between 1920 and 1923 was the contradiction existing between the violent rhetoric and militant structure of the party and its never clearly stated purpose of achieving power only with the cooperation of the police and the army. The discrepancy between its goal of national power and its actual strength made it necessary to enlist the aid of the armed forces, but one of the major attractions of the party was its claim to be an island of strength in a sea of national weakness. The problem which the contradiction raised was that the rank and file of the party during the course of 1923 exerted an increasing pressure for armed insurrection, while the party proved incapable of securing the conditions considered necessary for making such an uprising safe.

Hitler and the NSDAP might have been able to go on for some time talking of revolution and adding to their membership had not the French and Belgians occupied the Ruhr in January of 1923. The ensuing cry for national unity in the face of the common danger forced the party to take a stand, and it chose the highly unpopular one of refusing to cooperate with the government in Berlin. Hitler's argument was that no cooperation was possible with the "November criminals," and that once they were swept out of office by the national revolutionists, a government strong enough to deal with the French and the Belgians would control Germany.[84] This attitude may have had some merit, but it raised a number of serious problems. For one thing, the National Socialists had to clearly distinguish between their position and that of the Bavarian and Rhineland separatists, who also opposed Berlin but for much different reasons. Secondly, as economic conditions worsened during the course of the year, the pressure from the membership of the party to take some kind of action increased. Yet action depended upon the cooperation of the army and the police, and it cannot be said that Hitler did a great deal to enlist this support.

Twice during the year 1923 (on January 28th and on May 1st) Hitler staged demonstrations which were assumed by many of his followers to be the signal for a *Putsch*. The more serious of these demonstrations was that of May 1st on the Oberwiessenfeld of Munich when Ernst Roehm seized arms from the Munich barracks and distributed them to the waiting SA and other para-military organizations.[85] To these desperate men it seemed the signal for insurrection, and their disappointment was all the greater when their leader hesitated and then bowed to the demand of the army that the weapons be returned.[86] For Hitler the day had been one of humiliation in which his weakness and the weakness of the party had been made appallingly clear. Furthermore, he could not afford to call on his forces again if he did not intend to act, for any further demonstration of weakness could only lead to a catastrophic loss of party members. In addition to this, the unorthodox method by which the arms were seized did nothing to win the confidence of either the army or the police.

Such actions as Hitler did take during the year 1923 served only to limit his possibilities for political maneuver and to imperil his chances for a successful *Putsch*. But just as important as his actions were those measures which he failed to take. Most serious was his failure to act either before the government decided to end its resistance to the French (on September 26th) or immediately after that decision had been made. By failing to act before that courageous decision was taken, he lost the opportunity to take advantage of the chaos caused by the inflation; by failing to act immediately afterwards, he lost the advantage of the first indignant responses to Stresemann's policy change, and then allowed the government time to consolidate its position and win the all-important support of the *Reichswehr*.[87] Finally, Hitler allowed the initiative to pass into the hands of others, and particularly to von Kahr and the group of putative Bavarian separatists around him. From October on, the actions of the NSDAP followed the lead of Kommissar von Kahr without the advantage of close cooperation.

This was particularly true of the steps leading to the *Putsch* itself. The abortive plan for the 4th of November, the plan for the 12th of November, and the actual *Putsch* of November 8th and 9th were occasioned by meetings held by von Kahr and his associates, meetings which Hitler and the National Socialist leadership feared would either bring the proclamation of a National Revolution (without Hitler) or of Bavarian separation. Thus Hitler found himself led into the uprising by the actions and assumed intentions of another party.

From another side, Hitler found himself during the autumn forced to take some kind of action. The half-monthly reports of the Government *Präsidiums* in the various parts of Bavaria, as well as the police reports from the period of August through October, 1923, show that in many areas there was, even within the party ranks, dissatisfaction with Hitler's leadership which caused a number of men to leave the organization.[88] Possibly even worse, a sense of apathy had gripped the population, and this was most unwelcome to the prospective insurrectionists.[89] In such a situation one can understand the feelings of the SA leaders who were pressing for action. Ernst Roehm felt that time was working against the party—more and more of the experienced soldiers were dropping out.[90] SA leader Brueckner declared at the 1924 trial that he had urged Hitler to strike soon, since "the day is coming when I won't be able to hold the men back. If nothing happens now, they'll run away from us."[91] Kriebel reiterated this point in his testimony at the same trial.[92] The *Bund Oberland* officers told Roehm at the time that they could no longer hold their men in check.[93]

It was in response to these outside pressures, rather than the result of an inner conviction that the time was ripe, that caused Hitler finally to order the *Putsch* to take place. It occurred at a time not of his own choosing and under conditions which made its success unlikely if not altogether impossible. Yet one could hardly say that Hitler was not responsible for the situation. It was he who had given the SA and the *Kampfbund* the idea that an earnest revolution was in the making; it was he who had procrastinated throughout the spring, summer, and fall; it was he who had failed to win the confidence of the *Reichswehr,* the police, and the potentially friendly political leaders. Thus, when the *Putsch* was made, Hitler realized that it had to succeed completely in order to avoid utter failure. There was, it seemed, no halfway measure possible, and it was to be the supreme test not only of the political instrument which he had built but of himself as well.

The *Putsch* showed all of the signs of hasty, if sometimes brilliant, improvisation. From a tactical point of view basic errors were made; strategic locations such as the railroad and the telegraph offices were untouched so that it was easy to rally forces against the *putschists.* Yet in the *Bürgerbräu Keller* itself, Hitler handled the situation with the sureness which he would demonstrate on many a later occasion. Three things he did that night are of particular interest to us here. The first was his announcement that he would head the Reich government. Until now Hitler had been content to view himself as a sort of John the Baptist for the coming ruler of the Reich.[94] Now, in a desperate situation, he sought to overcome his problems by elevating himself from the realm of party politics to that of government leadership. It was a logical extension of his decision to revolt, which in itself was an admission that his party policies had failed. It was also the most extreme and least acceptable of the alternatives to that policy which he could have chanced upon.

The second thing of interest he did that evening was to leave the *Bürgerbräu Keller* and the three men whom he had coerced into working with him, von Kahr, von Lossow, and Seisser. For the moment he had achieved the appearance of political unity with these men, but by leaving them to their own devices he afforded them the opportunity to escape which they promptly took. This as much as anything sealed the doom of the affair. One can only wonder why, in a venture for such high stakes, Hitler could have committed such an elementary error of judgment.

Thirdly, Hitler declared that if he failed he would shoot himself. To emphasize his point he placed his pistol to his temple, saying, "If I am not victorious by tomorrow afternoon, I shall be a dead man." [95] Since the next afternoon he was neither victorious nor dead, there has been a strong tendency to write this off as merely an act, a bit of cheap theatrics to impress his unwilling collaborators. [96] Yet he repeated the statement before the whole assembly of the *Bürgerbräu Keller* and in later years said that he had not expected to survive. [97] Some would argue that he obviously was not serious since he avoided being shot down by the police at Odeonsplatz the next day and then fled the scene. Yet we have no right to consider his threat as a frivolous one, especially in view of his later suicide. The way in which he allowed himself to be pushed into the attempt at revolution, and the manner in which, after the flight of von Kahr and his associates, he allowed control of the affair to slip into the hands of Ludendorff, suggests that he had abandoned himself to whatever fate might hold.

It was Ludendorff who made the decision to stage the marching demonstration in a last desperate effort to sway the feelings of the army and the police. [98] At Odeonsplatz, when the shooting began, Hitler, who had been marching arm in arm with Scheubner-Richter, either fell to the ground or was pulled down when his comrade was struck.* In the confusion that

---

* Since Hitler wrenched his shoulder in the fall it seems more likely that he was pulled to the ground by Scheubner-Richter. An old front-line soldier might well react instinctively to shooting by seeking cover —but he would also know how to fall.

followed, friends were able to pull him into a waiting car and escape to the Haenfstaengl house in Utting (south of Munich). There, two days later, Hitler surrendered without protest to the police officer sent to arrest him.[99]

Throughout this affair it is remarkable to note the extent to which Hitler was led rather than leading. Scheubner-Richter and Rosenberg planned (if that is the word) the *Putsch*.[100] Ludendorff gave the order for the march. Hitler allowed himself to be pulled and pushed in every direction, and finally was arrested with never a sign of resistance. Like a man who knew that his doom was inevitable, he submitted to everything, only to discover a few days later that he was not dead, and that, though his political party was shattered, it too possibly had some life in it. Hitler had passed through the ordeal—not with success, but he had *at least* survived.

It may well be asked whether Hitler's policies in 1923 really courted disaster as much as we have intimated above. The refusal to become a part of the national front against the French, for instance, while containing elements of danger, might have been a feasible political stand as well as being consistent with the party ideology. Again, it may have been tactically wise to wait until after the surrender had been made before attacking the national government, though the long period of inaction after September 26th may have contributed to the failure of the *Putsch*. In other words, Hitler's actions in this crisis of 1923 are subject to various interpretations, though the simple fact that he was taking risks, even great risks, seems well established.

The most amazing feature of the *Putsch* is the fact that Hitler was able to rebuild his political fortunes. One would have thought that his career was broken, as were the careers of so many other men of the period. Yet, contrary to reasonable expectation, Hitler was able to achieve within a decade the goal of national leadership.

III

The steps by which Hitler recovered from the disaster of 1923 do not need to be traced here in any detail. Suffice it to say that he was able to retain a solid core of party support, to establish his absolute authority over that core, and to work out a program for the gaining of political power by legitimate means. Admittedly, divisions remained within the party, such as those between the northern and southern sections or between the political leadership and the SA, but by and large Hitler had been able to maintain control—mainly through the force of his personality.

Until 1932, however, he had not established any real program for the attainment of power. The astounding success of the NSDAP at the polls in September of 1930 (when their strength in the Reichstag leaped from 12 to 107 members) may have suggested to him that he could actually capture a majority of the electorate. More sober estimates of his potential strength indicated that it was probably something less than half of the total German electorate. Yet Hitler during the crisis year of 1932 continually acted as though he had a majority behind him. Thus for months he made no serious effort to establish a coalition with the other parties, such as the Center or the Nationalists, which might have given him a parliamentary majority. In his conversations with Hindenburg on August 13 and November 19 of 1932, he demanded powers justified neither by his popular vote nor by the confidence which Hindenburg had placed in him. Nor would he assent to cooperate in a cabinet headed by some other leader. Lastly, his inflammatory speeches stood at odds with his steadfast refusal to depart from legal means of gaining power.

Despite its eventual success, Hitler's policy during 1932 was an extremely risky one. His chances of gaining a majority of the vote were slim. His chances of gaining the support of the president were undermined by his arrogant demands and by the wild actions of the SA and SS. His policy of refusing to cooperate with the other parties proved ever more discouraging to the political leaders of his party who hungered after public office, and his refusal to authorize a *Putsch* threatened to drive his SA leaders mad with frustration. In other words, Hitler pursued a course of action which offered small chance of success and which threatened the destruction of the party in case of failure. The "all or nothing" quality of the venture has its parallel in the earlier events of Hitler's life which we have already touched upon—but there is one great difference: this time he succeeded.

The world-wide depression of 1929 brought the brief German recovery from the effects of war and defeat to the point of collapse. It proved impossible to secure working majority coalitions in the Reichstag and in 1930 the first of the presidential cabinets* came into being. The new misery of the depression coming so quickly on the heels of the inflation and military defeat broke the confidence of the German people in the powers of democratic government. Perhaps the outstanding feature of the political scene in the years immediately preceding Hitler's chancellorship was the fact that, whether Nazi, Communist, or extreme conservative, a majority of the German voters were opposed to democratic principles of government. Nor did the Brüning cabinet do anything to alter this attitude. The policy of fulfillment of foreign commitments was carried through at the price of increased misery for the German wage earner. Increased unemployment and decreased wages and salaries only served to sharpen the anger of the German voters

---

* One that governed without a majority in the Reichstag through the support of the President.

against a "system" which taxed its citizens in order to "demonstrate its national weakness" in foreign affairs by the continued payment of reparations. This attitude may have been unfair to Brüning's courageous policy, but one may well ask whether Brüning was wise to purchase success in foreign affairs at such a high domestic price.

Hitler and the NSDAP, of course, profited immensely from the troubles of the depression. Until 1929 they had been essentially forgotten, but the financial chaos made them prophets with honor in their own land. The National Socialist party leaped from the obscurity of a splinter group to the position of the second largest party in Germany. Yet between 1930, the year of transformation, and 1932, the year of crisis, Hitler did little to formulate a positive program for the seizure of power.[101] It is true that his SA groups increased in size and possibly even in ferocity, but if we accept the view that he intended to gain power by legal means, then the only real step which he made in that direction was the "Harzburg Alliance" of September, 1931, with a conglomeration of rightist groups. That this alliance was stillborn is indicated, however, by the fact that most of the important groups represented at the meeting put up separate candidates for the presidential elections of the following spring.

By far the most important political actions taken by Hitler during this period were negative in character. The success at the polls in 1930 was followed by other victories in provincial elections during 1931 with the result that Chancellor Brüning and other state and army leaders realized clearly how beneficial Hitler's cooperation would be. In one instance National Socialist cooperation was considered particularly vital: Brüning's cabinet depended upon President Hindenburg for support since it did not command a majority in the Reichstag. Unfortunately, Hindenburg's seven-year term of office was due to end in 1932, and it was not certain whether the old soldier could be persuaded to campaign for office again. For government leaders who feared not only economic collapse but civil war as well should Hindenburg leave, anything seemed preferable to an election campaign. The constitution provided that the Reichstag could, by a two-thirds vote, extend the President's term of office, but to gain the necessary two-thirds majority, National Socialist cooperation was needed. On two occasions, once in the fall of 1931 and again in January, 1932, Hitler was asked to cooperate. Not only did he refuse but he did so in such a manner as to anger Hindenburg enough so that he consented to run again for office.

The consequences of this decision were enormous and not entirely favorable to the Nazi cause. By refusing to cooperate in extending the presidential term of office, Hitler insured that a test of strength would take place. By doing it in such a manner that Hindenburg was angered, it insured that this trial would be fought against the most popular political figure in Germany. Furthermore, the pressure from the rank and file of the party, and particularly the SA, for Hitler's candidacy was immense. The Fuehrer fully realized the difficulties involved and hesitated a full month before finally deciding to announce his decision to run.[102] The real danger lay in the question of whether the party could survive the disappointment of the defeat of their leader (and defeat was to be expected); it was also questionable whether the party treasury could survive the costs of the campaign.

There seems no doubt that Hitler precipitated a crisis in which the odds against success were quite great. The chances of defeating Hindenburg were slight; once committed to the quest for a majority, the party would have to keep campaigning until it gained that end or until it had exhausted its reserves of votes and had begun to decline. But decline would be fatal, and would lead, most observers believed, to the breakup of the party through disappointment, defection, and bankruptcy. Thus Hitler staked everything on a gamble which had to end in victory in order to avoid total collapse.

Not all members of the party agreed with these tactics. The powerful party organization leader, Gregor Strasser, felt that it would be wiser to avoid a direct clash with the President and to seek partial power through the control of some cabinet posts. In other words, Strasser hoped to husband and build party strength and to seek alliances with other parties in the hope of eventually establishing a coalition government which would realize some, if not all, of the party's goals. Strasser's course of action would also have saved the German political structure from the exhausting effects of repeated election campaigns and might have allowed more time and energy for the solving of the economic crisis.

Despite such considerations as these, Hitler threw the party into the elections and conducted the campaigns with an energy and imagination hitherto unseen in German politics. Yet the effort was in vain, for the National Socialists were unable to crack the solid block of support for Hindenburg. Interestingly enough, the British Ambassador was able, two weeks before the election of March 13, 1932, to predict with considerable accuracy the probable number of votes for each party and even to predict the probable necessity of a run-off election.[103] Since Hindenburg did fail, by a small percentage, to gain the absolute majority needed, a second election had to be held on April 10th. The outcome was a foregone conclusion, but Hitler entered the campaign in the hope of increasing his total voting support. Furthermore, defeat in the first campaign had been disappointing to the ordinary party members, but failure to continue the contest might have been disastrous to morale. Berlin party leaders informed the British Ambassador that they could not afford to stand still.[104]

Even though the presidential campaign had been a failure, there was scarcely time to pause, for on April 24th provincial elections were scheduled for the state of Prussia. Again the National Socialists increased their share of the vote, but again there was an element of hope for those who favored Nazi defeat. The small parties of the Right lost heavily in numbers in this election when compared with their strength of a few years before, and apparently these voters had scurried over to the National Socialist ranks. By the same token, however, this reserve was now swallowed up, and the Nazis had failed to make any dent in the ranks of the large parties of the Left and Center. Thus a large expansion of the NSDAP was not to be expected. This, at least, was the attitude of well-informed opinion, and it seems to have been essentially correct.[105]

The National Socialist leadership did not seem to see this however. At least Hitler and Goebbels were pressing for the election of a new Reichstag. Admittedly, an election would give the NSDAP such increased numbers that in combination with some acceptable party they might form a majority.* To this extent the call for new Reichstag elections made a good deal of sense, but there is no evidence that Hitler made any real attempt to build such a coalition. What Hitler wanted was a clear majority of National Socialists. Failing that, he wanted, as leader of the strongest party, to be accepted by Hindenburg as the chancellor of a presidential cabinet. Yet the signs indicated that he could not win a majority, and his previous meetings with Hindenburg, together with the bitter accusations he had

---

* Actually, in the Reichstag elected July 31, 1932, the Nazis and the Center could have formed a majority bloc.

made against him during the presidential campaigns, practically insured that he would be unacceptable to the old soldier. Thus Hitler seemed to be destroying the foundations upon which his policy was erected.

Furthermore, the violent and confident tenor of the speeches of Hitler and the other National Socialist leaders, coupled with the pressures of steady campaigning and street fighting as well as the temporary police ban, had worked the SA troops to a height of excitement that made them very difficult to control. Worse (from Hitler's point of view), if the SA troops were bitterly disappointed by failure, they might leave the party in large numbers. Thus during the latter half of the year Hitler's policy of constant and hard campaigning threatened to break up his party. From June onward, Hitler was involved in a race against destruction which might well be considered the result of a situation of his own making.

On July 31, 1932, Germany went to the polls again, this time to elect a new Reichstag. Again the NSDAP was impressively successful in gaining votes (37.5% of the total), and again they failed in their efforts to secure a majority. Yet for a time Hitler apparently believed that he had done enough to earn the post of chancellor and confidently awaited the President's call. Just as confidently, subordinate members of the party prepared to take over power.

One can only wonder why such an apparently shrewd politician as Hitler should have allowed himself to be so deceived about the situation. Sir Horace Rumbold, writing on the 4th of August, could state bluntly,

> The National Socialists are now in a difficult position. It would appear that they have shot their bolt and have exhausted the reservoir from which they drew many of their adherents, and yet have failed to obtain an absolue majority in the Reichstag. Their Storm Troops will soon begin to ask themselves what their

marching . . . [is] leading to. In other words, the time is fast approaching when Hitler will be expected to deliver the goods.[106]

Certainly Hitler's sources of information were not less good than those of the British Ambassador. The fact is that Hitler was prepared to settle for nothing less than the chancellorship. When on August 12th he went to Berlin for his conference with von Papen, and later with Hindenburg, he went in full expectation of being granted all of his demands.

The disappointment of the interview with the Chancellor and the President was immense. All of Hitler's demands were rejected, and the offer of subordinate cabinet posts for certain National Socialists was unacceptable to Hitler.[107] It appeared for the moment at least that Hitler's program of legality had foundered on the rocks of his overambitious demands. The SA was furious. Kurt Luedecke and Joseph Goebbels reported that the Storm Troops were prepared to revolt against the government and could be held back with only the greatest difficulty.[108] A greater danger was that important groups within the party might decide (as some of them had thought in May, 1923) that Hitler could not or would not act and so might transfer their allegiance to other flags. Individual instances of this party breakup occurred in late August and early September.[109]

During August the National Socialists did make some motions in the direction of cooperation with the Center party. Characteristically, these advances did not seem aimed at building a coalition (which would have held a majority of seats in the new Reichstag); rather the negotiations were to be used as a threat to force the government to accede to Hitler's will.[110] Curiously, Hitler even suggested cooperation for the purpose of deposing the President and calling new elections.[111] Since most political observers expected that new elections would bring a decline in National Socialist support, it is difficult to see what purpose this maneuver would have served. The Center and the NSDAP did cooperate, however, to elect Hermann Goering president of the new Reichstag on August 30th.

The first working meeting of the Reichstag took place on September 12th and resulted in a curious farce in which that body, led by an alliance of Nazis and Communists, delivered a vote of censure for the government, while the Reichstag President ostentatiously refused to recognize Chancellor von Papen who held the order for the dissolution of the Reichstag. It was a curious scene not only by reason of the cooperation between the NSDAP and the Communists but also because von Papen and many of the National Socialist deputies probably did not want to see the Reichstag dissolved. Von Papen says that he wanted at least the opportunity to present his reform plans and to allow them to be debated. He had obtained the dissolution order in late August for use in case the Reichstag failed to support him.[112] A large number of the National Socialist deputies liked the salary which they were receiving and foresaw the likelihood of losing their seats in any new election. Gregor Strasser, in particular, was becoming disgusted with the program of opposition and constant electoral campaigns.[113]

It may well be that the dissolution of the Reichstag was due to a set of miscalculations. Apparently before the sessions began all of the other parties had agreed that nothing was to be gained by the Communist-sponsored proposal of censure. When it was introduced, the Nationalists were to oppose it and open the way to its defeat. Yet when the time came, the Nationalists were silent, and Frick, as leader of the NSDAP fraction, called for a half-hour recess. In a meeting at the Reichstag President's palace, Hitler, Frick, and Strasser apparently agreed that the Nationalist silence was part of a von Papen maneuver. They decided to outwit him by supporting the Communist proposal.[114] Von Papen says nothing of his purported cooperation with the

Nationalists.[115] Whatever the case, von Papen was angry over the defeat and, though Hitler (who apparently made the decision) was "beside himself in joy," Frick and Strasser were dismayed.[116]

Exactly why Hitler was so elated is not apparent. The National Socialists were now forced into the last great election of the year under most adverse circumstances. Money was short;[117] many of the leaders were disgruntled; and there was little hope that the party could improve its position. On the other hand, the danger of disillusionment among the rank and file of the party was great. If Hitler was trying to force the government into accepting his conditions, then there can be no doubt that the means used to accomplish this end threatened the destruction of all that he had so painstakingly built up.

The British Embassy reports of this period document the belief that the party was losing ground. Sir Horace Rumbold wrote that the action in the Reichstag on September 12 had done "further harm" to the National Socialist cause[118] and that in the next elections the party would lose ground.[119] Mr. Newton (for Ambassador Rumbold) predicted just before the elections that while the NSDAP would not lose heavily,[120] there was a possibility of a division within the party led by Gregor Strasser, and the Strasser group would be willing to work with the government.[121] All of these predictions proved accurate in the election of November 6, 1932.

The National Socialists lost two million votes from their July peak of thirteen million, and their seats in the new Reichstag dropped from 230 to 196. Furthermore, the decline in Center party representation ended the possibility of creating a majority through a coalition of the two parties. On the following day the *Muenchener Neueste Nachrichten* (conservative) reported that the results of the elections showed that NSDAP could be broken; the losses were fatal,[122] and on November 19, Sir Horace Rumbold remarked that the ". . . results of the elections . . . released the country from the Hitlerite incubus." [123] A more recent study of the period (1955) expresses much the same opinion. The limit of National Socialist expansion had been achieved, and it was now possible to proceed to a final collapse of Nazi power and to the restitution of parliamentary democracy.[124]

Von Papen's first step after the elections was to sound out the possibilities of forming a cabinet based on a parliamentary majority. These efforts met with cold response from most party leaders contacted, including Hitler, and led the Papen cabinet to conclude on November 17th that it should resign in order to leave Hindenburg free to discuss matters with the party leaders.[125] This Hindenburg did, speaking to the leaders of the Center and Right parties on the 18th (the Social Democrats refused to participate in a coalition government) and to Hitler on the 19th. Although the meeting was more cordial than the one of August 13th, the situation remained much the same save that Hindenburg was now willing to accept Hitler as chancellor—if he could form a majority coalition. The evidence shows that Hitler still wanted a presidential cabinet and did not even attempt to contact the other party leaders concerning the possibility of coalition.[126] By November 26th Hindenburg was forced to admit the impossibility of establishing a parliamentary majority and was forced to turn again to von Papen. At this point, however, von Schleicher, the defense minister (the man who had used the authority of the army to unseat Brüning and to make von Papen chancellor) intervened. The army, he said, feared the outbreak of civil war if von Papen remained in office, and he produced a Colonel Ott to present the army case. Whether valid or not, Hindenburg was impressed by the report and dropped his old friend von Papen. But the President now forced von Schleicher to move into the open by naming him chancellor on December 2nd.

In the National Socialist camp, Hitler's continued refusal to compromise led to the worst crisis which the party had faced since 1923. Units of the SA openly broke with the party or resorted to banditry;[127] the party treasury was practically exhausted; and Gregor Strasser, disgusted with Hitler's intransigence, now began discussions with von Schleicher for the purpose of lending him the support of part of the NSDAP. Provincial elections showed a drastic decline in National Socialist voting strength (40% in Thuringia). On the 6th of December, Goebbels noted in his diary that "the situation in the Reich is catastrophic." [128]

The final blow was dealt on the 8th of December when Gregor Strasser announced that he was resigning all of his party offices, a move which had been awaited for some time. Now it was expected that the former party organization leader would carry a large number of party officials into the Schleicher camp. Depression, even despair, prevailed among the leadership around Hitler, and the Fuehrer stated flatly to these men that "if the party disintegrates I'll make an end of it in three minutes with a pistol." [129]

Yet what else could Hitler have expected? Since early in 1932, he had used the party's energies and resources in a reckless gamble for power and had failed. Opportunities for moderate rewards, or at least for a respite, had been spurned. It can only be said that Hitler had chosen a road to power which showed little promise of success. The desperate situation of the party was largely of his own making. Unless he could almost immediately solve the enormous difficulties which he faced by gaining the power he craved, he and the party were doomed to an early failure, in which case he probably would have carried out his threat. But to surmount his difficulties would require something akin to a political miracle—and that is about what happened.

Hitler's political recovery from this shattering experience was accomplished with the aid of several pieces of amazingly good fortune. The first was the refusal of Gregor Strasser to fight Hitler for the leadership of the party. Why Strasser did not show more combativeness is hard to say. Bullock feels that his whole previous record showed that he lacked the toughness to stand up to the Fuehrer.[130] Strasser explained to his brother Bernhard that in a moment of weakness he had sworn an oath never to work against Hitler and now could not bring himself to break his word.[131] Whatever the reason, Strasser's failure to struggle for the party leadership allowed the men around Hitler to act quickly to repair the damage. New pledges of loyalty were exacted. Strasser's political organization was smashed and a new system erected. Hitler, Goebbels, and other leaders visited party groups all over the country and finally talked them back into line. It had been a near disaster, but the crisis had finally been resolved.

But this recovery only brought the NSDAP back to the point at which it had stood in early December, and that position had been far from favorable. However, during the month of January, a warm winter (with consequent low coal sales) and a falling price of butter conspired to raise discontent among the Ruhr workers and industrialists and farmers with dairy interests so that confidence in the von Schleicher cabinet was shaken. In addition to this, von Papen and others were able to change Hindenburg's mind sufficiently so that by the latter days of January he was finally prepared to accept a presidential cabinet headed by Hitler (but surrounded by supposedly safe men).

There are several points worth noting about Hitler's final success in 1933. Most important is the fact that he compromised in accepting the chancellorship to an extent he had never been willing to go to before. It may well be that a deal had been shaping up for more than a year and that all of Hitler's stubbornness was merely a part of the bargaining procedure. But the record seems to indicate that his expectations exceeded his party's capabilities and that Hitler's policy was so reckless as to very nearly destroy the party. Possibly recklessness was the only feasible policy to follow. Certainly one can hold that many political groups followed courses which did not bode well for success in this time. This can be said of the Communists, of the Social Democrats, and of Franz von Papen. All in their own ways were gambling, just as Hitler was gambling, against heavy odds.

This willingness to compromise reminds us of Hitler's attempt to contact the Bavarian Crown Prince in the early morning hours before the march which ended the *Putsch* of 1923. At that time the feeble gesture had completely miscarried. Now in 1932, after the moment of despair, Hitler's compromise lifted him into a new sphere of power from which he could master the inner dissensions of the party. It may be that the threat to commit suicide had been a "cry for help" (as discussed by Stengel and Cook) in which Hitler, no longer able to solve the problems of party division, called upon his followers to solve them for him. It may also be that the closeness of disaster on December 8th made Hitler fully conscious of the recklessness of his course and of the need for compromise.

Finally it should be noted that even as chancellor, Hitler did not overcome all of his problems with party dissension until the "Blood Purge" of June, 1934. At that time he finally tamed the SA, as he had conquered the political leadership in December, 1932. It is interesting to note that in the wake of the clash between the army and the SA which culminated in the Purge, Hitler again leaped into a new realm of power by combining the office of president with that of reichschancellor and making the Army take an oath of loyalty to his person. This ultimate accretion of power came as the result of a crisis between the army and the SA which Hitler had allowed to develop until it threatened to destroy his political regime.

The evidence from his private and public life shows that Hitler courted disaster as a method, that in the *Putsch* of 1923 and in the election year of 1932 he followed a course in which the probability of failure was high. In the events leading up to the "Blood Purge" of 1934, this is perhaps not so evident, but one wonders what would have happened if even ten per cent of the SA (or about 300,000 men) had chosen to resist. Any kind of civil war would have been extremely dangerous and probably even fatal to the Hitler regime. One of the problems in studying the life of this man is that of understanding how he could be so certain that he would prevail against the great odds which so often confronted him. In many cases this certainty does not seem to be derived from any detailed study of the plans or interests of his opponents (this was especially true in foreign affairs); perhaps it was built upon a secret joy in the knowledge that if he did not succeed he would at least fail completely.

IV

The next two instances in which Hitler referred to the possibility of doing away with himself (September 1, 1939, and November 23, 1939) are interesting in that they occur within three months of each other and both are somewhat oblique. It might be possible to overlook them entirely if it were not for the gravity of the situation which occasioned their utterance. Because of this, it is well to investigate, if only briefly, whether the crisis of the outbreak of war represented a collapse of Hitler's policy, as was the case with the previous suicide threats, and whether there existed any internal conflicts which he was trying to resolve by a flight into new responsibilities.

Ordinarily, one would assume that war represented the breakdown of policy, but there is enough evidence that Hitler actually craved a war to make it arguable that the conflict of 1939 represented the fruition rather than the failure of his plans. Certainly the furor occasioned by A. J. P. Taylor's *The Origins of the Second World War* give evidence that an important part of the scholarly world believes that *this* war was the intended result of Hitler's program.[132] Professor Taylor's contention that the war of 1939 was the result of a series of blunders committed both by the Germans and the other powers has not been happily received. It is not our purpose here to enter into the controversy but rather to attempt to determine what Hitler's policy was in the years prior to the outbreak of the war, and secondly to see whether the war he got was the one he wanted, if indeed he wanted war at all. Lastly, we must ask whether divisions within the Reich forced Hitler, in the manner that the SA unrest had plagued him in 1923 and 1932, to seek a solution which would give him a firmer control over all the departments of the party and Reich government.

From the time in 1934 that Hitler consolidated his hold over the German nation by assimilating the office of the president to that of the chancellor, his policies had been more and more directed towards the goal of altering the situation forced on Germany by the defeat of 1918. In the first instance this involved ending the restrictions placed upon German sovereignty in the field of military preparedness and territorial control. By 1937 that goal had been largely achieved. Conscription had been reintroduced, and the Versailles restrictions on military armaments had been rejected; the Rhineland had been remilitarized, and the Rhine waters were again under German control. Reparations payments were dropped. All of this had been accomplished with only the most feeble of protests from France and Great Britain.

For the historian, interpretation of these developments sets no serious problems. Hitler stated clearly what he intended to do, and he accomplished that purpose. The next period is, by contrast, exceedingly difficult to understand because there is a very considerable problem in determining what it was that Hitler wanted to accomplish. This may seem simple-minded in view of what he did do in the years from 1937 to 1939, but there is less than perfect assurance that what Hitler did conformed with his plans and his hopes. To many, the progression of events—the *Anschluss*, Munich, March of 1939, and the outbreak of war—seems to indicate that Hitler had a fixed "timetable" for conquest. Yet, so far as we know, no such timetable existed, nor, in the nature of things, could it have existed. Even the Hossbach conference of November 5, 1937—hailed as a "blueprint for aggression"—was hardly that.[133] Furthermore, the evidence which has come to light since the war shows the remarkable degree to which chance played a part in Hitler's moves. This is most obvious in the case of Austria, which far from being a long-planned affair was, in fact, a hasty improvisation.

We need not doubt that Hitler aspired to revise the map of Central Europe, but whether he had any far-reaching plans for accomplishing this end is certainly open to question. Perhaps the most that can be said is that he hoped to achieve his "free hand" in this area by breaking the will of France and Great Britain to resist such moves. Apparently this was to be done by threatening the West with violence in order to force negotiation. The method, though inelegant, did for a time achieve its purposes. It is vaguely reminiscent of the policy Hitler had followed in 1932. Then he had tried to gain the chancellorship by legal means, all the while threatening that if he were not appointed his Storm Troops might resort to civil war. The parallelism is not complete however. Then his political opponents were able to assess his voting strength and to realize that, though large, it by no means constituted a majority. Now Britain and France, faced with the potential power of a re-armed Germany, feared that war would be unbearably costly, if not disastrous. In 1932, the fear that the SA might revolt seems to have been well founded, but in 1938-39 the army, far from pressing Hitler to war, tended to shrink from the idea of conflict. However, the army did provide the element of internal opposition to Hitler's program such as Strasser had provided in 1932. In fact, Hitler might be said to have had two major problems facing him in the years before the war. The first was that of forcing the former Allies to allow and even to sanctify his expansion in Central Europe. The second was that of breaking the army to his will. At times it would seem that actions taken in the field of foreign affairs were motivated by the hope of surmounting internal difficulties.

The Austrian *Anschluss* is an illustrative example. Here the foreign adventure definitely served to quell unrest at home. In January and February of 1938, the major problem facing Hitler was that of pacifying the army. The dismissal of Defense Minister Blomberg and of Army Chief Fritsch (the latter on a false charge of homosexuality) left the army seething with discontent which was not alleviated by a reorganization of the armed forces that gave Hitler more direct control over them. It is at least conceivable that Fritsch's "court of honor," scheduled to convene on March 12, 1938, could have been the instance for an army revolt against the Fuehrer. Instead, events in Austria, not of Hitler's making, led to the annexation of March 11 which completely smothered the impact of the "court of honor." Hitler might have acted just as forcefully even if he had not faced unrest at home, but there is no doubt that the *Anschluss* served admirably the purpose of quelling the generals.

Concerning the relation of war to the solution of these

major problems, several alternative interpretations are possible. Without by any means exhausting the possibilities, we can mention five alternatives which Hitler had before him in the period from 1938 to 1939. The first was pursuit of a course of diplomatic activities which would have permitted him to expand German influence in Central and Eastern Europe without recourse to war. Secondly, if Hitler wanted war, or if he felt he could only accomplish his objectives by war, then he could limit the conflict to a "small" war against a secondary power such as Poland. Thirdly, if it proved to be impossible to isolate Poland from the Western powers, then he could pursue the war in such a manner that the belligerency of Britain and France would be only nominal and could be ended quickly by a peace conference. Fourth, he could enter the war with Poland in full recognition of the fact that England and France would become involved, but without any real plans for solving the difficulties thus raised. Fifth, he could begin the war with the avowed purpose of conquering Europe.

We cannot say for certain which, if any, of these alternatives was in Hitler's mind in the late summer of 1939, but we can show that he prepared the ground badly for the accomplishment of any one of them.

If Hitler wished to avoid war and to win his goals through diplomacy, a possibility which we must at least admit, then his method was singularly ill-adapted to his purposes. It is true that in 1938 he had been able to force Great Britain and France into making great concessions, and thus to break the will of the Czechs, by increasing the military tension in Europe. Effective as such a method may be, it allows for only two alternatives should the diplomatic adversary fail to bow. Either the threatening power must make good its threats or it must face the humiliation of backing down. In 1939 Hitler faced in Poland such a determined adversary.

Thus, if Hitler's goal was a diplomatic triumph without war, or if it was, as A. J. P. Taylor suggests, the settlement of differences over Danzig as a preliminary step to German-Polish cooperation against Russia,[134] the method chosen was far too rigid. The method was made even more inflexible by Hitler's refusal to engage in diplomatic parlays during the spring and summer of 1939 (both he and Ribbentrop were largely unavailable). Furthermore, Hitler imposed upon his military preparations a deadline of September 1, 1939. This date, established on April 3rd, had no intrinsic importance, but by reason of its selection it was to become an insuperable barrier to further discussion. There was certainly no need for such inflexibility, just as there was probably no military need for the ordering of preparations so long in advance.[135]

If we assume, for the moment, that Hitler's intentions were consistently peaceful, then we can only explain his orders for military preparations and his warlike speeches to his generals on May 23rd and August 22nd as parts of a game of bluff which had to be carried through not only against his adversaries but against his own subordinates as well.[136] When such bluffing tactics are linked with a rigid timetable, then any hesitancy at the decisive moment can cause consternation and loss of confidence in the ranks of the subordinates. When the attack order for August 26, 1939, was canceled a few hours after it was given (August 25, 1939), one witness reported the following reaction from Admiral Canaris of Wehrmacht intelligence:

> . . . Canaris and Thomas and all of our friends were now under the impression that this withdrawal of an order to march was an incredible loss of prestige for Hitler. Oster thought that never before in the history of warfare had a supreme commander withdrawn such a decisive order in the throes of a nervous breakdown. And Canaris said to me, "Now the peace of Europe is saved for 50 years, because Hitler has lost the respect of the generals." [137]

There is no other evidence that Hitler did lose the confidence of the generals by this action (Halder's diary, for example, says nothing about this incident [138]), but the possibility existed and Canaris may have had information that is no longer available.

It must also be noted that the treatment accorded Czechoslovakia gave Poland every reason to resist concessions even to Hitler's "reasonable" demands. Even if we give Hitler the benefit of the doubt and suppose that his occupation of Prague was occasioned by a collapse of Czech authority and was meant to avert the occupation of Slovakia by Hungarian troops,[139] could the Poles have hoped for any better fate? Once the authority of the Polish government was shaken, could a fourth partition of Poland be long avoided? The Polish government thought not, and the Russian government apparently concurred.[140]

Thus, from a number of points of view, if a peaceful solution was desired the means employed were singularly inappropriate. But much of the evidence indicates that Hitler really wanted war, at least against Poland.[141] If we assume that he wanted to isolate Poland, could he have prepared the ground any better? Certainly the pact with Russia was a master stroke but, as events proved, insufficient for the task of cutting off Poland from the Western powers. The isolation of Poland from the West depended primarily upon maintaining English and French confidence in the Munich settlement and forcing Poland to appear as the intransigent or even belligerent party in the negotiations over the Corridor. Neither of these tasks was accomplished or even seriously attempted.

In the weeks following Munich, actions on the part of Hitler and the National Socialist party conspired to destroy hopes of friendship between Germany and England. Hitler's attack upon Chamberlain was not only in bad taste but alienated those members of English government who hoped for a settlement with Germany on the basis of the Munich pact. Furthermore, the outbreak of violence against Jewish persons and property in November, 1938, again shocked the sensibilities of the Western states. This insane outburst sharpened the image of the National Socialists as a criminal organization. Instead of cultivating the tendency of people to forget the less desirable features of a society, Hitler deliberately flouted them and in the process obscured Poland's own bad record in matters of minority rights and democratic institutions. Perhaps these internal affairs should have had no influence upon the conduct of international relations, but that they did is unquestionable.

The fatal blow to the Munich settlement, however, was the seizure of the Bohemian portions of Czechoslovakia and the final dismemberment of that state on March 15, 1939. Whatever reasons Hitler may have had for this move,[142] it destroyed all confidence in his pledged word and led directly to the British extension of guarantees to Poland on March 31, 1939. Whether justified or not, Britain, France, and the United States now concluded that no state in Central Europe was safe from German aggression, and the speculation was voiced with increasing frequency that Hitler wanted to conquer all of Europe (or the world). Thus Hitler's actions even before he had decided to attack Poland gravely lessened the possibility that such an attack could be an isolated one.

If Hitler accepted the theory that a war with Poland would involve him in war with the West, he may still have thought that such a conflict would be more nominal than real. In this case one could expect demonstrations along the German-French borders, mobilization orders, and then, after the unavoidable fate of Poland had been settled, a peace conference which would patch up the differences and sanctify Germany's free hand in Central Europe. It might even have led to cooperation against Russia. This prospect was not altogether illusory since the Western powers intended to do, and indeed could do, little to aid Poland.[143] Such an outcome would depend upon German moderation in Poland both as to demands for territory and in the treatment of the population. Neither of these stipulations was fulfilled. SS units in Poland during the early days of the campaign established the pattern of control which was to eventuate in the annihilation centers of Auschwitz and Treblinka.[144] German territorial claims far exceeded those propounded in the spring, and the establishment in Poland of the German-run Government General was more a slap in the face than a sop to Allied feelings.[145]

Perhaps even worse was the fact that the German-Soviet pact opened the way for Russian occupation of the eastern third of Poland. Even if Hitler had been willing to scale down his claims in Poland for the sake of peace with England and France, there was little that he or they could do about the Russian seizures. Hitler's peace offer of October 6, 1939, may well have been sincere, but under the conditions prevailing he had little to offer the Allies but humiliation.[146] The pact with the Soviets probably destroyed any hope of a nominal war with the West, whether Hitler realized it at the time or not.

But perhaps Hitler was convinced of the necessity for a showdown with the West. Certainly he had spoken of it for a long number of years at various times. Both in *Mein Kampf* and in his unpublished work of 1928, he saw no possibility of peace with France.[147] He alluded to it again in the Hossbach Conference of November 5, 1937, and in his speeches to the generals of May 23 and August 22, 1939.[148] Despite this long history of belief that a war with France could not be avoided, it would seem that Germany in the year 1939 was in many ways unprepared for such a war. Absurd as this statement may seem in the light of the victory of the next spring, it is nonetheless true that Germany in her military preparations and economic preparations was not yet in condition to wage a war against major opponents. The army had scarcely finished the period of rapid expansion which followed upon the reintroduction of conscription in 1935. Many new units had been formed, but some of these were not as yet well trained. The army had certainly improved since the fall of 1938, when (it is now judged) it would have had a great deal of difficulty in dealing with the Czech army.[149] The armored units were being rapidly formed but as yet were largely untried. Certainly the bulk of the tanks (Mark I's and Mark II's) were not powerful weapons, and in number they did not exceed those available to the Western Allies.[150]

This is not to say that the German army in 1939 was not a good army; it was very good. The senior commanders were certain that it could deal easily with the antiquated Polish army, but they did not feel that it was as yet either large enough or well trained enough to achieve victory against France and England. And if that decisive victory could not be gained, then, in their eyes, the war was lost.[151] Nor did the generals feel warranted in assuming that German tactics and German leadership were so superior as to assure victory, an attitude which is even more dangerous than it is immodest.

The Luftwaffe's case was different. In 1939 it was undoubtedly the most powerful air force in the world. Furthermore, its weaknesses were not as yet clearly recognized. Its lack of long-range strategic bombers would only make itself felt during the battle against Britain in 1940-41. On the other hand, neither was it fully recognized to what extent control of the air would affect the issue on the ground, so that in assessing their chances for success cautious generals may have tended to underestimate the effectiveness of the Luftwaffe. In any case, modern air warfare was as yet largely unproved and many were skeptical of the claims of its most ardent proponents.[152]

Of the German navy there could also be no doubt. It was definitely inferior to the navies of Britain and France. Admiral Raeder was brought close to despair by the outbreak of the war, and it was really not until 1941 that the U-boat fleet became a factor of major importance in the German war effort.[153]

If the condition of the armed forces was such as to raise serious doubts about the possibility of defeating the Allies, the state of the economy was not more heartening. In August, as the war drew near, the economics expert for the OKW (Oberkommando der Wehrmacht), General Thomas, protested violently but to no avail against beginning the war with such inadequate industrial preparations.[154] Germany's supply of strategic raw materials stood at a dangerously low level,[155] production of weapons was also low, and, surprisingly, weaponry remained at these low levels through 1941.[156] Again, as compared with the condition of its adversaries the German picture may not have been too bad, but was it good enough to insure victory? The answer seems to be that it was not.

General Thomas, in his critique of Hitler's prewar military and economic policies, charged that the Fuehrer sacrificed the possibility of building a stronger weapon by rearming in "width" rather than in "depth." By this Thomas meant that Hitler chose to create an imposing force out of the materials available to him rather than to reinforce the industrial base upon which that force was built. The end result of this policy was that, in 1939, Hitler had an instrument of considerable power, but one which was inadequate to the demands of a long war.[157] And it was this type of war which the generals expected to fight if they became engaged with the French and the British.

Thus if Hitler entered into the war against Poland under

the assumption that he would have to deal also with an England and France determined to carry the war to a finish, it can only be said that he did so under conditions which were inauspicious for success. The only real excuse for deliberately incurring such a situation would be the existence of some plan for the quick dispatch of the Western Allies so as to avert a prolonged struggle. The evidence is, however, that no such plan existed. Despite the fact that Hitler had stated on May 23rd that in case the Polish difficulties would lead to war with England and France, he would attack the West first, no arrangements were actually made to meet such an eventuality.[158] The first military dispositions of the year as given in the OKH (Oberkommando des Heeres) directive of January 18th were defensive.[159] These defensive dispositions towards the West were reiterated in the first OKW directives for the conduct of the war (August 31 and September 3, 1939),[160] and were repeated again in the OKW directive of September 17 handling the redisposition of troops from Poland to the West.[161]

It was not until the 10th of October, in a memorandum dated from the previous day, that Hitler finally called for the preparation of an offensive to be undertaken in the West that fall.[162] The plan of attack which eventuated from this memorandum ("Case Yellow," October 19, 1939) has usually been labeled an unimaginative reissue of the von Schlieffen plan. In actuality, as both Telford Taylor and Jacobsen have demonstrated, "Case Yellow" was something quite different.[163] As the memorandum states:

> . . . the German attack is to be so constituted that it can lead to the destruction of the French Army, but in any case to gain a better attack position and thereby create a situation for further successful prosecution of the war.[164]

The rest of the memorandum makes it clear that Hitler was

concerned more with the protection of the Ruhr and with gaining positions from which an aerial attack on England could be launched than with winning the war at one blow.[165] A comparison of this memorandum with some of his speculations voiced in the spring and late summer show that Hitler's concept of war with the West had for some time been one of limited objectives. Perhaps he believed that England and France could be "brought to reason" by a few sharp blows and without a fight to the finish.[166]

The OKW directive which resulted from the memorandum, and was issued the same day, makes even more emphatic the limited nature of this offensive.

> The goal of this attack operation is to strike the strongest possible part of the French army and that of her allies and at the same time to capture the greatest possible territory in Holland, Belgium and Northern France as a base for . . . air . . . and sea operations against England and as a defensive zone for the Ruhr.[167]

This is in no sense of the word a reissue of the von Schlieffen plan aimed at the rapid destruction of the French army.

Ten days later the first plan, "Case Yellow," arising from this directive was issued, and on the 29th of October a second revised plan was issued.[168] Although there were misgivings about this plan and although Hitler himself toyed with its alteration,[169] it was not until the 24th of February, two-and-a-half months before the attack began, that the decision was finally made to attempt to destroy the French army.[170] In other words, Hitler not only entered the war with a military and economic instrument badly suited to the conduct of a long war, he also had at the beginning of the war, and for six months thereafter, no plans directed towards the gaining of a quick decision.

Thus we see that whatever his expectations may have been, in eventualities ranging from the maintaining of peace to the conquest of Europe, Hitler had stacked the cards against his success. The fault was not wholly his, but he cannot escape a great part of the responsibility.

Lastly we must turn to the relationship between Hitler and his generals. There seems to be little doubt that tensions between the political leadership and the military represented the most dangerous challenge to Hitler's authority in the period following his assumption of full powers in 1934. This conflict broke into the open in early 1938 with the dismissal of Blomberg and Fritsch and the reorganization of the armed forces. Temporarily smoothed over, it came perilously close to revolt at the time of the Czech crisis and the resignation of the army chief of staff, Beck.[171] The generals were mollified, even humbled, by the results of the Munich conference, but as the danger of war increased in the summer of 1939 the restiveness of the generals reappeared, and after the war broke out it led to a number of plots against the life of Hitler scheduled for enactment in the fall of 1939. In fact, with regard to his generals, Hitler found himself in a most difficult position in August, 1939. If he were to back down from his demands, he would have been damned as irresponsible and weak; if his war turned out badly, he would be damned as irresponsible. Most observers expected it to turn out badly.

Thus September 1, 1939, represented for Hitler exactly what November 8-9, 1923, and December 8, 1932, had represented, a culmination of all his mistakes, for the point was brought home to him that he must either succeed entirely or fail completely. Hitler realized this (if only instinctively) and stated during the course of his speech to the Reichstag on September 1, 1939, what must have been for him the simplest matter of fact: "I have again put on that coat [the soldier's coat] which for me was the holiest and the dearest. I shall not take it off until victory or—I will not see the finish." The meaning is scarcely veiled—the terms for Hitler were victory or destruction, and, implicitly, the terms for Germany were the same.[172]

In 1923 destruction had come, but Hitler, after his initial despair, had survived. In 1932 came victory. In both cases his suicide threat had been more direct than in 1939, though probably not more sincere. It is curious that as Hitler approached the time of his death his suicidal threats became less direct. In 1943 he could only wonder why others (von Paulus in particular) did not shoot themselves.[173] For the present (September 1939) Hitler's threat could be viewed more as a warning to the country that their leader would desert them should they fail him. It was serious but only in the sense that it was a cry for help—this time uttered to the entire nation. Yet one cannot escape the conviction that it was a cry for help voiced by a man who had created the conditions of his own destruction.

Two days later in Berlin the British Ambassador handed in his credentials preparatory to a declaration of war. As he left, Hitler turned to Ribbentrop and asked, "What do we do now?" [174] The dreaded consequences of the outbreak of war had come to pass. The problem was now what to make of the situation. Instead of enjoying a "free hand in Central Europe" with the blessing of the West, he found himself limited in the East by his Russian alliance and at war with England and France.

It may well be that the alternatives which were suggested, ranging from peace to conquest of Europe, were not mutually exclusive but rather represented progressive states of Hitler's attitude towards the problem confronting him. That is, he could well have begun the diplomatic negotiations with Poland under the impression that they could be concluded peacefully, though possibly under intense pressure, and he may have maintained this attitude up to the point of the outbreak of war. Coincident with the latter weeks of this period, and possibly ranging back as far as the spring of the year, he may have considered war with Poland a feasible and even desirable outcome of the crisis. Certainly on the 31st of August he must have been willing to accept the probability that England and France would declare war, though he may have thought, even *probably* thought, that this would constitute only a nominal state of hostilities. Hence he could look forward to a peace conference in October, though this possibility was seemingly shattered by the Russian occupation of eastern Poland. Hitler made the offer of peace on October 6, 1939, but he must have sensed the futility of the gesture because he ordered preparations for the Western offensive even before receiving Chamberlain's reply.[175]

It must be noted that he did not abandon hope that England and France would be willing to avoid a fight to the finish, as can be seen from an examination of the development of the plans for the Western offensive. Still there was a tone of desperation in a conference of the 23rd of November, 1939, in which, after a rather sober beginning, he proceded to give vent to all of his native violence:

> No one has created what I have made. My life plays no role here. I have led the German people to greater heights, even though they hate us in the world I shall gamble this entire creation. I have to choose between victory and destruction. I choose victory.
>
> I will not shrink from anything and I'll destroy everyone that opposes me. . . . I shall destroy the enemy. . . . I will stand or fall in this war. I shall not survive the collapse of my people.[176]

Strangely prophetic was this outburst of hatred, and again the clear implication is present that he would commit suicide if things went amiss. Scarcely less clear was the implication that if he were destroyed, so would Germany be destroyed. Like his previous threats of suicide, this occurred at a time when he was committed to a course the outcome of which was doubtful. If he had little faith in the total success of the offensive which was to begin on December 3rd, his generals had none at all.[177] He spoke of destroying his enemies, but the plan he was employing did not envisage such a destruction.

In November of 1939, Hitler was in a corner largely of his own making. His diplomacy had failed; his limited war had not remain limited. His outburst was essentially correct—he had arrived once again at a point where he could only escape destruction through a total victory, a point where he had to flee into a wholly new realm of power in order to escape destruction in the present one. Thus it was that he had forced upon himself the role of European conqueror by leaving himself such desperate alternatives.

The escape was brilliant but only partially successful, and though it brought Hitler to the apex of his powers, it left him faced with the same insoluble difficulties from which he had been trying to flee. The campaigns of the spring of 1940 were shattering in their impact upon Europe and the world. In the face of the strongest navy in the world, the German armed forces were able to carry out a successful invasion of Norway. A month later they opened their stunning attack against the Lowlands and France. Drastic revisions had changed the limited offensive of the previous fall into the master stroke of the spring. By the middle of June all of Western Europe north of the Pyrenees was under Hitler's control. Only Great Britain remained, and she was in a sadly battered condition.

We cannot say with any certitude when Hitler formulated his plans to become master of Europe. It may have been as early as the 1920's when he sat in his prison cell writing his autobiography. But on the other hand it may have developed only after the fall of France. His hesitation during the battle of Flanders, the failure to make any preparation for the eventuality of invading England, even the expansion into the Scandinavian countries point to a strategy based on a longer war against England. It is true that this war was being fought for the purpose of gaining a free hand in Central and Eastern Europe, but it is perfectly possible to doubt that Hitler had developed any grand strategy for the conquest of Europe before the summer of 1940.

It is usually asserted that Hitler turned against Russia because of his inability to destroy English power. This is only partially true. If Hitler's only purpose was to destroy English power, he could have done so more effectively by attacking in Africa, the Middle East and Gibralter, or by building his air and sea strength for a direct assault on the British Isles. It is true that the conquest of Russia would have given Hitler a mighty concentration of power to hurl against the British, but this was certainly not the most direct method of approaching the problem. Furthermore, a very considerable part of Russian raw materials was available for the use of the German war machine during the period 1939–41. It should also be noted that the first discussions of a possible offensive against Russia took place on July 13, 1940, before Hitler's peace offer to the British (July 19th) had been made and rejected, and before the air offensive against England had failed.

We would like to suggest that the attack against Russia was only a part of a more general assault launched by Hitler, and that this more general assault grew out of the collapse of Hitler's policy of extending his influence in Central Europe which had foundered on the rock of Polish obstinacy. The parts of the problem thus engendered included not only the continuing conflict against England but also the frustrations of forming a "New Order" in Europe following the battle of France, and also the problem of establishing and maintaining his ascendancy over his generals. Thus the period after September, 1939, represented the movement by Hitler from one realm of power, that of chief of state, to another, that of European conqueror. In this respect it parallels the earlier leaps which Hitler had made, such as that from the party leader of 1932 to the chief of state of 1934. As in the earlier situations, Hitler was as much fleeing from an intolerable condition of his own making as he was seizing opportunities which existed.

In the period between 1940 and 1942 the German leader greatly expanded the area of conflict. What had begun as a European war was, during this time, extended into Africa, across the seas, and deep into the heart of Russia. At the same time the racial struggle propounded by the National Socialists was expanded into a war of annihilation, and in a set of parallel actions Hitler finally established his full control over the German state and over the officer corps. The steps by which these things were accomplished were not planned in advance, though Hitler may have had in mind general goals towards which he was working. Rather, the change grew out of the opportunities thrust in his path and the frustrations which arose in the course of prosecuting the war.

Undoubtedly the most dramatic of Hitler's decisions during this period was that of attacking Russia. It is also undoubtedly true that he underestimated the strength of the Russian enemy, a mistake which was to imperil the whole venture of European conquest. The blow at Russia followed not so much from the frustrations over the failure of Britain to surrender as from the change in attitude about the possibilities for victory which is reflected in the February 24, 1940, alterations of "Case Yellow." [178] On that date the plans to make the war more difficult in order to force England and France to a compromise peace were exchanged for a plan which sought victory in one blow. In other words, Hitler realized that the collapse of his effort to win

Middle Europe by threats necessitated a new strategy which would give him dominance over the continent. As soon as he reached this conclusion, it became obvious that he would have to deal somehow with Russia.

But the years 1940–41 saw also the development of the concept of the "final solution" of the "Jewish problem." Despite the terrible conditions existing in the prewar concentration camps, they involved, by later standards, a relatively small number of victims and were not annihilation centers. "The war," said Joseph Goebbels, "opened up new possibilities. . . ." for the National Socialists.[179] Possibilities which had not existed in peacetime (or had not been perceived) now revealed themselves. The jargon of the Nazis could become a reality. Even here the change was not immediate. Jews and other undesirables were thrust into ghettos; then the ghettos were concentrated. Plans were made for the expulsion of European Jewry or the establishment of a Jewish colony on Madagascar. It appears to have taken some time for the leaders to realize that it was literally possible to "kill the Jews." The period in which this conclusion was reached coincided exactly with the period in which the decision to attack Russia was made.[180]

The least understandable of Hitler's major decisions during this time was the declaration of war on the United States. For well over a year the Americans had been moving away from their declared position of neutrality towards one of open war against the Germans. There can be no doubt that the Roosevelt administration wanted war with the Germans, though apparently Congress was much less interested in the project.[181] Roosevelt would have been happy to have the Germans declare hostilities or to commit some act which would provide a *casus belli*, but throughout 1941 Hitler showed remarkable patience in the face of repeated American provocation.[182] Then at the moment when the United States had become suddenly and deeply involved in a war with Japan, and at a time when the German army was in grave trouble in Russia, Hitler declared war against the U.S.A.[183] Why he did so is by no means clear. He was certainly not obligated to Japan to this extent, and by so doing he may have enabled the United States to concentrate upon the war with Germany much earlier than would otherwise have been the case.[184] The truth is that Hitler gratuitously brought into the ranks of his enemies the most powerful and implacable country in the world.

The reasons for this incredible mistake are difficult to find. Certainly Hitler consistently underestimated the strength of the United States, and he may not have realized the power he now had directed against himself. Or he may have thought that the United States was ready to declare war in any case, though this was not so apparent in Washington. Again, he may have been simply exasperated. But possibly a part of the answer is to be found in Hitler's ideological view of the world. It will be noted that 1941 was the year in which Hitler declared war upon all the major enemies of human survival (by National Socialist standards): international Marxism, international finance capitalism (represented by the United States), and behind both the apocalyptic figure of the international Jew.

If this is the case, and the texts of his war declarations against both the Soviet Union and the United States indicate that he was thinking along these lines, then the new realm of power into which he had climbed becomes more clear. As reichschancellor in 1939, his policy of limited expansion had collapsed on the rocks of Polish and English resistance. Because of this he was vulnerable to attack from that other leading power of the state, the army. But as overlord of Europe and Fuehrer of the supreme struggle against the ideological enemies he had no peers. In the years 1941–42 he successfully destroyed the foundations of all rivals who did not operate on the ideological level. Only the SS remained as the truly powerful organization in Hitler's Europe.

During the years 1940 through 1942, Hitler exerted ever greater influence over the leadership of the armed forces, a process which culminated in his assumption of personal control over the conduct of the war in December, 1941. Ever since the Polish campaign, Hitler had interfered with operations from time to time, the most notable instance being the famous "stop order" issued to the Panzer units rolling towards Dunkirk in May of 1940.[185] Again, in August of 1941 he ordered Panzer units preparing for the march on Moscow to turn south for a battle of encirclement near Kiev. The time lost by this change of direction may well have cost the Germans Moscow.[186]

Yet, exasperating as these interferences were to the generals, they were qualitatively different from the change which Hitler effected in the military leadership during December of 1941. With the failure of the last German offensive of that year, Adolf Hitler assumed *personal* control of the armed forces and now effectively controlled *all* of the movements of the Wehrmacht. Temporarily this policy achieved some degree of success. Hitler's order that the army should not retreat before the Russians may have prevented a debacle.[187] Later the memory of the success of this stubborn tactic would lead Hitler to order foolish and even impossible holding actions. The long list of positions held without hope forms a dismal litany for the final years of the Third Reich and without a doubt contributed significantly to its collapse.[188] Thus Hitler was able finally to gain absolute superiority over the generals, but the price was an imposition upon the war effort of a limited and rigid tactical concept.

This assumption of personal control over the armed forces was paralleled by a final seizure of total power over all of the various facets of life within the Reich. On April 26, 1942, Hitler asked for and received a Reichstag decree which stated:

There exists no doubt that the Fuehrer, at the present time in the war in which the German people are battling over the question of existence or non-existence, must possess the right to do everything which serves to win the war or aids that purpose. The Fuehrer must, without being bound by established legal regulations—in his capacity as Fuehrer of the nation, as commander-in-chief of the armed forces, as governmental leader and supreme possessor of executive power, as supreme judge and as Fuehrer of the party—at all times be in the position in the case of necessity to (force) every German to fulfill his duty—whether he is a simple soldier or an officer, an inferior or higher official, a judge, a leading or subordinate party functionary, a worker or a salaried person—and if this duty is not fulfilled, after conscientious examination but without consideration for so-called well established laws, to relieve (the offending person) of his office, his rank and his position.[189]

This law, which Hitler did not take full advantage of until 1944, made him supreme dictator and judge over all German actions.[190] It consummated the trend begun by the Enabling Act of March 24, 1933. Without explicitly stating so, it gave Hitler complete control over the lives of all individuals within the Reich because it left them without protection against the arbitrary decisions of the Fuehrer. This distinction is not an academic one. Those who consider the Hitler regime a reign of terror from beginning to end miss the important point that the terror developed gradually. Just as there is more than a subtle distinction between the Nuremberg Laws of 1935 and the "final solution" of 1941–42, so there is a distinction between the original establishment of authoritarian rule in 1933 and its culmination in the totalitarian regime of 1942–45.

A comparison of Hitler's position in 1942 with that of 1939 shows the manner and direction in which he temporarily solved his problems. In 1939 he was a statesman who, having pursued a dangerous course, found that his policies had failed.

Instead of opening the way to a Middle European Empire, he had saddled himself with a war against Great Britain and France. His first reaction was the qualified despair voiced in his suggestion of suicide on September 1, 1939, and echoed two days later in his "What shall we do now?" when he received the news that Britain was declaring war.[191] During the ensuing months he apparently developed three lines of thought on the solution of his problems. The first and least hopeful was that of concluding peace once the Polish campaign was finished. As we have seen, this was dropped almost without serious pursuit. The second involved the delivery of a serious military blow against France and England with the hope of forcing them into a compromise peace.[192] The third policy, and the one eventually adopted, was that of a full attack against the West with the prospect of bringing these states to their knees. The idea of such a project can be dimly glimpsed in Hitler's suggestion of an armored thrust through the Ardennes,[193] and is more pronounced in his speech to the generals on November 23, 1939, when he said that he would destroy his enemies or—reiterating his suicide threat—he would not survive the German defeat.

The two suicide threats are different in character. The one was made in the wake of a collapse of policy, the other at the birth of a new line of action. Both were appeals for help— appeals which were, for the moment, reassuringly answered. They differ from Hitler's previous threats in that they are covert and in that the problem was divided into two parts, an end and a beginning, as it had not been in the previous threats.

The transformation of Hitler from a statesman into a master of the battlefield and supreme judge was gradual. One could not altogether foresee the rapid defeat of France or the determination of England to fight on. The defeat of the one afforded the possibility of European domination; the resistance of the other made it imperative. Nor was it only the strategic situation which forced Hitler's transformation; he was drawn on by his ideology. Hence a war which had begun with diplomatic blunders eventuated in a conflict motivated by the ideological interests of defeating the cosmic enemies of National Socialism: international Marxism, international capitalism, and, most importantly, the international capitalistic-Communistic Jew.

Yet the seeds of defeat were laid in the very drawing of the lines. Both in his choice of enemies and in his assembly of the means Hitler created a situation which almost certainly assured his defeat. Though he may not have realized it, the forces ranged against him were overwhelming both in numbers and destructive power. Secondly, his policy of destroying whole groups of people, and in particular the Jews of Europe, helped created the will to use this power unreservedly. Lastly, the means which Hitler marshaled to counter this mighty effort fell short of what was necessary, and for long did not approximate what was possible. His leadership of the armed forces from 1942 to 1945 borders on the incredible, for seldom have good troops been so ill-used as those in Stalingrad, the Courland, and Normandy.[194] The internal counterpart of this misuse was the failure to encourage German production to perform to its limits. Despite the work of Speer, German industry never produced what it was capable of producing, and while the tanks, planes, and weapons rose greatly in number during the last year of the war, they appeared too late to affect the outcome. It was, in fact, only with the officers' uprising of 1944 that any attempt was made to establish a total war program.

Wherever one looks in these years, one sees the sure evidences of a policy of ruin. Hitler had created the necessity for success upon a European or world-wide level, and he consistently destroyed the possibility of its realization. His shortsighted insistence upon making bombers out of fighters delayed the appearance of the jet fighters by a good year and a half.[195]

Similarly, his vacillation in the matter of the V-2 rockets made it impossible to use them effectively.[196] It cannot be asserted that if Hitler had had these weapons in time he would have won the war, but he would most certainly have made it much more difficult for the Grand Alliance to win and might have forced a compromise peace.

Towering above these failures (which went relatively unnoticed) were the great public failures of Stalingrad, Tunisia, and the loss of the war at sea. The spring of 1943, which is generally marked as the turning point in the war, saw the destruction of the Axis forces in Africa and the beginning of the long retreat from Russia. By June the U-boats could no longer operate in the North Atlantic. In July the terrible destruction of Hamburg foreshadowed the fate of many another German city. The spring also marked the beginning of another of those periods of hesitancy or even lassitude which had been such a characteristic of Hitler's career since the early days in Munich. "The hardest thing," wrote Joseph Goebbels at this time, "is to get the Fuehrer to make a decision." [197] Goebbels, who had been pressing for a total war program since 1942, assumed that the crisis following the loss of Stalingrad was the ideal time for instituting such measures. But the Propaganda Minister was doomed to disappointment, for Hitler showed something less than avid interest in the idea and finally divided responsibility in such a manner that nothing much was accomplished.[198] According to Guderian, Hitler showed much the same lack of interest in the Kursk offensive of the summer of 1943.[199]

Thus Hitler let the crucial year 1943 slip away without action on his part. Only in the Italian crisis did he show any decisiveness, and this was essentially a reaction to a situation not of his making. The first half of 1944 passed and witnessed the virtual destruction of the Luftwaffe, the successful landings in Normandy, and the collapse of whole German armies at

Minsk. Yet none of this roused Hitler from his lethargy. Instead, his indecisiveness was ended only when a group of officers, in despair over Hitler's conduct of the war, attempted to assassinate him. The failure of the July 20th revolt elicited from Hitler decisions which had hung fire for a year or more. A "total war program" of sorts was initiated, though the ardor of its prosecution was not matched by its effectiveness.[200] Shortly afterwards a recruitment of all remaining manpower was made for the front and grouped into a last-ditch force called the *Volkssturm*.[201] All production which could not furnish results within a year's time was ordered stopped. In short, the assassination attempt produced a fanatical reaction among the National Socialist leaders which caused them to prepare a defense of the Reich with the means available. Against the conspirators no mercy was shown and thousands went to their deaths after incredible trials before the "People's Court."

Thus it seemed that once again Hitler had staked everything on success. Into the defense of the Reich he threw (or wanted to throw) every remaining resource of the German nation. But it is at this point that a serious question arises concerning Hitler's intentions. There can be no doubt that his decisions in the period following the fall of France had contributed greatly to the desperate position in which he now found himself. In this the situation did not differ from previous periods of crisis in Hitler's career. As in 1923, 1932, and 1939, Hitler, and the group under his control, found themselves faced with the necessity of either succeeding or failing completely. The middle ground of compromise had been removed. In the latter two crises, Hitler had been able to save himself and the movement by breaking through into a greater realm of power. But now the greater realm of power was closed to him by reason of the overwhelming strength and determination of the Allies. Thus it seemed, to judge from his actions in the months from

August, 1944, to April, 1945, that the icily logical Hitler hoped for the remaining alternative, total defeat.

This is not altogether clear regarding the Ardennes offensive of December, 1944, which was aimed at severely hampering the Anglo-American effort, possibly with the intention of driving them out of the war. But Hitler's decisions from January onwards are difficult to explain if one assumes that he was still seeking to win the war. This is especially true with regard to his conduct of the war on the Eastern front, where he seems deliberately to have ordered troops away from the crucial Polish front in the days before the beginning of the Russian offensive on January 12, 1945.[202] Nor did his repeated statement that "the Eastern front would have to take care of itself" offer either consolation to the hard-pressed commanders or credibility to any assumption that he was trying to win the war against the Russians.[203]

Instead, the conviction grows, as one reads the evidence, that Hitler was preparing a disaster of vast proportions for Germany. These Germans who were not, as he had said in July, 1944, "worthy of my greatness" were to be faced with conditions which would assure their destruction.[204] The climax of this effort to destroy his own forces came on March 18, 1945, when Hitler ordered the blowing up of all bridges, factories, water stations, and other usable installations to prevent their capture by the enemy. When Albert Speer pointed out to him that this would mean death for millions of Germans, Hitler was unmoved:

> If the war should be lost, the nation too will be lost. That would be the nation's unalterable fate. Then there is no need to consider the basic requirements that people need in order to continue to live a primitive life. On the contrary, it is better ourselves to destroy such things, for the nation will have proved itself the weaker and the future will belong to the stronger Eastern

nation. Those who remain alive after the battles are over are in any case only inferior persons, since the best have fallen.[205]

On March 19, 1945, the orders were issued to carry out this destruction and were followed by an order of March 23rd, over Bormann's signature, that the German population in threatened areas was to be transported to the interior of Germany or would have to march there on foot. If such actions had been carried out, it is probable that a disaster of immense proportions would have resulted. Fortunately these orders were thwarted by Speer and the military authorities and those of the Gauleiters who had sense enough to see that the war was irretrievably lost.[206]

It is ironic that Hitler was able neither to succeed as greatly as the situation demanded nor to fail as catastrophically as he might have wished. Unable to achieve destruction on so grand a scale, he seems to have spent his last month in a setting of ultimate unreality awaiting some sign that the time had come to end his own life. In the bunker, with all of the accoutrements of a modern command post—the clattering typewriters, the unending click of telegraph keys, the coming and going of messengers, the conferences and the shouted orders—nothing was accomplished. Nor could anything be accomplished, for the lines of communications led nowhere. Phantom armies were marched and countermarched; attacks were ordered but never made, for the men and arms were missing; and, finally, a new government was appointed for a state which had ceased to exist. Nowhere is the insanity of the system better illustrated than in these last days within the bunker when all that was unnatural and bizarre in National Socialism was brought out starkly under the white lights of the bunker lamps playing on concrete walls.

The sign for which he had been waiting came on April 22nd, when news was received that Heinrich Himmler had attempted to negotiate an armistice with the Western Allies. Yet, though he resolved that afternoon to kill himself, he waited nine days before carrying out his intention and during that time continued to repeat his threat both verbally and in writing. One might almost feel that Hitler was appealing for help in this, his last and most desperate predicament. Yet no help was forthcoming. Instead, those about him, led by Joseph Goebbels, encouraged him to go through with his plans. So it was that on April 30th, at about three-thirty in the afternoon, Adolf Hitler finally took his life as he had so often threatened to do.

In preparation for his suicide Hitler dictated on the 29th of April his will and his political testament. What is of interest is the fact that in form they are much like the genuine suicide notes studied by Shneidman and Farberow.[207] The comparison between genuine suicide notes and simulated ones indicates that the true notes differ considerably from ones written by non-suicidal persons trying to imagine the situation.

> The total number of thought units was significantly higher in the 33 real notes than in the fictitious notes, indicating that the genuine-note writers apparently feel the need to say more in this last communication.
>
> With respect to "discomfort" statements, or the statements of guilt, blame, tension, aggression, and the like, we found some difference between the prorated number of discomfort units expressed by the genuine-suicide-note writers and those expressed by the simulated-note writers. We noted that the discomfort statements in the simulated suicide notes were only mildly negative but that similar statements in the genuine notes were characterized by deeper and more intense feelings of hatred, vengeance, demand, and self-blame. . . .
>
> As for the number of "relief" statements, or statements which were pleasant, warm, loving, and which denoted relief from tension, we found no quantitative difference between the genuine notes and the simulated notes.
>
> It was in regard to the "neutral" statements, the statements free of expressions either of tension or of release from tension, that

the notes revealed the greatest significant difference. The genuine suicide notes contained much the higher percentage of neutral thought units. On inspection, we found them to be mostly statements giving instructions and admonitions and sometimes listing things to do. . . .

The genuine note-writer has, as one part of his thinking, apparently accepted and incorporated the idea that within a short time he will not be alive. In this connection he instructs and admonishes in relation to the many details of continued living which he will not be able to pursue himself. . . . It is as though he were exercising power and command in these directions, as if somehow he were making sure his plans would be carried out. It is a kind of unrealistic feeling of omnipotence and omnipresence on the part of the suicidal individual which may reflect in part some of the confused, illogical, and paradoxical motivations in the entire act.[208]

This description of the genuine suicide note fits quite accurately the character of both Hitler's last will and his last political testament. The testament begins with a justification of his own actions and moves quickly to a last attack upon the Jews, whom he again accuses of having started the war. On the other hand, he dies "with a happy heart aware of the immeasurable deeds and achievements of our soldiers at the front," but this thankfulness does not extend to the general staff, who, in an appendix to the political testament, are accused of disloyalty and incompetence.[209] In the testament, Hitler also gives a detailed list of the men who are to head the National Socialist government, and these men are charged with maintaining a "merciless opposition to the universal poisoner of all peoples, international Jewry."

Hitler's will is a calmer document which expresses a sense of relief at finally ending the long struggle and deals with the disposition of his personal property. Both the will and the testament are quite detailed and indicate Hitler's intention to control affairs even after his death. They are filled both with self-pity and with hatred for others, attitudes characteristically Hitlerian but just as characteristically suicidal.

Like many another suicide, Hitler seems to have created the situations which led to his death. It is probably too much to say that this suicidal tendency was the one key factor in Hitler's career—there have been, after all, many suicides but only one Hitler, and a leaning towards self-destruction does not account for the undoubted creative talents which enabled this man to build the Third Reich and very nearly to conquer Europe. Yet many of Hitler's actions remain inexplicable unless we assume that he did not (either consciously or unconsciously) always intend to succeed. It is often pointed out that Hitler was a gambler; if such was the case, he was a very bad gambler since he consistently played the long shot. We suggest rather that Hitler was not so much a gambler as a man bent on doing injury to himself, for unknown reasons, either by subjecting himself to unnecessary ordeals or through actual self-destruction.

There are several alternative interpretations which can be given to Hitler's suicide. The simplest and most popular is to assume that it was a "rational" suicide, that is, he chose death because continued living was, both subjectively and objectively speaking, too horrible to bear.[210] While Hitler's situation on April 30, 1945, would seem to argue for this view his previous record would seem to indicate that this is too simple an answer to be satisfactory.

A more interesting possibility in the light of his previous suicide threats is that this began as the last of the "cries for help"; that, in fact, Hitler's threat to commit suicide on the 22nd of April was intended chiefly to obtain the kind of results that these threats had obtained in the past—purposeful and successful action. Instead, something happened which had never happened before—his subordinates agreed with the Fuehrer that suicide was the only solution. Hitler repeated his threat nine times but failed to receive a satisfactory response, so that at last, crushed by an insensitive world, he was forced to go through with an act he had never really intended to carry out.[211]

A variation of this "attempted suicide" theme would be the supposition that the war represented the last of a series of ordeals to which he had subjected himself, allowing Fate or Providence to pass upon his right to live. Having failed this last ordeal he recognized the necessity of ending his life and did so with complete equanimity.[212]

All of these interpretations assume that Hitler recognized his defeat. But it is just possible that this last gesture represented to him an ultimate weapon in the struggle for victory. Charles Wahl in his article, "Suicide as a Magical Act," suggests that often in attempting to face insurmountable problems persons will indulge in retrospective scrutiny of their own pasts to discover "aiding memories of those times and places" in which they were able to cope with such situations. This phenomenon of regression, Wahl continues, can lead one back, when under terrible pressure, to the stage of infantile omnipotence. At this stage of development the child cannot differentiate himself from the persons or objects of his world. Later this feeling persists in the sensation of cosmic identification, as though all things were part of one's self.

> The suicide achieves, as does the infant, a kind of cosmic identification. . . . Therefore to kill oneself is to kill everything that there is. . . . Not only . . . is the suicide committing an aggressive act against . . . himself and against the introjected parents whom he wished to murder, but also against that extension of the parents—society, which the aggrieved individual has found to be nonnurturant and nonsuccoring. . . . In an immense moment of fantastic grandiosity he lays them, and all the world, to ruin.[213]

We shall never know exactly why Hitler killed himself, but the prospect of finally achieving absolute domination over his enemies by a leap into this new realm of power may well have appealed to him. Perhaps then in one blinding moment he did destroy the world; hours later he was simply a charred corpse in the chancellery courtyard of a ruined city. If for a moment he was the supremely powerful being of his universe, a short while later he was the complete nonentity, recognizable only from his dental records.

"He would have wanted it that way."

NOTES

1. The basic account of Hitler's death is still H. R. Trevor-Roper's *The Last Days of Hitler* 3rd ed. (London: Macmillan, 1958), pp. 119–251. In his Introduction to the third edition of his book (originally published in 1947), Trevor-Roper discusses the information which has since come to light and especially the problem of what the Russians knew about the death of Hitler. Cornelius Ryan's conversations with the Russians in the spring of 1964 confirmed many of Trevor-Roper's deductions.

2. See Doc. 3569–PS (Hitler's will, April 29, 1945), *Nazi Conspiracy and Aggression* (Washington: U. S. Govt. Printing Office, 1946), VI, 259; see also Karl Koller, *Der Letzte Monat* (Mannheim: N. Wohlgemuth Verlag, 1949), p. 31; quoted in Alan Bullock, *Hitler: A Study in Tyranny* (New York: Harper and Bros., 1952), p. 716, and Trevor-Roper, *op. cit.*, p. 121.

3. On the relationship between urbanization and suicide see E. R. Ellis and G. N. Allen, *Traitor Within* (Garden City, N. Y.: Doubleday and Co., 1961), p. 28; Hans Fuchs, *Selbstmordversuche im Grossstadtraum* (Vienna: Oesterreichisches Statistisches Zentralamt, 1959), pp. 7 ff.; Hans Fuchs, *Selbstmordhandlungen* (Vienna: Oesterreichisches Statistisches Zentralamt, 1961), pp. 9 ff., 21 ff., and 50 ff. (hereafter SMH); on age groups see Ellis and Allen, *op. cit.*, pp. 17–19.

4. Ellis and Allen, *op. cit.*, p. 19, gives the male frequency as three to four times that of female suicide. Fuchs, *SMH*, shows a male frequency twice that of female. C. S. Kruijt, *Zelfmoord* (Assen: Van Gorcum and Co., 1960), p. 5, and Georg Siegmund, *Sein oder Nichtsein* (Trier: Paulinus Verlag, 1961), p. 108, both note the greater frequency of male suicide though pointing out that female suicide is on the increase. Werner Ringel, *Der Selbstmord* (Vienna: Verlag fuer medizinische Wissenschaften, 1953), p. 91, denies that suicide is in actuality a sex-linked characteristic.

5. Kruijt, *op. cit.*, pp. 366–67, presents graphs showing that the years from 45 to 55 are particularly dangerous. F. Dubitscher, *Der Suicid* (Stuttgart: Georg Thieme, 1957), pp. 33–34, shows that the peak years for suicide in Germany were those between 45 and 60. Siegmund, *op. cit.*, p. 80, notes an increase after 45, and Fuchs, *SMH*, p. 35, shows that in Vienna in recent years the 51-60 age group is the most likely to commit suicide.

6. The figures are the World Health Organization statistics cited in Siegmund, *op. cit.*, p. 181. Ellis and Allen, *op. cit.*, p. 41, state that suicide is the seventh-ranked cause of death in Germany.

7. Siegmund, *op. cit.*, pp. 97, 104 (table), 112; Fuchs, *SMH*, p. 80. See also Franco Ferracuti, "Suicide in a Catholic Country," *Clues to Suicide*, eds. E. S. Shneidman and N. L. Farberow (New York: McGraw-Hill, 1957), pp. 70–77; Joseph Hirsh, "Demography of Suicide," *Mental Hygiene*, Oct. 1959, p. 523.

8. Ellis and Allen, *op. cit.*, p. 24.

9. Kruijt, *op. cit.*, p. 90; Siegmund, *op. cit.*, pp. 89–90; E. Stengel and Nancy G. Cook, *Attempted Suicide* (London: Chapman and Hall, 1958), pp. 108–9, show an underrepresentation of the more well-to-do classes in their samples but because of the method of selection attach no significance to this fact. Ringel, *op. cit.*, p. 60, reports a similar situation. Other studies, such as E. Stengel and Nancy G. Cook, "Contrasting Suicide Rates in Industrial Communities," *Journal of Mental Science*, Nov. 1961, pp. 1011–19, and An-

drew F. Henry and James F. Short, *Suicide and Homicide* (Glencoe, Ill.: The Free Press, 1954), show that the relationship between class status and suicide is by no means clear.

10. Ellis and Allen, *op. cit.*, p. 21 (no figures). Dubitscher, *op. cit.*, p. 68, gives a low rate (0.7).

11. *Ibid.*, pp. 37, 38.

12. Ellis and Allen, *op. cit.*, pp. 5, 6, lists eighteen prominent political figures who have committed suicide. Interestingly enough, Hitler's name is not included. Dubitscher, *op. cit.*, p. 68, gives a high incidence for public officials (19.2) but a very low one for party politicians (0.2).

13. The suicide rate for Berlin at the present time is: West Berlin, 33.9; Soviet sector, 35.0. See Siegmund *op. cit.*, p. 181. For Vienna the present rate is 30.7 (1956–59). See Fuchs, *SMH*, p. 15. Cities have long had high rates. Kruijt, *op. cit.*, p. 27, connects suicide with urbanization; Siegmund, *op. cit.*, p. 84, states that urban rates are three times as high as rural rates. Vienna's rate in 1959 was 32.4 as against 22.3 for the rest of Austria. See Fuchs, *SMH*, p. 18.

14. Ellis and Allen, *op. cit.*, p. 21; Kruijt, *op. cit.*, p. 423; Fuchs, *SMH*, p. 40; Dubitscher, *op. cit.*, pp. 66–67 (table). Ringel's study, *op. cit.*, also shows that among married persons attempting suicide, those having marital difficulties are high: pp. 37–38, 40–54; Hirsh, *op. cit.*, p. 521, suspects that the rates for married individuals are higher than reported. See Siegmund, *op. cit.*, p. 187, for a discussion of *Shinju*.

15. Ellis and Allen, *op. cit.*, pp. 155, 160; Fuchs, *SMH*, p. 48 (note the marked percentage of orphans among Vienna suicides); Ringel, *op. cit.*, pp. 16–18, considers this to be of the greatest importance. Stengel and Cook, *Attempted Suicide*, pp. 16–17. Gregory Zilboorg, "Considerations on Suicide with Particular Reference to that of the Young," *The American Journal of Orthopsychiatry*, Jan., 1937, p. 22, states flatly, "Only those individuals who appear to have

identified themselves with a *dead* person and in whom the process of identification took place during childhood or adolescence, at a time when the incorporated person was already dead, are most probably the truly suicidal individuals." 95% of the suicidal patients in one group had lost either parents, siblings, or mates. See Leonard M. Moss and Donald M. Hamilton, "The Psychotherapy of the Suicidal Patient," *American Journal of Psychiatry*, April, 1956, p. 815.

16. Ellis and Allen, *op. cit.*, p. 20; Siegmund, *op. cit.*, p. 121; Fuchs, *SMH*, p. 103; Henry and Short, *op. cit.*, *passim*.

17. See Trevor-Roper, *op. cit.*, pp. 186–87.

18. Ellis and Allen, *op. cit.*, p. 156; Siegmund, *op. cit.*, p. 121; Fuchs, *SMH*, p. 103; Zilboorg, *op. cit.*, p. 16 ff.; Edwin S. Shneidman and Norman L. Farberow, "The Logic of Suicide," in *Clues to Suicide*, pp. 31–49; Ringel, *op. cit.*, p. 141.

19. American men: Ellis and Allen, *op. cit.*, p. 126; German soldiers: Dubitscher, *op. cit.*, p. 36; Austria: Fuchs, *SMH*, p. 84.

20. Fuchs, *SMH*, pp. 137–38 (table).

21. Ellis and Allen, *op. cit.*, p. 83.

22. *Ibid.*

23. *Ibid.*, pp. 76–79.

24. The dates of these previous threats are 1905; Nov. 8–9, 1923; Dec. 8, 1932; Sept. 1, 1939; and Nov. 23, 1939. Each will be discussed in detail below. On the seriousness of suicide threats see Shneidman and Farberow, "Clues to Suicide," in *Clues to Suicide*, p. 9; Ringel, *op. cit.*, p. 127; Joseph Hirsh, "Suicide: Part 4: Predictability and Prevention," *Mental Hygiene*, July, 1962, p. 384; Lewis J. Siegal and Jacob H. Friedman, "The Threat of Suicide," *Diseases of the Nervous System*, Feb., 1955, pp. 37–46.; E. Stengel, "Recent Research into Suicide and Attempted Suicide," *American Journal of Psychiatry*, Feb., 1962, pp. 725–26.

25. Stengel and Cook, *Attempted Suicide*, p. 17. In fact, it is problematical whether any method of approach tried thus far "works." See Ellis and Allen, *op. cit.*, Chapter II and Appendix on National Save A Life League in New York and the *Friends* program in Miami. See also Ringel, *op. cit.*, pp. 199–230 for a discussion of similar programs in Austria. A. E. Bennett, "Suggestions for Suicide Preventions," Shneidman and Farberow, *Clues to Suicide*, pp. 187–93, also includes a section on prevention.

26. The basic ideas for the psychoanalytic description of suicide were advanced by Freud in his paper "Mourning and Melancholia" (1917). See Sigmund Freud, *Collected Papers* (London: Hogarth Press, 1949), IV, 152–70. Perhaps the fullest discussion is still Karl Menninger, *Man Against Himself* (New York: Harcourt, Brace and Co., 1938), 1961 (Harvest Books). Menninger's book forms the basis for this section. Other, somewhat similar, formulations can be found in Ringel, *op. cit.*; Siegal and Friedman, *op. cit.*, pp. 38–39; Herbert Hendin, "Suicide," *Psychiatric Quarterly*, April 1956, pp. 267–82.; Joseph Hirsh, "Dynamics of Suicide," *Mental Hygiene*, April, 1960, pp. 274–80; and Moss and Hamilton, *op. cit.*, p. 814. For the components of the self-destructive impulse see Menninger, pp. 23–17; see also Zilboorg, *op. cit.*, p. 28.

27. Menninger, *op. cit.*, pp. 30 ff.; Moss and Hamilton, *op. cit.*, p. 816; Siegal and Friedman, *op. cit.*, p. 38; Ringel, *op. cit.*, 127 ff.

28. Menninger, *op. cit.*, pp. 59–63; Hendin, *op. cit.*, p. 274.

29. Menninger, *op. cit.*, p. 70; Zilboorg, *op. cit.*, pp. 16–19, prefers to avoid using the concept of the "death instinct" while not entirely denying its validity; Hendin, *op. cit.*, 270, cites Zilboorg's reservations with approval; Ringel, *op. cit.*, p. 133, states that while the death instinct is by no means normal it is present in cases of suicide and attempted suicide. More wholehearted support for the concept is offered by Benson D. Carmichael, "The Death Wish in Daily Life," *Psychiatric Review*, Jan., 1943, pp. 59–66; Kate Friedlander, "On the 'Longing to Die,'" *International Journal of Psycho-*

analysis, Oct., 1940. pp. 416–26; and A. A. Brill, "The Concept of Psychic Suicide," *International Journal of Psychoanalysis*, July-Oct., 1939, pp. 246–51.

30. Menninger, *op. cit.*, pp. 77–198; Zilboorg, *op. cit.*, p. 20; Ringel, *op. cit.*, pp. 104–53; Melvin L. Selzer and Charles E. Payne, "Automobile Accidents, Suicide, and Unconscious Motivation," *American Journal of Psychiatry*, Sept., 1962, pp. 237–40.

31. Dubitscher, *op. cit.*, pp. 202–4; Ringel, *op. cit.*, pp. 131 ff., 139; Hendin, *op. cit.*, pp. 274–78; Menninger, *op. cit.*, pp. 109–18.

32. Menninger, *op. cit.*, pp. 118 ff.; Siegal and Friedman, *op. cit.*, p. 38; Hendin, *op. cit.*, p. 274.

33. Stengel and Cook, *Attempted Suicide*, p. 22.

34. Franz Jetzinger, *Hitler's Youth*, trans. Lawrence Wilson (London: Hutchinson, 1958). (Hereafter: Jetzinger)

35. Konrad Heiden, *Der Fuehrer*, trans. Ralph Mannheim (Boston: Houghton Mifflin Company, 1944). (Hereafter: Heiden)

36. August Kubizek, *Adolf Hitler: Mein Jugendfreund* (Goettingen: Leopold Stocker Verlag, 1953). (Hereafter: Kubizek)

37. Josef Greiner, *Das Ende des Hitler Mythos*. (Vienna: Almathea Verlag, 1947).

38. Jetzinger, p. 136.

39. *Ibid.*, p. 67.

40. See *ibid.*, p. 57; Heiden, p. 44; Walter Goerlitz and Herbert A. Quint, *Adolf Hitler: eine Biographie* (Stuttgart: Steingruben Verlag, 1952), p. 22. (Hereafter: Goerlitz and Quint)

41. Jetzinger, p. 58; Heiden, p. 44, assumes that Hitler took all of

his schooling here at Lambach at the monastery; Goerlitz and Quint, p. 23, reports Hitler's deportment as wild.

42. Jetzinger, pp. 59–60; Heiden p. 44; Goerlitz and Quint, pp. 24, 30; Adolf Hitler, *Mein Kampf* (New York: Reynal and Hitchcock, 1940), Chapter 1 (Hereafter: *Mein Kampf*); Adolf Hitler, *Hitler's Secret Conversations* (New York: Farrar, Straus and Young, 1953), pp. 155–57, 289, 566–67. (Hereafter: *Secret Conversations.*)

43. Jetzinger, p. 64.

44. *Ibid.*, p. 67.

45. *Ibid.*, p. 67.

46. *Mein Kampf*, p. 24; Jetzinger, p. 89–90.

47. Jetzinger, p. 66.

48. *Mein Kampf*, pp. 14, 27–28.

49. This is brought out by Kubizek, pp. 45, 48, 72 ff.

50. On father's death: Jetzinger, pp. 52–53; Edmund's death: *ibid.*, p. 43; (Kubizek, p. 53, gives an incorrect date of June 29, 1900, for Edmund's death); Angela Hitler's marriage to Raubal: Jetzinger, p. 42; Hitler's hatred for Leo Raubal: Kubizek, p. 47; of Angela: attitude toward Jetzinger, p. 97.

51. Jetzinger, p. 69.

52. *Ibid.*, pp. 89–90; Kubizek reports a long illness in 1905, pp. 73–74.

53. Kubizek, p. 45.

54. *Ibid.*, pp. 24, 34.

55. Jetzinger, p. 75 (red Indians); Jetzinger pp. 72, 88–89 (on school at Steyr); Kubizek, p. 20 (meeting in 1904).

56. Kubizek, pp. 181–82.

57. Jetzinger, pp. 109–14, shows that from the time of his mother's death until his twenty-third year Hitler received an orphan's pension of 25 kronen a month. In addition his patrimony yielded 58 kronen per month. Jetzinger demonstrated that it was possible to live on this sum, thus undercutting Hitler's story of complete indigence.

58. Kubizek, Chapter "Zeichen, Malen, Bauen" pp. 116–32.

59. *Ibid.*, pp. 23–24.

60. *Ibid.*, pp. 76–89; Jetzinger, pp. 105–8.

61. Kubizek, pp. 83 ff.

62. *Ibid.*, pp. 72 ff.

63. *Ibid.*, pp. 161–73; Jetzinger, pp. 103–5.

64. Heiden, pp. 52–53, gives a copy of the notices of rejection for both 1907 and 1908.

65. Kubizek, pp. 199–200.

66. *Mein Kampf*, p. 27.

67. Kubizek, pp. 207–14.

68. *Mein Kampf*, p. 27.

69. He still had his orphan's pension. Jetzinger, p. 114.

70. Kubizek, pp. 302–16.

71. Here self-interest might have spurred Raubal on. If Hitler took work, then his half of the orphan's pension would revert to his sister Paula who was at this time living with the Raubals. Jetzinger, pp. 112–13, 137–40.

72. *Ibid.*, p. 134.

73. William A. Jenks, *Vienna and the Young Hitler* (New York: Columbia University Press, 1960); Jetzinger, pp. 130–37.

74. Jetzinger, p. 152.

75. *Ibid.*, p. 153.

76. *Mein Kampf*, p. 163.

77. Jetzinger, p. 145.

78. The full account of this episode is contained in Jetzinger, pp. 144–57. The German police were called in at the instance of the Austrian Consul.

79. For the record of this regiment in World War I see Fridolin Solleder (ed.) *Vier Jahre Westfront:* Geschichte des Regiments List R.I.R. 16 (Munich: Verlag Max Schick, 1932); also Adolf Meyer, *Mit Adolf Hitler in Bayrischen Reserve-Infanterie Regiment 16 List* (Neustadt-Aisch/Mfr.: Georg Aupperle, 1934).

80. *Mein Kampf*, p. 215.

81. *Ibid.*, p. 269.

82. *Ibid.*, pp. 299–300.

83. The account of the lottery ticket incident is given in Kubizek, pp. 127 ff.

84. Bullock, *op. cit.*, pp. 82–85; Heiden, p. 164; S. William Halperin, *Germany Tried Democracy* (New York: Crowell Co., 1946), p. 254; Goerlitz and Quint, p. 178; Adolf Hitler, *My New Order*, ed. Raoul de Roussy de Sales (New York: Reynal and Hitchcock, 1941), pp. 47–70, has excerpts from Hitler's speeches from this period.

85. Goerlitz and Quint, pp. 181–82; Ernst Roehm, *Die Geschichte eines Hochverraeters*, 2nd ed. (Munich: Franz Eher nachf., 1930), p. 180; Bullock, *op. cit.*, pp. 86–88.

86. Heiden, pp. 173–74.

87. Harold J. Gordon, *The Reichswehr and the German Republic, 1919–1926* (Princeton: Princeton University Press, 1957), pp. 275–83.

88. These reports are contained in Ernst Deuerlein, *Der Hitler Putsch: Bayrische Dokumente zum 8/9 November, 1923* (Stuttgart Deutsche Verlags Anstalt, 1962), Doc. Nos. 4, 18, 29, 50, 51.

89. *Ibid.*, Doc. Nos. 19, 77, 83.

90. Roehm, *op. cit.*, p. 194.

91. Bullock, *op. cit.*, p. 95.

92. *Der Hitler Prozess vor dem Volksgericht in Muenchen.* 2 pts. (Munich: Knorr and Hirth, 1924), Part I, p. 51.

93. Roehm, *op. cit.*, p. 209.

94. Goerlitz and Quint, *op. cit.*, pp. 196, 203. It had been assumed by most persons up to this moment that Hitler would become the chief propagandist for a government under the leadership of the "national dictator" Ludendorff.

95. *Hitler Prozess*, Part I, p. 4.; "Generalstaatskommissar Kahr an Ministerpraesident Knilling. Muenchen 12. 12. 1923." Doc. No. 182. Deuerlein, *op. cit.*, p. 496.; Bullock, *op. cit.*, p. 97; Heiden, p. 188.

96. Otto Strasser, *Hitler und Ich* (Constance: Johannes Asmus Verlag, 1948), pp. 61–64. It might be noted that many a would-be suicide has relented when threatened with another form of death.

97. Bullock, *op. cit.*, p. 102.

98. See General Ludendorff, *Auf dem Weg zur Feldherrnhalle* (Munich: Ludendorffs Verlag, 1938), pp. 65–68.; Bullock., pp. 99–100; Heiden, p. 195.

99. Doc. No. 100, Deuerlein, *op. cit.*, p. 336.

100. Heiden, pp. 184–85.

101. To be specific, Hitler made no moves to cement relations with the other parties during these two years and seemed content to wait for the chancellorship to be dropped into his lap, a prospect which at the time did not seem too likely.

102. Goebbels recounts the agony of waiting in his *Vom Kaiserhof zur Reichskanzlei* (Munich: Franz Eher nachf., 1934/1941), pp. 16–50.

103. See Doc. No. 95, "Sir H. Rumbold to Sir J. Simon. Berlin. Mar. 1, 1932" in *Documents on British Foreign Policy 1919–1939*. eds. E. L. Woodward and Rohan Butler. 2nd series (London: His Majesty's Stationery Office, 1948), III, 101–2. (Hereafter: *DBFP* 2 III).

104. Doc. No. 97, "Sir H. Rumbold to Sir J. Simon," Berlin, Mar. 24, 1932, *DBFP* 2 III, pp. 108–9.

105. Doc. No. 106, "Sir H. Rumbold to Sir J. Simon," Berlin, April 27, 1932, *DBFP* 2 III, p. 126.

106. Doc. No. 9, "Sir H. Rumbold to Sir J. Simon," Berlin, August 4, 1932, *DBFP* 2 IV, pp. 20–23.

107. See von Papen's account in Franz von Papen, *Memoirs*. trans. Brian Connell (London: Andre Deutsch, 1952), pp. 195–98. See also the accounts in Bullock, *op. cit.*, pp. 197–201; Heiden, pp. 480–84; and Goerlitz and Quint, pp. 347–48.

108. Kurt Luedecke, *I Knew Hitler* (London: Jarrolds, 1938), pp. 348, 351, 355; Goebbels, *Vom Kaiserhof . . .*, p. 148.

109. Goebbels, *Vom Kaiserhof . . .*, p. 158.

110. *Ibid.*, pp. 142–43.

111. Bullock, *op. cit.*, p. 204.

112. Von Papen, *op. cit.*, pp. 199, 207–9.

113. Heiden, pp. 490–91, 493.

114. Bullock, *op. cit.*, p. 205.

115. Von Papen, *op. cit.*, pp. 207–9.

116. Heiden, p. 493.

117. Goebbels, *vom Kaiserhof* . . . , p. 167.

118. Doc. No. 24, *DBFP* 2 IV, pp. 49–52.

119. Doc. No. 26, *ibid.*, p. 54.

120. Doc. No. 30, *ibid.*, pp. 65–66.

121. Doc. No. 31, *ibid.*, pp. 66–69.

122. *Muenchener Neueste Nachrichten* (No. 303, Nov. 7, 1932, p. 1, col. 1.

123. Doc. No. 37, *DBFP* 2 IV, p. 79.

124. Karl Dietrich Bracher, *Die Aufloesung der Weimarer Republik* (Stuttgart: Ring Verlag, 1955), p. 657.

125. Von Papen, *op. cit.*, pp. 211–14.

126. *Ibid.*, p. 215; Bullock, *op. cit.*, pp. 211–12; Heiden, p. 497; Goerlitz and Quint, pp. 353–54.

127. Heiden, pp. 500, 507–8, 516.

128. Goebbels, *Vom Kaiserhof* . . . , pp. 217–18.

129. *Ibid.*, p. 220.

130. Bullock, *op. cit.*, p. 217.

131. P. Bernhard Strasser, *Gregor und Otto Strasser* (Munich: Bund fuer Deutschlands Erneuerung, 1954 [?]), p. 11.

132. A. J. P. Taylor, *The Origins of the Second World War* (New York: Atheneum, 1962). The most important attack upon this book thus far is perhaps that of H. R. Trevor-Roper, "A. J. P. Taylor, Hitler, and the War," *Encounter*, July, 1961, pp. 88–96.

133. Hossbach Conference Doc. 386-PS, International Military Tribunal, *The Trial of the Major War Criminals before the International Military Tribunal*. Proceedings and Documents (Nuremberg: 1947) (Hereafter: IMT) XXV, 402–13. Most of the situation envisioned by Hitler did not, in fact, arise. Nor does it seem likely that, in a document which he said could be considered as his "last will and testament" in the event of his death, he would have neglected to mention the "Jewish question."

134. A. J. P. Taylor, *op. cit.*, pp. 210, 216.

135. Doc. C-120, *IMT*, XXXIV, 380–422.

136. Doc. 798-PS, *IMT*, XXVI, 338–44; Doc. 079-L, *IMT*, XXXVII, 546–56.

137. Gisevius testimony, *IMT*, XII, 224–25.

138. Generaloberst Halder, *Kriegstagebuch* (Stuttgart: W. Kohlhammer, Verlag, 1962), I, 30–49, (entries 21–26, August, 1939.)

139. A. J. P. Taylor, *op. cit.*, pp. 200–3.

140. The Assistant Commissar for Foreign Affairs told French Ambassador Coulondre at the time of the Munich agreement that ". . . For us I see no other way out than a fourth partition of Poland." Coulondre, *De Staline a Hitler* [?], p. 16. Quoted in A. J. P. Taylor, *op. cit.*, p. 192. Certainly the Poles seemed to feel that their only salvation from another partition was to maintain a policy favoring neither of Poland's great neighbors, and in the end even this proved fatal.

141. See Doc. C-120, *IMT*, XXXIV, 380–422; Doc. 798-ps, *IMT*, XXVI, 341; Doc. 1014-ps *IMT*, XXVI, 523–24.

142. A. J. P. Taylor, *op. cit.*, pp. 187–214, suggests that after the Munich settlement Czechoslovakia was falling apart and Hitler's seizure of Prague was essentially a defensive move to fill a political vacuum. For a more conventional interpretation of the events of March 15, 1939, see L. B. Namier, *Diplomatic Prelude, 1938–1939* (London: Macmillan, 1948).

143. Neither the British nor the French were psychologically or militarily prepared to take effective action in the case of a German invasion of Poland. For the preparation of the French see Telford Taylor, *The March of Conquest* (New York: Simon and Schuster, 1958). See also General Gamelin, *Servir*. 3 vols. (Paris: Plon, 1946). For the status of British offensive capabilities in September, 1939, see Sir Charles Webster and Noble Frankland, *The Strategic Air Offensive Against Germany, 1939–1945* (London: Her Majesty's Stationery Office 1961), I. That the Germans had in mind cooperation with the Poles against the Russians is indicated to some small degree by Ribbentrop's memorandum of a conversation with Beck. Doc. 126, Germany, Auswaertiges Amt, *Documents on German Foreign Policy*. Series D (Washington: Dept. of State, 1953). V, 167–68.

144. Telford Taylor, *op. cit.*, pp. 64–75. For a later view of the occupation of Poland see Alexander Hohenstein, *Warthelaendisches Tagebuch, 1941/42* (Munich: Deutscher Taschenbuch Verlag), 1963.

145. The laws governing the areas annexed to the Reich and the law establishing the General Gouvernment of Poland are contained in Heinrich Schoenfelder, *Deutsche Reichsgesetze* 12 ed. (Munich: C. H. Beck'sche Verlagsbuchhandlung, 1944 [?]). See 19d, "Gesetz ueber die Wiedervereinigung der Freien Stadt Danzig mit dem Deutschen Reich"; 19e, "Erlass des Fuehrers und Reichskanzlers ueber Gliederung und Verwaltung der Ostgebiete"; and 19f, "Erlass des Fuehrers und Reichskanzlers ueber die Verwaltung des besetzten polnischen Gebiete."

146. For the text of this speech see *Voelkischer Beobachter* (South German ed.), Oct. 7/8, 1939, pp. 2–3.

147. *Mein Kampf*, p. 987; Adolf Hitler, *Hitler's Secret Book* (New York: Grove Press, 1961), pp. 128–32.

148. See Record of the Hossbach Conference, Nov. 5, 1937, Doc. 386-ps, *IMT*, XXV, 408; Hitler's speech of May 23, 1939, Doc. 079-L, *IMT*, XXXVII, 546–56; Hitler's speech of Aug. 22, 1939, Doc. 798-ps, *IMT*, XXVI, 339.

149. This was particularly true of the period of May, 1938, when Hitler first made the decision to dismember Czechoslovakia. See Waldemar Erfurth, *Die Geschichte des deutschen Generalstabes von 1918 bis 1945* (Berlin: Musterschmidt Verlag, 1960), I, 211, 212; Walter Goerlitz, *History of the German General Staff* (New York: Praeger, 1953), p. 327; J. W. Wheeler-Bennett, *The Nemesis of Power* (London: Macmillan, 1954), pp. 398–404; B. H. Liddell Hart, *The German Generals Talk* (New York: Berkley Editions, 1958), p. 30.

150. See United States Strategic Bombing Survey, Munitions Division, *Tank Industry Report* (Washington: U. S. Govt. Printing Office, 1947). See also Telford Taylor, *op. cit.*, p. 17.

151. Jodl Testimony, *IMT*, XV, 350. See also General von Leeb's estimate of defensive capabilities in Hans-Adolf Jacobsen, *Dokumente zur Vorgeschichte des Westfeldzuges. 1939–1940* (Frankfurt: Musterschmidt Verlag, 1956), pp. 80–85. See further Hans-Adolf Jacobsen, *Fall Gelb* (Wiesbaden: Franz Steiner Verlag, 1957), pp. 1–11.

152. See General Bodenschatz' estimate of air capabilities in 1939. *IMT*, IX, 27.

153. Telford Taylor, *op. cit.*, p. 10.

154. See General Thomas, "Grundlagen fuer eine Geschichte der deutschen Wehr- und Ruestungswirtschaft," Doc. 2353-ps, *IMT*, XXX, 259–80.

155. On September 1, 1939, Germany had on hand 3.1 month's war supply of aviation gasoline, 1.9 month's supply of motor gasoline, and 2.4 month's supply of rubber. See United States Strategic Bombing Survey, Oil Division, *Oil Division Final Report* (Washington: U. S. Govt. Printing Office 1947), p. 1.

156. Dr. Rolf Wagenfuehr, *The Rise and Fall of German War Economy. 1939–1945* (unpublished study).

157. General Thomas, *op. cit.*, p. 262.

158. Doc. 798-PS, *IMT*, XXVI, 338–44; 079-L, *IMT*, XXXVII, 546–56.

159. Jacobsen, *Dokumente . . .* , "Aufmarschweisung 'Fall West' vom 18.1.39. (OKH)," pp. 31–32.

160. *Ibid.*, "OKW Weisung Nr. 1 fuer die Kriegsfuehrung vom 31.8.39," p. 1; "Weisung Nr. 2 fuer die Kriegsfuehrung vom 3.9.39," p. 2.

161. *Ibid.*, "Weisung fuer die Umstellung des Heeres auf den Abwehrkrieg in Westen vom 17.9.39," pp. 35 ff.

162. Doc. 052-L, *IMT*, XXXVII, 466–86; See also Jacobsen, *Fall Gelb*, pp. 12 ff.

163. Jacobsen, *Fall Gelb*. pp. 25 ff.; Telford Taylor, *op. cit.*, pp. 155–56; for comparison with "Case Yellow" see "Schlieffens Grosse Denkschrift vom Dezember 1905" in Gerhard Ritter, *Der Schlieffenplan* (Munich: Verlag R. Oldenbourg, 1956), pp. 140–60.

164. Doc. 052-L, *IMT*, XXXVII, 480.

165. *Ibid.*, pp. 466–86.

166. This point is certainly debatable, for in his speech of May 23, 1939, Hitler speaks of the necessity of striking with all weapons

against the real foe, England, and of bringing her to her knees (Doc. 079-L, *IMT*, XXXVII, 552–54). Yet his practical suggestions seem much more limited since he speaks of occupying Holland and Belgium in order to protect the Ruhr (*ibid.*, p. 550), and speaks of a maturing of armament plans only in 1943–44 (*ibid.*, pp. 555–56). Perhaps the whole point of his speculation about a war to the finish with England is to underline the necessity of isolating Poland (*ibid.*, p. 549). On August 22, 1939, Hitler seemed almost certain that the Western powers would not intervene (Doc. 798-PS, *IMT*, XXVI, 341) and that the war would not be a long one (*ibid.*, p. 343). In May he had suggested that the war might be very long indeed (079-L, p. 551). Finally, in his memorandum of the 9th of October, 1939, he speaks of the necessity of destroying the armies of England and France (Doc. 052-L, *IMT*, XXXVII, 468), but his practical suggestions are limited again to a seizure of Holland and Belgium for the protection of the Ruhr and for the prosecution of the air war against England (*ibid.*, pp. 473, 474–76; 483). In this paper Hitler appears to be much concerned about the dangers to Germany of a long war, as he was not in the spring (*ibid.*, p. 472; 079-L, p. 551). On inspection it would seem that there is a contradiction between Hitler's various, more grandiose statements in these three documents and the manner in which he attempted to implement his more limited, stated aims with action as in the case of the isolation of Poland or the original "Case Yellow" which envisaged a simple thrust into Belgium and Holland.

167. Doc. 062-L, *IMT*, "Weisung Nr. 6 fuer die Kriegsfuehrung. 9.10.39."

168. Jacobsen, *Dokumente* . . . , Aufmarschweisung 'Gelb' vom 19.10.39," p. 41; "Aufmarschweisung 'Gelb' vom 29.10.39," p. 46.

169. Telford Taylor, *op. cit.*, pp. 66–67.

170. Jacobsen, *Dokumente* . . . , "Neufassung der Aufmarschweisung 'Gelb' vom 24.2.40," p. 64.

171. Wheeler-Bennett, *op. cit.*, pp. 398 ff.

172. *Voelkischer Beobachter*. (South German ed.), Sept. 2/3, 1939, p. 2, col. 4.

173. Heinz Schroeter, *Stalingrad* (New York: E. P. Dutton, 1958), p. 260.

174. Dr. Paul Schmidt, *Statist auf displomatischer Buehne. 1923–1945* (Bonn: Athenaeum Verlag, 1953), p. 473.

175. Wheeler-Bennett, *op. cit.*, p. 464; Jacobsen, *Dokumente . . . ,* 21–23. Hitler's decision to attack in the West was made on the 10th of October. Chamberlain's reply to the "peace proposal" was made on the 12th. Daladier had replied separately on the 10th but Hitler's memorandum was dated October 9th though it was delivered on the 10th.

176. Doc. 789-PS, *IMT*, XXVI, 327–36.

177. Wheeler-Bennett, *op. cit.*, p. 469.

178. See p. 206 in essay.

179. Paul Joseph Goebbels, *The Goebbels Diaries* (Garden City, N. Y.: Doubleday and Co., 1948), p. 148.

180. Reitlinger places the real beginning of the action against the Jews in the period November, 1941-July 1942. See Gerald Reitlinger, *The Final Solution* (London: Vallentine, Mitchell, 1953), pp. 95 ff.

181. See William L. Langer and Everett S. Gleason, *The Undeclared War* (New York: Harper and Bros., 1953), pp. 732–35. The authors believe that it would be correct to state that Roosevelt, while still not convinced that an invasion of continental Europe by American forces was necessary, did feel that American naval and air forces would have to become engaged in order to insure the defeat of the Axis powers. Winston Churchill states his belief that in the fall of 1941 Roosevelt wanted to bring the United States into the war.

Winston Churchill, *The Grand Alliance* (Boston: Houghton Mifflin Co., 1950), p. 539.

182. As evidence of American provocation, the "destroyer deal" and the "Lend-Lease" program could be cited. These were indirect, though not the less important for that. A more straighforward case of provocation was the "Greer" incident in 1941. It was following this incident that the "shoot-on-sight" order was given. See Langer and Gleason, *op. cit.*, pp. 743–44 for a discussion of this.

183. The text of Hitler's declaration of war is given in Dr. Johannes Hohlfeld (ed.), *Dokumente der deutschen Politik und Geschichte von 1848 bis zur Gegenwart* (Munich: Giersch & Co., 1954 [?]) Band V. Doc. #140.

184. If Hitler had not declared war it might have been some months before the Administration could have convinced a Congress and people aroused against Japan that Germany should also be actively engaged. It was even possible that it might not have been able to secure a declaration of war against Germany.

185. Telford Taylor, *op. cit.*, pp. 252–65; Heinz Guderian, *Panzer Leader* (New York: Dutton, 1952), pp 117–20.

186. Guderian, *op. cit.*, pp. 189–226; Seymour Freidin and William Richardson (eds.), *The Fatal Decisions* (New York: William Sloane Associates, 1956), pp. 60–62.

187. Friedin and Richardson, *op. cit.*, p. 78.

188. Stalingrad is only the most famous of these positions. One may add to the list Tunisia, the Courland, Normandy, and many others.

189. Hohlfeld, *op. cit.*, p. 365.

190. Hannah Arendt. *The Origins of Totalitarianism* (New York: Harcourt, Brace and Co., 1951), pp. 301–429.

191. See p. 208 in essay.

192. The blow was aimed particularly at England, which Hitler thought to be the major contestant. Hence the seizure of Holland and the thrust into Belgium and northern France were intended to establish bases for air attack against England more than as vital thrusts against the French army and industry.

193. Telford Taylor, *op. cit.*, p. 166; Jacobsen, *Fall Gelb*, p. 51. The suggested alteration in the attack plan is mentioned in Jodl's diary (30.10.39). Apparently Hitler arrived independently at the same conclusion which Mannstein reached: namely, that victory could not be gained by a drive to the coast through central Belgium.

194. Hitler seems to have had the notion that by designating an area a "fortress" the defensive capacities of the position were greatly heightened. This "fortress fixation" seems to have developed during the severe winter fighting of 1941–42 when holding fast did indeed yield positive results. This fixation resulted, during the last days of the war, in the designation of certain cities as fortresses without any relation to the realities of the battle situation, or to each other, or, apparently, to anything which existed outside of the mind of the Fuehrer. One suspects that he derived a secret joy in the knowledge that men would stand and die in their tracks at his command.

195. Werner Baumbach, *The Life and Death of the Luftwaffe* (New York: Coward McCann, 1960), pp. 290–98; Adolf Galland, *Die Ersten und die Letzten* (Darmstadt: Franz Schneekluth, 1953), pp. 335–48.

196. Walter Dornberger, *V–2: Der Schuss ins Weltall* (Esslingen: Bechtle Verlag, 1952).

197. Goebbels, . . . *Diaries*, 20.11.1943, p. 539.

198. *Ibid.*, pp. 259–315. This section deals principally with Goebbels' attempts to obtain a "total war effort." Actually there is considerable doubt whether Goebbels had any real comprehension of what was involved in such a program.

199. Guderian, *op. cit.*, pp. 308–9.

200. The story of the attempt to put into effect a total mobilization of manpower for the war effort in August and September of 1944 can be gleaned from such sources as Wilfred von Oven, *Mit Goebbels bis zum Ende* (Buenos Aires: Duerer Verlag, 1949), Vol. II; Martin Bormann *The Bormann Letters*, ed. H. R. Trevor-Roper (London: Nicolson and Weidenfeld, 1954); and the testimony and documents of Albert Speer, *IMT*, Vols. XVI and XLI. In essence, a number of powerful figures including Goebbels, Bormann, Speer, and Himmler worked at cross purposes to take people out of unessential industries for war work and out of war work for the front. The end result was a temporary unemployment crisis in September of 1944 which caused the Propaganda Minister to exclaim "Total War—really total nonsense!" von Oven, *op. cit.*, II, 1939.

201. The problems involved in mobilizing the *Volkssturm* were similar to those involved in the total war effort. Furthermore they were complicated by resistance at the local level to sending out old men and young boys. See Ernst von Salomon, *Fragebogen*, (Garden City, N. Y.: Doubleday and Co., 1955), p. 303; and Karl Wahl, *. . . es ist das deutsche Herz* (Augsburg: Im selbstverlag Karl Wahl, 1954).

202. This failure is related in considerable detail by Guderian in his *Panzer Leader, op. cit.*, pp. 383–85.

203. *Ibid.*, pp. 387–88.

204. Trevor-Roper, *The Last Days . . .* , pp. 31–32; Wheeler-Bennet, *op. cit.*, pp. 645–46.

205. Exhibit Speer 23, *IMT*, XLI, 420–25; Exhibit Speer–24, *IMT*, XLI, 425–29; Speer Testimony, *IMT*, XVI, 499–501.

206. Guderian, *op. cit.*, p. 424; Trevor-Roper, *The Last Days of Hitler* (1st ed., 1947), p. 74.

207. Shneidman and Farberow, "Clues to Suicide," *op. cit.*, pp. 3–9; see also their "Logic of Suicide," *op. cit.*, pp. 31–40.

208. Shneidman and Farberow, "Clues to Suicide," *op. cit.*, p. 7.

209. Office of U. S. Chief of Counsel for Prosecution of Axis Criminality, *Nazi Conspiracy and Aggression* (Washington: U. S. Govt. Printing Office, 1946–47). The reconstructed appendix is given in Trevor-Roper, *The Last Days of Hitler* (1st ed., 1947), pp. 194–95.

210. Siegal and Friedman, "The Threat of Suicide," *op. cit.*, p. 38.

211. See Stengel and Cook, *Attempted Suicide.*

212. *Ibid.*

213. Charles W. Wahl, "Suicide as a Magical Act," *Bulletin of the Menninger Clinic*, May, 1957, pp. 91–98.

BIBLIOGRAPHY

DOCUMENTS

Deuerlein, Ernst. *Der Hitler Putsch:* Bayrische Dokumente zum 8/9 November, 1923. Stuttgart: Deutsche Verlags Anstalt, 1962.

Germany, Auswaertiges Amt. *Documents on German Foreign Policy.* (Series D.) Washington: Department of State, 1953.

Halder, Generaloberst Franz, *Kriegstagebuch,* ed. Hans-Adolf Jacobsen. Stuttgart: W. Kohlhammer Verlag, 1962.

Der Hitler Prozess vor dem Volksgericht in Muenchen. 2 parts. Munich: Knorr und Hirth, 1924.

Hohlfeld, Dr. Johannes (ed.). *Dokumente der deutschen Politik und Geschichte von 1848 bis zur Gegenwart.* Vol 5. Munich: Giersch und Co., 1954 [?].

Jacobsen, Hans-Adolf. *Dokumente zur Vorgeschichte des Westfeldzuges, 1939–1940.* Frankfurt: Musterschmidt Verlag, 1956.

International Military Tribunal. *Trial of the Major German War Criminals.* Nuremberg: 1947.

Office of United States Chief of Counsel for Prosecution of Axis Criminality. *Nazi Conspiracy and Aggression.* 8 vols. Washington: U. S. Govt. Printing Office, 1946–47.

Schoenfelder, Heinrich. *Deutsche Reichsgesetze.* (12th ed.). Munich: C. H. Beck'sche Verlagsbuchhandlung, 1944 [?].

United States, Munitions Division. *Tank Industry Report.* Washington: U. S. Govt. Printing Office, 1947.

United States Strategic Bombing Survey, Oil Division. *Oil Division Final Report.* 2 vols. Washington: U. S. Govt. Printing Office, 1947.

Woodward, E. L., and Rohan Butler (eds.). *Documents on British Foreign Policy 1919–1939.* 2nd Series, Vols. 3 and 4. London: His Majesty's Stationery Office, 1948.

MEMOIRS, SECONDARY WORKS, ETC.,

Arendt, Hannah. *The Origins of Totalitarianism*. New York: Harcourt, Brace and Co., 1951.

Baumbach, Werner. *The Life and Death of the Luftwaffe*. New York: Coward McCann, 1960.

Bezzel, Oskar. *Das Koenigliche Bayrische Reserve-Infanterie Regiment Nr. 6*. Munich: Verlag Max Schick, 1938.

Binding, Rudolf G. *Wir fordern Reims zur Uebergabe auf*. Frankfurt/M: Ruetten und Loening Verlag, 1935.

Blueher, Hans. *Fuehrer und Volk in der Jugendbewegung*. Jena: Eugen Diederichs, 1917.

―――. *Wandervogel: Geschichte einer Jugendbewegung*. Prien/Obb.: Anthropos Verlag, 1919.

Bormann, Martin. *The Bormann Letters*, ed. H. R. Trevor-Roper. London: Nicolson and Weidenfeld, 1954.

Bracher, Karl Dietrich. *Die Aufloesung der Weimarer Republik*. Stuttgart: Ring Verlag, 1955.

Brandt, Heinrich. *Trommelfeuer*. Hamburg: Fackelreiter Verlag, 1929.

Braun, Otto. *Von Weimar zu Hitler*. Hamburg: Hammonia Norddeutsche Verlagsanstalt, 1949.

Brenner, Hildegard. *Die Kunstpolitik des Nationalsozialismus*. Hamburg: Rowohlt deutsche Enzyklopaedie, 1963.

Bullock, Alan. *Hitler, A Study in Tyranny*. New York: Harper and Bros., 1952.

Churchill, Winston. *The Grand Alliance*. Boston: Houghton Mifflin Co., 1950.

Cohen, Max. *Der Aufbau*. Berlin: Bund deutscher Gelehrter und Kuenstler [Buchabteilung], 1919.

Coper, Rudolf. *Failure of a Revolution*. Cambridge: At the University Press, 1955.

Dehio, Ludwig. *Deutschland und die Weltpolitik im 20. Jahrhundert*. Munich: Verlag R. Oldenbourg, 1955.

Dornberger, Walter. *V-2: Der Schuss ins Weltall*. Esslingen: Bechtle Verlag, 1952.

Dubitscher, Fred, Dr. med. *Der Suicid*. Stuttgart: Georg Thieme, 1957.

Ellis, Edward R., and George N. Allen. *Traitor Within*. Garden City, N. Y.: Doubleday and Co., 1961.

Erfurth, Waldemar. *Die Geschichte des deutschen Generalstabes von 1918 bis 1945*. Berlin: Musterschmidt Verlag, 1960.

Eyck, Erich. *Geschichte der Weimarer Republik*. 3 vols. Stuttgart: Eugen Rentsch Verlag, 1954.

Fischer, Louis. *Gandhi: His Life and Message for the World*. New York: Signet Key Books, 1954.

Flex, Walter. *Die schwimmende Insel*. Munich: C. H. Beck'sche Verlagsbuchhandlung, 1925.

————. *Sonne und Schilde*. Berlin: Georg Westerman, 1918.

————. *Der Wanderer zwischen beiden Welten*. Munich: C. H. Beck'sche Verlagsbuchhandlung, 1917.

Frank, Hans. *Im Angesicht des Galgens*. Munich: Friedrich Alfred Beck Verlag, 1953.

Franziss, Franz. *Wir von der Somme*. Freiburg: Herder und Co., 1936.

Freidin, Seymour, and William Richardson (eds.). *The Fatal Decisions*. New York: William Sloane Associates, 1956.

Freud, Sigmund. *Collected Papers*. Vol. 4. London: Hogarth Press, 1949.

Fuchs, Hans. *Selbstmordhandlungen*. Vienna: Oesterreichisches Statistisches Zentralamt, 1961.

————. *Selbstmordversuche im Grossstadtraum*. Vienna: Oesterreichisches Statistisches Zentralamt, 1959.

Galland, Adolf. *Die Ersten und die Letzten*. Darmstadt: Franz Schneekluth, 1953.

Gamelin, General. *Servir*. 3 vols. Paris: Plon, 1946–47.

Gaupresseamt der NSDAP, Gauleitung Westfalen-Nord (ed.). *Mit dem Fuehrer*. 1943. [n.p.].

German Library of Information. *A Nation Builds*. New York: German Library of Information, 1940.

Gilbert, Felix (ed.). *Hitler Directs His War*. New York: Oxford University Press, 1950.

Gisevius, Hans Bernd. *Bis zum bittern Ende*. Zurich: Fretz und Wasmuth, 1946.

Goebbels, Joseph. *The Goebbels Diaries*. Garden City, N. Y.: Doubleday and Co., 1948.

———. *Vom Kaiserhof zur Reichskanzlei*. Munich: Franz Eher nachf., 1934, 1941.

Goerlitz, Walter. *History of the German General Staff*. New York: Praeger, 1953.

———, and Herbert A. Quint. *Adolf Hitler: eine Biographie*. Stuttgart: Steingrueben Verlag, 1952.

von der Goltz, Joachim. *Der Baum von Cléry*. Munich: Albert Langen, 1934.

Gordon, Harold J. *The Reichswehr and the German Republic, 1919–1926*. Princeton: Princeton University Press, 1957.

Greiner, Josef. *Das Ende des Hitler Mythos*. Vienna: Almathea Verlag, 1947.

Guderian, Heinz. *Panzer Leader*. New York: E. P. Dutton and Co., 1952.

Halperin, S. William. *Germany Tried Democracy*. New York: Crowell Co., 1946.

Harms, Heinrich. *Die Geschichte des Oldenburgischen Infanterie-Regiments Nr. 91*. Oldenburg/Berlin: Druck und Verlag von Gerhard Stahling, 1930.

Heiden, Konrad. *Der Fuehrer*. Boston: Houghton Mifflin Co., 1944.

Henderson, Sir Nevile. *Failure of a Mission*. New York: G. P. Putnam's Sons, 1940.

Henry, Andrew F., and James F. Short. *Suicide and Homicide.* Glencoe, Ill.: The Free Press, 1954.

Hierl, Konstantin. *Im Dienst fuer Deutschland. 1918–1945.* Heidelberg: Kurt Vowinckel Verlag, 1954.

Hitler, Adolf. *Hitler's Secret Book.* New York: Grove Press, 1961.

———. *Hitler's Secret Conversations.* New York: Farrar, Straus and Young, 1953.

———. *Mein Kampf.* Munich: Franz Eher nachf., 1940.

———. *Mein Kampf.* New York: Reynal and Hitchcock, 1940.

———. *My New Order.* New York: Reynal and Hitchcock, 1941.

Hohenstein, Alexander. *Warthelaendisches Tagebuch, 1941/42.* Munich: Deutscher Taschenbuch Verlag, 1963.

Howe, Frederick C. *European Cities at Work.* New York: Charles Scribner's Sons, 1913.

———. *Socialized Germany.* New York: Charles Scribner's Sons, 1915.

International Council for Philosophy and Humanistic Studies. *The Third Reich.* London: Weidenfeld and Nicolson, 1955.

Jacobsen, Hans-Adolf. *Fall Gelb.* Der Kampf um den deutschen Operationsplan fuer West Offensive 1940. Wiesbaden: Franz Steiner Verlag, 1957.

Jenks, William A. *Vienna and the Young Hitler.* New York: Columbia University Press, 1960.

Jetzinger, Franz. *Hitler's Youth.* London: Hutchinson and Co., 1958.

Juenger, Ernst. *Der Arbeiter.* Hamburg: Hanseatische Verlagsanstalt, 1932.

———. *Der Kampf als inneres Erlebnis.* Berlin: E. S. Mittler und Sohn, 1929.

——— (ed.). *Krieg und Krieger.* Berlin: Junker und Duenhaupt, 1930.

———. *In Stahlgewittern.* Berlin: E. S. Mittler und Sohn, 1926/27.

———. *The Storm of Steel.* London: Chatto and Windus, 1929.

Kamp, Dr. Kurt. *Die Haltung des Frontkaempfers.* Wurzburg: Konrad Triltsch Verlag, 1940.

Knickerbocker, H. R. *The German Crisis.* New York: Farrar and Rinehart, Inc., 1932.

Kordt, Erich. *Wahn und Wirklichkeit.* Stuttgart: Union Deutsche Verlags Anstalt, 1948.

Krebs, Albert. *Tendenzen und Gestalten der NSDAP.* Stuttgart: Deutsche Verlags Anstalt, 1959.

Kruijt, C. S. *Zelfmoord.* Assen: Van Gorcum and Co., 1960.

Kubizek, August. *Adolf Hitler: Mein Jugendfreund.* Goettingen: Leopold Stocker Verlag, 1953.

———. *The Young Hitler I Knew.* Boston: Houghton Mifflin Co., 1955.

Langbehn, Julius. *Rembrandt als Erzieher.* (37th edition) Weimar: Alexander Dunker Verlag, 1922.

Langer, William L., and Everett S. Gleason. *The Undeclared War.* New York: Harper and Bros., 1953.

Liddell Hart, B. H. *The German Generals Talk.* New York: Berkley Editions, 1948.

Ludendorff, General Erich. *Auf dem Weg zur Feldherrnhalle.* Munich: Ludendorffs Verlag, 1938.

Luedecke, Kurt G. W. *I Knew Hitler.* London: Jarrolds, 1938.

Mann, Golo. *Deutsche Geschichte des Neunzehnten und Zwanzigsten Jahrhunderts.* Frankfurt/M: S. Fischer Verlag, 1958.

Mau, Hermann, and Helmut Krausnick. *Deutsche Geschichte der juengsten Vergangenheit.* Stuttgart: J. B. Metzlersche Verlagsbuchhandlung, 1953.

Meinecke, Friedrich. *The German Catastrophe.* Cambridge, Mass: Harvard University Press, 1950.

Menninger, Karl. *Man Against Himself.* New York: Harcourt, Brace and Company [Harvest Books], 1938, 1961.

Meyer, Adolf. *Mit Adolf Hitler im Bayrischen Reserve-Infanterie Regiment 16 List.* Neustadt-Aisch/Mfr.: Georg Aupperle, 1934.

Michaelis, Dr. Herbert, and Dr. Ernst Schnaepler. *Ursachen und Folgen vom deutschen Zusammenbruch 1918 und 1945 bis zur staatlichen Neuordnung Deutschlands in der Gegenwart.* 8 vols. Berlin: Dokumenten-Verlag Dr. Herbert Wendler & Co.

Moeller, Eberhard Wolfgang. *Die Briefe der Gefallenen.* Munich: Albert Langen/Georg Mueller, 1935.

Moeller van den Bruck, Arthur. *Das dritte Reich* (3rd ed.). Hamburg: Hanseatische Verlagsanstalt, 1931.

————. *Germany's Third Empire.* London: George Allen and Unwin Ltd., 1934.

————. *Der preussische Stil.* Munich: R. Piper and Co., 1916.

Mueller, Major d.R.D., Oberst a.D. v. Fabeck, and Oberstleutnant a.D. Kiesel. *Geschichte des Reserve-Infanterie-Regiments Nr. 99.* Zeulenroda-Thuringen: Verlag Bernhard Sporn, 1936.

von Muellern-Schoenhausen, Dr. Johannes. *Die Loesung des Raetsel Adolf Hitler.* Vienna: Verlag zur Forderung wissenschaftlichen Forschung, 1959.

Namier, L. B. *Diplomatic Prelude. 1938–1939.* London: Macmillan, 1948.

Nationalsozialistische Deutsche Arbeiterpartei. *Erster Parteitag Grossdeutschlands.* Munich: Franz Eher nachf., 1938.

Neumann, Franz. *Behemoth.* New York: Oxford University Press, 1942.

von Oven, Wilfred. *Mit Goebbels bis zum Ende.* 2 vols. Buenos Aires: Duerer Verlag, 1949.

von Papen, Franz. *Memoirs.* London: Andre Deutsch, 1952.

Pfeiler, William K. *War and the German Mind.* New York: Columbia University Press, 1941.

Poppe, Richard. *Jungdeutschland.* Waldenburg-in-Schlesien, 1912.

Pross, Harry. *Vor und Nach Hitler.* Freiburg: Walter-Verlag, 1962.

Reitlinger, Gerald. *The Final Solution.* London: Vallentine, Mitchell, 1953.

Remarque, Erich Maria. *All Quiet on the Western Front*. Boston: Little, Brown and Co., 1929, 1945.

————. *Im Westen Nichts Neues*. Frankfurt/M: Ullstein Buecher, 1958.

————. *The Road Back*. Boston: Little, Brown and Co., 1931.

von Rheinbaben, Werner Freiherr. *Viermal Deutschland*. Berlin: Argon Verlag, 1954.

Richter, Hans Werner (ed.). *Bestandsaufnahme*. Munich: Kurt Desch Verlag, 1962.

————. *Du sollst nicht toeten*. Frankfurt/M.: Ullstein Verlag, 1962.

Riess, Curt. *Joseph Goebbels*. London: Hollis and Carter, 1949.

Ringel, Werner. *Der Selbstmord*. Vienna: Verlag fuer medizinische Wissenschaften, 1953.

Ritter, Gerhard. *Der Schlieffenplan*. Munich: Verlag R. Oldenbourg, 1956.

————. *Staatskunst und Kriegshandwerk*. 2 vols. Munich: Verlag R. Oldenbourg, 1954, 1960.

Rittich, Dr. Werner. *New German Architecture*. Berlin: Terramare, 1941.

Roehm, Ernst. *Die Geschichte eines Hochverraeters* (2nd ed.). Munich: Franz Eher nachf., 1930.

Romains, Jules. *Death of a World*. New York: Alfred Knopf, 1938.

————. *Verdun*. New York: Alfred Knopf, 1939.

Rosenberg, Alfred. *Memoirs of Alfred Rosenberg*. Chicago: Ziff-Davis Publishing Co., 1953.

Roth, W. A. *Die siegreiche Technik Deutschlands*. Berlin: Verlag Reimar Hobbing, 1917.

Sailler, Friedrich. *Bruecke ueber das Niemandsland*. Leipzig: Wilhelm Goldmann Verlag, 1938.

von Salomon, Ernst. *Fragebogen*. New York: Doubleday and Co., 1955.

Sassoon, Siegfried. *Memoirs of an Infantry Officer*. New York: Coward, McCann and Co., 1930.

Schippel, Max. *Die Gewerkschaften, der Krieg, und die Revolution*. Berlin: Bund deutscher Gelehrter und Kuenstler [Buchabteilung], 1919.

Schmidt, Dr. Paul. *Statist auf diplomatischer Buehne. 1923–1945*. Bonn: Athenaeum Verlag, 1953.

Schmidt-Pauli, Edgar. *Geschichte der Freikorps. 1918–1924*. Stuttgart: Robert Lutz nachf. Otto Schramm, 1936.

Schorske, Carl. *German Social Democracy 1905–1917*. Cambridge: Harvard University Press, 1955.

Schramm, Percy Ernst (ed.). *Kriegstagebuch des Oberkommandos der Wehrmacht*. 4 vols. Frankfurt/M., 1961.

Schuwer, Camille. *La Signification Metaphysique du Suicid*. Paris: Aubier, 1949.

Schwab-Felisch, Hans (ed.). *Der Ruf. Eine deutsche Nachkriegszeitschrift*. Munich: Deutscher Taschenbuch Verlag, 1962.

Shirer, William L. *The Rise and Fall of the Third Reich*. New York: Simon and Schuster, 1960.

Shneidman, E. S., and N. L. Farberow (eds.). *Clues to Suicide*. New York: McGraw-Hill, 1957.

Siegmund, Georg. *Sein oder Nichtsein*. Trier: Paulinus Verlag, 1961.

Solleder, Dr. Fridolin. (ed.). *Vier Jahre Westfront* Geschichte des Regiments List R.I.R. 16. Munich: Verlag Max Schick, 1932.

Spann, Dr. Othmar. *Der Wahre Staat* (4th ed.). Jena: Verlag von Gustav Fischer, 1938.

Spengler, Oswald. *Der Mensch und die Technik*. Munich: C. H. Beck'sche Verlagsbuchhandlung, 1952.

———. *Preussentum und Sozialismus*. Munich: C. H. Beck'sche Verlagsbuchhandlung, 1934. (1st edition 1919.)

Stengel, E., and Nancy G. Cook. *Attempted Suicide*. London: Chapman and Hall Ltd., 1958.

Stern, Fritz. *The Politics of Cultural Despair*. Berkeley: University of California Press, 1961.

Strasser, P. Bernhard. *Gregor und Otto Strasser*. Munich: Bund fuer Deutschlands Erneuerung, 1954.

Strasser, Gregor. *Freiheit und Brot*. Berlin: Kampf Verlag, 1928.

Strasser, Otto. *Aufbau des deutschen Sozialismus*. Leipzig: Wolfgang Richard Lindner Verlag, 1932.

———. *Hitler und Ich*. Constance Johannes Asmus Verlag, 1948.

Stuehmke, Generalmajor a.D. *Die 26 Infanterie-Division im Weltkrieg 1914–18*. Stuttgart: Bergers Litarisches Buero und Verlagsanstalt, 1927.

Taylor, A. J. P. *The Origins of the Second World War*. New York: Atheneum, 1962.

———. *The Struggle for the Mastery of Europe*. Oxford: Clarendon Press, 1954.

Taylor, Telford. *The March of Conquest*. New York: Simon and Schuster, 1958.

Tenenbaum, Joseph. *Race and Reich*. New York: Twayne Publishers, 1956.

von Tirpitz, Admiral. *My Memoirs*. New York: Dodd, Mead and Co., 1919.

Trevor-Roper, H. R. *The Last Days of Hitler* (3rd ed.). London: Macmillan, 1958.

von Unruh, Fritz. *Opfergang*. Frankfurt/M.: Societaets Verlag, 1931.

Vermeil, Edmond. *L'Allemagne Contemporaine*. 2 vols. Paris: Aubier, 1953.

Viereck, Peter. *Metapolitics: From Romanticism to Hitler*. New York: Alfred Knopf, 1941.

Vogt, Hannah. *Der Arbeiter* (2nd ed.). Groene-Goettingen: August Schoenhuette und Soehne, 1947.

Wagenfuehr, Dr. Rolf. "The Rise and Fall of the German War Economy. 1939–1945." Unpublished study.

Wahl, Karl. . . . *es ist das deutsche Herz*. Augsburg: In Selbstverlag Karl Wahl, 1954.

Waite, R. G. L. *Vanguard of Nazism*. Cambridge: Harvard University Press, 1952.

Webster, Sir Charles, and Noble Frankland. *The Strategic Air Offensive Against Germany, 1939–1945*. London: Her Majesty's Stationery Office, 1961.

Wheeler-Bennett, John W. *The Nemesis of Power*. London: Macmillan, 1954.

Wiechert, Ernst. *Die Novellen und Erzaehlungen*. Munich: Verlag Kurt Desch, 1962.

Winnig, August. *Der Arbeiter im dritten Reich*. Berlin: Buchholz und Weisswange Verlagsbuchhandlung, 1934.

————. *Der englische Wirtschaftskrieg und das werktaetige Volk Deutschlands*. Berlin: Verlag Reimar Hobbing, 1917.

————. *Europa*. Berlin: Eckart Verlag, 1938, 1952.

————. *Der Glaube an das Proletariat*. Munich: Milavida-Verlag, 1926. Neue Fassung.

————. *Vom Proletariat zum Arbeitertum*. Hamburg: Hanseatische Verlagsanstalt, 1930.

————. *Volkspolitik und Parteipolitik*. Berlin: Verlag fuer praktische Politik und geistige Erneuerung, 1921.

————. *Der Weite Weg* (2nd ed.). Hamburg: Hanseatische Verlagsanstalt, 1932.

————. *Der Weltkrieg vom Standpunkt des deutschen Arbeiters*. Hamburg: Verlag Deutscher Bauarbeiterverband, 1915.

Wuelfing, Walter. *Peter Krafts Kampf*. Reutlingen: Enslin und Laiblins Verlagsbuchhandlung, 1936.

Zoeberlein, Hans. *Der Befehl des Gewissens*. Munich: Franz Eher nachf., 1937.

Zoller, A. (ed.). *Hitler Privat*. Duesseldorf: Droste Verlag, 1949.

ARTICLES

Arendt, Hannah. "Ideologie und Terror," *Offener Horizont. Festschift fuer Karl Jaspers*. Munich: R. Piper and Co., 1953.

Brill, A. A. "The Concept of Psychic Suicide," *International Journal of Psychoanalysis*, (July-October, 1939).

Carmichael, Benson D. "The Death Wish in Daily Life," *Psychiatric Review* (January, 1943).

Freund, Michael. "Geschichte ohne Distanz," *Deutscher Geist zwischen Gestern und Morgen*. Stuttgart: Deutsche Verlags Anstalt, 1954.

Friedlander, Kate. "On the 'Longing to Die,'" *International Journal of Psychoanalysis* (October, 1940).

Hendin, Herbert. "Suicide," *Psychiatric Quarterly* (April, 1956).

Hirsh, Joseph. "Demography of Suicide," *Mental Hygiene* (October, 1959).

———. "Dynamics of Suicide," *Mental Hygiene* (April, 1960).

———. "Suicide: Part 4: Predictability and Prevention," *Mental Hygiene* (July, 1962).

Juenger, Ernst. "Vorwarts," *Der Kampf um das Reich*. Essen: Deutsche Vertrieb (stelle) "Rhein und Ruhr" Wilhelm Kamp, 1932.

Mau, Hermann. "Die 'Zweite Revolution'—Der 30 Juni 1934," *Vierteljahrshefte fuer Zeitgeschichte* (April, 1953).

Moss, Leonard M., and Donald M. Hamilton, "The Psychotherapy of the Suicidal Patient," *American Journal of Psychiatry* (April, 1956).

Selzer, Melvin L., and Charles E. Payne. "Automobile Accidents, Suicide, and Unconscious Motivation," *American Journal of Psychiatry* (September, 1962).

Siegal, Lewis J., and Jacob H. Friedman. "The Threat of Suicide," *Diseases of the Nervous System* (February, 1955).

Stengel, E. "Recent Research into Suicide and Attempted Suicide," *American Journal of Psychiatry* (February, 1962).

Stengel, E., and Nancy G. Cook. "Contrasting Suicide Rates in Industrial Communities," *Journal of Mental Science* (November, 1961).

Strasser, Otto. "Von Sinn des Krieges," *Die Gruenen Hefte der "N. S. Briefe."* Berlin: Kampf-verlag, 1930.

Wahl, Charles W. "Suicide as a Magical Act," *Bulletin of the Menninger Clinic* (May, 1957).

Whiteside, Andrew G. "The Nature and Origins of National Socialism," *Journal of Central European Affairs* (April, 1957).

Zilboorg, Gregory. "Considerations on Suicide with Particular Reference to That of the Young," *The American Journal of Orthopsychiatry* (January, 1937).

NEWSPAPERS

Muenchener Neueste Nachrichten

Voelkischer Beobachter (North German edition and South German edition)